™

References for the Rest of Us!®

BESTSELLING BOOK SERIES

Are you intimidated and confused by computers? Do you find that traditional manuals are overloaded with technical details you'll never use? Do your friends and family always call you to fix simple problems on their PCs? Then the *...For Dummies*® computer book series from IDG Books Worldwide is for you.

...For Dummies books are written for those frustrated computer users who know they aren't really dumb but find that PC hardware, software, and indeed the unique vocabulary of computing make them feel helpless. *...For Dummies* books use a lighthearted approach, a down-to-earth style, and even cartoons and humorous icons to dispel computer novices' fears and build their confidence. Lighthearted but not lightweight, these books are a perfect survival guide for anyone forced to use a computer.

> *"I like my copy so much I told friends; now they bought copies."*
>
> — Irene C., Orwell, Ohio

> *"Quick, concise, nontechnical, and humorous."*
>
> — Jay A., Elburn, Illinois

> *"Thanks, I needed this book. Now I can sleep at night."*
>
> — Robin F., British Columbia, Canada

Already, millions of satisfied readers agree. They have made *...For Dummies* books the #1 introductory level computer book series and have written asking for more. So, if you're looking for the most fun and easy way to learn about computers, look to *...For Dummies* books to give you a helping hand.

IDG BOOKS WORLDWIDE

1/99

Internet Marketing
FOR
DUMMIES®

Internet Marketing FOR DUMMIES®

by Frank Catalano
and Bud Smith

IDG Books Worldwide, Inc.
An International Data Group Company

Foster City, CA ◆ Chicago, IL ◆ Indianapolis, IN ◆ New York, NY

Internet Marketing For Dummies®

Published by
IDG Books Worldwide, Inc.
An International Data Group Company
919 E. Hillsdale Blvd.
Suite 400
Foster City, CA 94404
www.idgbooks.com (IDG Books Worldwide Web Site)
www.dummies.com (Dummies Press Web Site)

Library of Congress Control Number: 00-107257

ISBN: 0-7645-0778-8

Printed in the United States of America

10 9 8 7 6 5 4 3 2 1

1B/QX/RR/QQ/IN

Distributed in the United States by IDG Books Worldwide, Inc.

Distributed by CDG Books Canada Inc. for Canada; by Transworld Publishers Limited in the United Kingdom; by IDG Norge Books for Norway; by IDG Sweden Books for Sweden; by IDG Books Australia Publishing Corporation Pty. Ltd. for Australia and New Zealand; by TransQuest Publishers Pte Ltd. for Singapore, Malaysia, Thailand, Indonesia, and Hong Kong; by Gotop Information Inc. for Taiwan; by ICG Muse, Inc. for Japan; by Intersoft for South Africa; by Eyrolles for France; by International Thomson Publishing for Germany, Austria and Switzerland; by Distribuidora Cuspide for Argentina; by LR International for Brazil; by Galileo Libros for Chile; by Ediciones ZETA S.C.R. Ltda. for Peru; by WS Computer Publishing Corporation, Inc., for the Philippines; by Contemporanea de Ediciones for Venezuela; by Express Computer Distributors for the Caribbean and West Indies; by Micronesia Media Distributor, Inc. for Micronesia; by Chips Computadoras S.A. de C.V. for Mexico; by Editorial Norma de Panama S.A. for Panama; by American Bookshops for Finland.

For general information on IDG Books Worldwide's books in the U.S., please call our Consumer Customer Service department at 800-762-2974. For reseller information, including discounts and premium sales, please call our Reseller Customer Service department at 800-434-3422.

For information on where to purchase IDG Books Worldwide's books outside the U.S., please contact our International Sales department at 317-572-3993 or fax 317-572-4002.

For consumer information on foreign language translations, please contact our Customer Service department at 1-800-434-3422, fax 317-572-4002, or e-mail rights@idgbooks.com.

For information on licensing foreign or domestic rights, please phone +1-650-653-7098.

For sales inquiries and special prices for bulk quantities, please contact our Order Services department at 800-434-3422 or write to the address above.

For information on using IDG Books Worldwide's books in the classroom or for ordering examination copies, please contact our Educational Sales department at 800-434-2086 or fax 317-572-4005.

For press review copies, author interviews, or other publicity information, please contact our Public Relations department at 650-653-7000 or fax 650-653-7500.

For authorization to photocopy items for corporate, personal, or educational use, please contact Copyright Clearance Center, 222 Rosewood Drive, Danvers, MA 01923, or fax 978-750-4470.

About the Authors

Frank Catalano is a veteran marketing consultant and analyst. He's the principal of Catalano Consulting, a strategic marketing firm advising Internet and technology companies. His consulting assignments include stints as Managing Director for PC Data's Internet Monitoring Division, VP Marketing for McGraw-Hill Home Interactive, VP Marketing for iCopyright, and VP Marketing for Apex Computer. He also was a marketing manager for Egghead Software and for the Apple Programmers and Developers Association. When not consulting, Frank provides tech industry analysis and commentary for KCPQ-TV Fox Seattle and is the author of the long-running Byte Me columns for *Seattle Weekly* and others. His essays and short fiction about technology have appeared in a wide variety of print and broadcast media, including ClickZ, Omni, Inside Multimedia, and Analog. He resides in the Seattle area with his wife, son, cat, and Golden Retriever, but often lives on Alaska Airlines flights between Seattle and Silicon Valley.

Bud Smith's experience is split between the technical and marketing sides of the computer and Internet industries. Bud was a Jack in the Box fry cook before starting in the computer industry at age 21. He was a data entry supervisor, programmer, and technical writer before working as a competitive analyst and QuickTime marketing manager at Apple Computer. He has been a full-time writer and has joined Frank in several consulting projects. Bud is currently Director of Marketing at AllPublish, a venture-funded Silicon Valley startup. Bud's writing experience is all on the nonfiction side and includes computer and medical articles as well as a dozen computer books, including *Creating Web Pages For Dummies,* 5th Edition, with Arthur Bebak, and the recently published *Push Technology For Dummies,* both from IDG Books Worldwide, Inc.

ABOUT IDG BOOKS WORLDWIDE

Welcome to the world of IDG Books Worldwide.

IDG Books Worldwide, Inc., is a subsidiary of International Data Group, the world's largest publisher of computer-related information and the leading global provider of information services on information technology. IDG was founded more than 30 years ago by Patrick J. McGovern and now employs more than 9,000 people worldwide. IDG publishes more than 290 computer publications in over 75 countries. More than 90 million people read one or more IDG publications each month.

Launched in 1990, IDG Books Worldwide is today the #1 publisher of best-selling computer books in the United States. We are proud to have received eight awards from the Computer Press Association in recognition of editorial excellence and three from Computer Currents' First Annual Readers' Choice Awards. Our best-selling *...For Dummies®* series has more than 50 million copies in print with translations in 31 languages. IDG Books Worldwide, through a joint venture with IDG's Hi-Tech Beijing, became the first U.S. publisher to publish a computer book in the People's Republic of China. In record time, IDG Books Worldwide has become the first choice for millions of readers around the world who want to learn how to better manage their businesses.

Our mission is simple: Every one of our books is designed to bring extra value and skill-building instructions to the reader. Our books are written by experts who understand and care about our readers. The knowledge base of our editorial staff comes from years of experience in publishing, education, and journalism — experience we use to produce books to carry us into the new millennium. In short, we care about books, so we attract the best people. We devote special attention to details such as audience, interior design, use of icons, and illustrations. And because we use an efficient process of authoring, editing, and desktop publishing our books electronically, we can spend more time ensuring superior content and less time on the technicalities of making books.

You can count on our commitment to deliver high-quality books at competitive prices on topics you want to read about. At IDG Books Worldwide, we continue in the IDG tradition of delivering quality for more than 30 years. You'll find no better book on a subject than one from IDG Books Worldwide.

John Kilcullen
Chairman and CEO
IDG Books Worldwide, Inc.

Eighth Annual Computer Press Awards ≥ 1992

Ninth Annual Computer Press Awards ≥ 1993

Tenth Annual Computer Press Awards ≥ 1994

Eleventh Annual Computer Press Awards ≥ 1995

IDG is the world's leading IT media, research and exposition company. Founded in 1964, IDG had 1997 revenues of $2.05 billion and has more than 9,000 employees worldwide. IDG offers the widest range of media options that reach IT buyers in 75 countries representing 95% of worldwide IT spending. IDG's diverse product and services portfolio spans six key areas including print publishing, online publishing, expositions and conferences, market research, education and training, and global marketing services. More than 90 million people read one or more of IDG's 290 magazines and newspapers, including IDG's leading global brands — Computerworld, PC World, Network World, Macworld and the Channel World family of publications. IDG Books Worldwide is one of the fastest-growing computer book publishers in the world, with more than 700 titles in 36 languages. The "...For Dummies®" series alone has more than 50 million copies in print. IDG offers online users the largest network of technology-specific Web sites around the world through IDG.net (http://www.idg.net), which comprises more than 225 targeted Web sites in 55 countries worldwide. International Data Corporation (IDC) is the world's largest provider of information technology data, analysis and consulting, with research centers in over 41 countries and more than 400 research analysts worldwide. IDG World Expo is a leading producer of more than 168 globally branded conferences and expositions in 35 countries including E3 (Electronic Entertainment Expo), Macworld Expo, ComNet, Windows World Expo, ICE (Internet Commerce Expo), Agenda, DEMO, and Spotlight. IDG's training subsidiary, ExecuTrain, is the world's largest computer training company, with more than 230 locations worldwide and 785 training courses. IDG Marketing Services helps industry-leading IT companies build international brand recognition by developing global integrated marketing programs via IDG's print, online and exposition products worldwide. Further information about the company can be found at www.idg.com. 1/26/00

Dedication

This book is dedicated by Frank to his wife, Dee Dee, who had no idea what she was getting into by marrying a compulsive writer, and to his son, Michael, who lent his Dad to the first edition of this book for an unexpectedly large number of long days and nights, with only one break for a visit to Disneyland, where they both could be 10 years old.

Acknowledgments

Bud would like to acknowledge Michael Mace, formerly of Apple and now of Palm Computing, Inc., for his initial on-the-job tutorial in marketing and strategic planning. He would also like to acknowledge Ken Williams' ongoing efforts to keep him updated on the goings-on in the Wintel world during Bud's many years at Apple and since.

Frank would like to acknowledge Adam Boettiger of I-Advertising for being an idea trampoline on all things Internet advertising (and for having a damned fine e-mail discussion list). He would also like to acknowledge Pam Miller of The KMC Group for serving a similar purpose for Internet PR and making sure that there were no gaping omissions. Ralph Sims of Winstar Northwest Nexus deserves thanks for his role in sorting out gray technical areas of Usenet newsgroups for the first edition.

Both authors would like to acknowledge the Internet community as a whole, which continues to provide answers to questions of all sorts, detailed Frequently Asked Questions documents (FAQs), and much more, even as the Internet changes in ways that aren't always what was intended or even imagined by the people who started it all.

Both authors would also like to thank Riley Wells, who updated the Directory with our input and many hours of his own research, and the editorial staff at IDG Books Worldwide, Inc., for bringing this project back on track and across the finish line, including Steve Hayes, Acquisitions Editor, Susan Christophersen, Project Editor, and Judy Apostol and Steve Gold, Technical Editors.

Publisher's Acknowledgments

We're proud of this book; please register your comments through our IDG Books Worldwide Online Registration Form located at http://my2cents.dummies.com.

Some of the people who helped bring this book to market include the following:

Acquisitions, Editorial, and Media Development

Project Editor: Susan Christophersen
(Previous Edition: Clark Sheffy)

Acquisitions Editor: Steven H. Hayes

Copy Editor: Susan Christophersen

Proof Editor: Teresa Artman

Technical Editors: Judy Apostol and Steve Gold

Permissions Editor: Carmen Krikorian

Editorial Manager: Constance Carlisle

Media Development Manager: Heather Heath Dismore

Editorial Assistant: Candace Nicholson

Production

Project Coordinator: Maridee Ennis

Layout and Graphics: Amy Adrian, Jackie Bennett, Jeremey Unger

Proofreaders: Laura Albert, Susan Moritz, York Production Services, Inc.

Indexer: York Production Services, Inc.

Special Help
Amanda M. Foxworth

General and Administrative

IDG Books Worldwide, Inc.: John Kilcullen, CEO; Bill Barry, President and COO; John Ball, Executive VP, Operations & Administration; John Harris, CFO

IDG Books Technology Publishing Group: Richard Swadley, Senior Vice President and Publisher; Mary Bednarek, Vice President and Publisher; Walter R. Bruce III, Vice President and Publisher; Joseph Wikert, Vice President and Publisher; Mary C. Corder, Editorial Director; Andy Cummings, Publishing Director, General User Group; Barry Pruett, Publishing Director

IDG Books Manufacturing: Ivor Parker, Vice President, Manufacturing

IDG Books Marketing: John Helmus, Assistant Vice President, Director of Marketing

IDG Books Online Management: Brenda McLaughlin, Executive Vice President, Chief Internet Officer; Gary Millrood, Executive Vice President of Business Development, Sales and Marketing

IDG Books Packaging: Marc J. Mikulich, Vice President, Brand Strategy and Research

IDG Books Production for Branded Press: Debbie Stailey, Production Director

IDG Books Sales: Roland Elgey, Senior Vice President, Sales and Marketing; Michael Violano, Vice President, International Sales and Sub Rights

◆

The publisher would like to give special thanks to Patrick J. McGovern, without whom this book would not have been possible.

◆

Contents at a Glance

Cartoons at a Glance

By Rich Tennant

page 7

page 173

page 99

page 229

page D-1

page 277

Fax: 978-546-7747
E-mail: richtennant@the5thwave.com
World Wide Web: www.the5thwave.com

Table of Contents

Introduction

● ●

*T*he Internet is the subject of great excitement these days — and of great anxiety. Businesses have wonderful new opportunities to grow and to extend their relationships with customers — and new types of competitors that may take those customers away. This book will help you make sure that the Internet is your friend.

Marketing, broadly defined, is everything that happens from the initial idea for a product or service until it is created, tested, sold, updated, repriced, promoted, and eventually retired from inventory. Marketing differs from sales in that marketing responds to customer needs and creates demand for a product or service; sales fulfills that demand. However, this book is not a marketing primer; for that, see *Marketing For Dummies*, by Alexander Hiam (IDG Books Worldwide, Inc.). The job of this book is to tell you and show you how to market your products and services effectively on the Internet.

About This Book

Most people know that the Internet includes the World Wide Web, and if you've ever surfed the Web, you've no doubt stumbled across a great deal of marketing content; a large part of this book is therefore devoted to marketing on the Web. But in this book we also show you that the online world is much more than the Web. Online services, Usenet newsgroups, e-mail, personal organizers with Net connections, even cell phones are all part of the Internet's reach and are all potentially useful for your Internet marketing strategy.

We, the authors of this book, have many years of marketing and Internet experience, and we draw on all of it to tell you how to best use each and every one of these Internet services — and how to prioritize and combine your efforts to create the most effective Net presence possible.

Well-Attended Conventions

In this book, a convention is not necessarily something you have to book a hotel room for. Our *conventions* are standard ways of structuring specific types of information that you find in this book, such as steps and instructions. (One example of the use of a convention is the use of italics for the word *convention* when it appeared in the second sentence of this paragraph; when you see a term in italics, a definition of it may soon be following.) Here are the major conventions for this book:

- ✔ Things that you, the reader, are asked to type, as well as specific instructions that you need to follow in a set of numbered steps, are shown in bold.
- ✔ New terms are printed in italics.
- ✔ Information used in specific ways is formatted in a specific typeface. This book uses a special typeface for URLs (Uniform Resource Locators), which are the addresses used to specify the location of Web pages and other Internet resources. For example, the URL for the . . .*For Dummies* site is as follows:
- ✔ `http://www.dummies.com`
- ✔ In most of this book, we omit the `http://` from Web addresses because you don't actually have to type that part of the Web address into your Web browser.
- ✔ Related, brief pieces of information are displayed in bulleted lists, such as the bulleted list that you're reading right now.
- ✔ Right-clicking means clicking something on-screen while using the right mouse button. (That's right, mouse button as in "the mouse button on the same side of the mouse as your right hand," not "the mouse button that isn't the wrong one.") If you are left-handed or for some other reason have changed your mouse settings, you may need to use a different mouse button to achieve the effect of right-clicking something. Also, right-clicking doesn't have a direct equivalent on the Macintosh, which has only a single button on the mouse. For the Macintosh, the commands you choose by right-clicking in Windows are usually available via program menus.

How This Book Is Organized

To make finding things in this book easier for you, we divide it into parts that separate chapters into easily located, related groups. Here's a quick guide to the parts in this book.

Part I: Getting Started with Internet Marketing

You need to know a few basics to use the Internet effectively for marketing. For example, you need to know what Internet services are available for you to deliver your marketing messages; just as important, you need to know who's out there in the online world for you to reach with your marketing effort.

The Internet is a place not only for you to do marketing but also to find information for all your marketing planning, both online and offline. (We use the term *offline* to mean everything that isn't online, such as all your traditional marketing efforts.) As soon as you know who's there and how to reach them, you're ready to plan your online marketing effort. We give you a step-by-step description of how to create just such a plan.

Ever wonder why some companies have a great URL (online address) that's easy to remember, and others don't? We finish Part I by telling you how to get the right URL for your online marketing work.

Part II: Marketing on the World Wide Web

Part II is your tour — we think it's a tour de force — of how to establish an effective presence on the most popular Internet service of all, the one that's captured imaginations (and investments) around the world, the World Wide Web. In four easy-to-follow chapters, we tell you how to build your own Web presence, either as a DIY — that's British for a "Do It Yourself" project — or working with other professionals, whether employees of your company or hired consultants. After reading this part, you'll know just how to get what you want from your Web marketing effort.

Part III: Marketing with E-Mail

E-mail is the secret weapon of Internet marketing. Every e-mail message your company sends out is a marketing piece, and you can harness this power for your benefit or let it undermine your efforts. This part tells you how to pay attention to the basics that make single e-mail messages work; then it expands to tell you how to handle bulk e-mail messages and Internet e-mail lists (one of the most effective "secret" marketing techniques on the Internet).

Part IV: Even More Internet Marketing

This part takes you over the finish line to knowing all the angles in Internet marketing. Usenet newsgroups and other discussion groups can be a big help or give your marketing efforts a big hurt. Chat and online services are two more ways to learn from your (potential) customers and to get the message out.

Internet advertising is a whole other realm of communication. As Web marketing managers, we've learned a great deal about what works and what doesn't. And public relations is free (except for all the work you do); we show you how to use PR effectively on the Net.

The Internet Marketing For Dummies Internet Directory

The funky yellow color of the pages used for this part tells you that something different is going on here. This part consists of a directory of Internet resources — including Web sites, Usenet newsgroups, and e-mail lists — to help you in your online marketing efforts. Each entry in the directory gives you an address and a quick description of a site or service that offers valuable information for the online marketer.

Part V: The Part of Tens

The chapters in the Part of Tens are fun but have serious information about things to do in Internet marketing, things not to do, and pointers to some of the best *offline* resources to use in creating your online marketing presence.

Icons Used in This Book

You're ready to begin using this book, but let us quickly tell you one last thing. Like many computer books, this one uses icons, or little pictures, to flag things that don't quite fit into the flow of things. The . . .*For Dummies* books use a standard set of icons that flag these little digressions, such as the following:

This icon is just a friendly reminder to do something.

This icon is a friendly reminder *not* to do something.

This icon points out nerdy technical material that you may want to skip.

This icon points out a tip or provides a bit of useful information.

This icon signifies a reference to another . . .*For Dummies* book that you'll find helpful.

Part I
Getting Started with Internet Marketing

The 5th Wave   By Rich Tennant

BUNGCO
BUNGEE CABLE
COMPANY

"Come on Walt—time to freshen the company Web page."

In this part . . .

The Internet world is a whole new arena for marketing, one with many opportunities — but also with its own history and rules. Use this part to become familiar with using Internet resources effectively, learn more about who's online, figure out how to get a good domain name, and find out how to start extending your marketing efforts to reach this new audience.

Chapter 1

Getting Net-Savvy

· ·

· ·

*T*he Internet is new; it's been only 30 years since Al Gore invented it — and the Net has been used for business only since the early '90s. (No political lobbying intended — that "Al Gore" part was a joke.) Marketing is old, "the second oldest profession," as some of us would have it. Guess which is more misunderstood — the Internet, or marketing?

The answer is "marketing." It can mean anything from pure public relations to all the stuff you do in running a company. We use a broad definition because we think marketing is really, really important.

Marketing, in our definition, is part of just about everything you do in creating a product. Identifying something that people might want to buy is a marketing activity, even if the one coming up with the idea is an engineer, salesperson, executive, or secretary. (Want a six-word description of how to get rich? "Find a need and fill it." That's the first step in marketing.)

So you've identified a need and want to fill it. Creating a specific definition of your product or service is also a marketing activity. Product development people might then take the ball and run with it for a while, creating a prototype of the product or service. But deciding when the product or service is acceptable and ready to sell is marketing, too.

The marketing department then sets the initial price and hands the whole thing off to the sales department. Sales's job is to sell; marketing tracks the progress of sales and tweaks the product and price for maximum profit. Promotions, public relations, and packaging are also part of the marketing effort.

Marketing also influences areas that don't directly involve business. Politics has been revolutionized — for better or worse — by marketing-type practices. Job hunting is increasingly understood to mean marketing yourself. Even nonprofit organizations hire specialists to help them identify and reach target markets of donors and recipients of aid and services.

Companies vary widely in what areas they call "marketing" and what they call product development, engineering, or something else, and that's fine with us. Our point is not to say that marketing should take over everything in a company, but to point out that marketing either determines or affects almost everything a company does. If you care about making something — anything — happen in this big, wide, wonderful world of ours, you care about marketing.

In this chapter, we introduce the Internet and how it fits the needs of marketers (which means just about all businesspeople). *Hint:* You've probably never thought of some aspects of the Net the way we do, so be ready to learn something. We then justify the need for marketing on the Internet — so you can tell your boss why you're suddenly spending so much time Web surfing — and show you how to find the market for your products or services online. We finish by telling you how to use Internet marketing resources.

Marketing on the Internet

What is the Internet? It's a big mess — a mix of good and bad ideas, shaken, stirred, half-heated, and served buffet-style. More seriously, the Internet means many things to many people, but luckily we can give you a simple answer as to what it really is.

The Internet is simply an *inter-network* (which is where we get the word "Internet"); that is, a way to connect many smaller computer networks and computers with one another. The reason folks call it *the* Internet, and not just *an* internet, is that the Internet is the one network that connects most of the computers on Earth, so it deserves to be recognized as one specific thing. What makes all this connecting possible is that the Internet has a set of unifying standards. Though doing so is simplistic, you can think of the Internet as just a whole bunch of wires that carry messages that are compatible with each other.

Each different kind of content that goes over the Internet is called an Internet *service;* e-mail is one Internet service, and the Web is another. An Internet service meets agreed-on, public standards so that any computer on the Internet can access the particular service, using any of a variety of available software packages. These standards are based on *protocols,* each of which is like a language that the computers on the Internet speak when they want to transfer a particular kind of data. When people talk about the Internet today, they're not just talking about the underlying wiring; they're talking about the various Internet services and protocols that they use or have heard about.

The Internet versus the Web

In many cases, people use terms such as *the online world*, *Internet*, and *World Wide Web* more or less interchangeably. That's okay, and it reflects some interesting realities about the Internet. (Okay, you got us already: When we say "the Internet" or "the Net," we mean the whole thing — the Web, e-mail, traditional online services such as America Online, and all else that depends on being wired. Basically the online world is anything that you can connect to with your computer, or with a smaller device such as a Palm handheld organizaer, and a modem.)

At present, the World Wide Web is the most exciting place on the Internet, and your company or product Web site should be both the starting point and the linchpin of your Internet marketing effort. However, you need to use other Internet services, especially e-mail, plus traditional online services, to complement and support your Web presence. So don't be confused when you see terms such as *Internet*, *Web*, and *online services* all used more or less interchangeably; they're just different parts of the online elephant that everyone is trying to put to work for themselves.

An Internet service is different from an online service such as America Online, which has its own proprietary standards controlled by a single company, not open standards agreed on by all players like the Internet.

One such Internet service is used to transfer any kind of file between computers. This service is known commonly as *FTP*, which stands for File Transfer Protocol. The kinds of files that you can send with FTP include text documents, computer programs, graphics, sound files — just about anything. E-mail and newsgroups, each using their own specific protocols, emerged as early, text-only Internet services. The Web, another service with, again, its own protocol, became wildly popular by adding graphics to the mix. And Internet usage is growing even faster as people use small, wireless devices such as cell phones and Palm-based handhelds to communicate over the Internet. Expect to see more new Internet services, and lots of growth and change in existing ones, over the next few years.

Introducing the Web

The World Wide Web (or just *Web* for short) is the most talked-about online invention ever. Hyped beyond belief in the world press, and the force behind rags-to-riches stories like that of Netscape Communications, Inc. and hundreds of other startups, the World Wide Web is one of the great business stories of all time.

Luckily, the sizzle does come with some real steak. As we explain in detail later in this chapter, the Web has hundreds of millions of real users who collectively spend millions of hours a day surfing the Web.

Using the Web is made possible by software programs called *Web browsers,* the runaway leaders being Microsoft Internet Explorer and Netscape Navigator. In this book, we show Internet Explorer in our screen shots because it's more widely used and because, in our opinion, it's a somewhat better browser than Netscape Navigator. The things that we like best about it relate to the fact that it integrates different functions very well; for instance, searching, seeing a list of sites you've visited recently, and making your browser work well with Windows are all easier from within Internet Explorer. But Netscape Navigator is also an excellent tool, and we hope that the two will continue to compete aggressively for years to come.

From a marketer's point of view, the Web is best understood as a collection of shopping services, news sources, and glossy company reports that can be accessed by a large and fast-growing group of unusually influential people. But side-by-side with the company and product information are college course materials; personal home pages that describe hobbies, children, and pets; online pornography; political advertising; and anything else that you care to name. A glossy corporate home page is shown in Figure 1-1, and a personal home page is shown in Figure 1-2. The Web is a wild world.

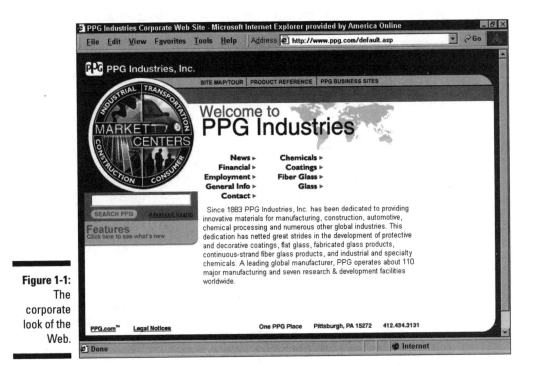

Figure 1-1: The corporate look of the Web.

Figure 1-2:
The
personal
look of the
Web.

The Web is one of the best tools ever invented for marketing. Unlike television commercials, which force themselves on the viewer, Web sites are accessed only by users who *want* to see them — your message is reaching people who want it. But to get people to stay with you, you need to use an enticing style.

Shouting above the noise on the Web is impossible. You can't get in people's faces on the Web the way you can with a television or radio commercial or even a print ad; people can click the Back buttons on their browsers to leave a site even faster than they can turn the page of a magazine or find the TV remote control hidden in the crevices of their couches. The trick is to put up a competent, easy-to-use Web site and then help the people who want to find you do so. (Speaking of making sure that your Web site is found, in Chapter 8 we show you how to get your site registered with the various search engines. Chapter 2 covers using search engines in order to find marketing-related information on the Web.)

Belying the hype about its importance, and despite the efforts of some people to spice up Internet marketing with audio and video, the Web is for the most part a *cool* medium: quiet, informative, and useful. To use it effectively, lead with information mixed with just enough graphical eye candy to attract a reader. An effective Web site works much like the *advertorial* inserts that you see in magazines such as *Time* or *Newsweek*, mixing *adver*tising and edi*torial* content. Count on the Web being an increasingly important part of your marketing efforts in the years to come. Chapters 4–8 cover the ins and outs of building and publicizing your marketing Web site.

E-mail and mail lists: Unsung online heroes

E-mail is probably the biggest single reason the Internet has become the success that it is today. A long, long time ago (about ten years ago, that is), people had e-mail accounts with services such as *BIX, CompuServe,* and *MCI Mail,* each with its own proprietary network and separate protocols. But people on each online service wanted to be able to send e-mail to friends and colleagues who used other services. To allow this interaction, the proprietary online services had to add *Internet gateways* (connections to the Internet) for e-mail to flow through from one person on one network to another person on another network. Businesses then connected their in-house e-mail systems to the Internet, and the Internet grew rapidly, setting the stage for the Web and other online resources.

Even in this age of the multimedia Web, most e-mail is still text-only, with no formatting (such as **bold**, underline, or *italics*) and no graphics; it even retains quaint and annoying problems such as a tendency to break a message up into many shorter lines. *HTML mail* is becoming more popular. HTML mail is a message that's like a Web page, with graphics and formatted text, that can be viewed by many popular e-mail clients such as recent versions of Microsoft Outlook, Yahoo! mail, and Hotmail. In both text and HTML forms, e-mail is an increasingly important communications medium and a key part of online marketing.

Like real mail (or *snail mail* — the kind delivered by the U.S. Postal Service), e-mail is a tempting channel for marketing. People have become used to getting advertising offers in their postal mail, though *junk mail* is the disparaging term for this kind of mailing, showing what many people think of it. But e-mail, unlike much regular mail, feels very special to people; they seem to take their e-mail Inbox more personally than they do their postal mailboxes. So when you're using e-mail for marketing to lots of people, proceed with caution, as we explain in detail in Chapter 10.

When you're selling on the Internet

More and more, the Internet is being used as a sales tool — sometimes for real-world products that are delivered to the customer shortly after the order, sometimes for products (such as some computer software) that are delivered over the Internet itself. To find out how to sell products on the Internet, get *Selling Online For Dummies,* by Leslie Lundquist (IDG Books Worldwide, Inc.). Then come back to this book to learn how to market your Internet-based products using the Internet to create demand for the products that sales fulfills.

The most important things to remember when using e-mail for online marketing are two dos and a don't:

- ✔ **Do make sure that you and your company respond to all e-mail you receive.** We know, it's hard to manage your e-mail Inbox; and if you put an e-mail address on a popular Web site, you can easily get flooded with e-mail. Make sure that you don't ignore any contacts or prospective customers you bring in and that they receive quick and appropriate responses.

- ✔ **Do try to ensure that e-mail sent to people outside your company is positive and informative.** Every e-mail sent by anyone in your company is, at least in part, a marketing message.

- ✔ **Don't send unwanted e-mail, such as the mass e-mail *spam* that some companies send to prospective (that is, soon to be *ex*-prospective) customers.** Most recipients ignore spam e-mail; others respond aggressively, with angry notes or even *mail bombs,* automated mass mailings back to the sender that can choke the sender's mail system.

Listservs, or *mail lists,* are one of the most useful forms of e-mail, especially from a marketing point of view. A mail list is simply a list of people who ask to be informed about a given topic. A short exchange of messages from a mail list is shown in Figure 1-3.

Both e-mail messages and mail lists are marketing tools that are best used with a light touch, not explicitly as marketing vehicles but as technical and information pieces that also support your marketing messages. We describe the effective use of e-mail and creating, maintaining, and influencing a mail list in Chapters 9, 10, and 11.

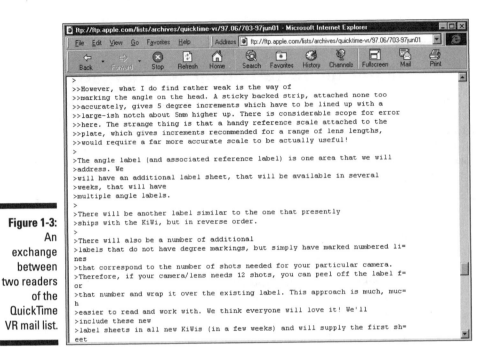

Figure 1-3:
An
exchange
between
two readers
of the
QuickTime
VR mail list.

Newsgroups: The threat and the promise

Any chance that you still remember the Pentium scare from winter 1994?
A university-based PC user tested the math functions on his new Pentium
computer and found that the Intel chip produced a series of errors in certain
unusual but not-unheard-of circumstances. Some of the people he corre-
sponded with used *Usenet newsgroups* — online discussion areas for messages on specific topics — to post his findings and ask others to repeat his
tests. They did. They confirmed the problems and then asked Intel what it
was going to do.

The folks at Intel ignored the postings at first. Then they responded, clumsily.
Then they tried to belittle the problem. Then they tried a software fix. Then
an exchange plan. Finally, Intel had to offer to recall and replace all the
Pentiums sold up to that point, a huge expense both in dollars and in damage
to the positive public image Intel had enjoyed.

Such is the exciting world of Usenet newsgroups. (Although similar forums
exist on online services and on Web sites, Usenet is the biggest, with tens of
thousands of newsgroups and millions of messages posted.) Employees of

different companies, acting with little or no supervision, slander one another and each others' products with abandon. Crazy conspiracy theories circulate, companies overreact, underreact, lie, and threaten users.

Of course, a lot of good things go on in newsgroups as well. Problems get solved, customers get reassured, people have a good time, and no one gets (physically) hurt. Figure 1-4 shows a newsgroup posting. But the potential problems are what first compel the attention of online marketers.

To effectively use newsgroups to respond to customer concerns and get your marketing information out to the world, you have to ask people in your company to see themselves as representatives of your company to the outside world, to avoid being negative, to be attentive, to be positive and helpful, and to let others inside the company know of any problems they hear about. (Imagine that anything you say in a newsgroup will be placed on the front page of the *Wall Street Journal* and you begin to appreciate the potential effect of newsgroup messages.) You can help yourself by making sure that your marketing messages are at least as well understood by people in your company as they are by the press and customers for whom you create them. You may also want to assign someone in your company to monitor postings in newsgroups relevant to your company and products. We describe in detail how to find and use newsgroups in Chapter 12.

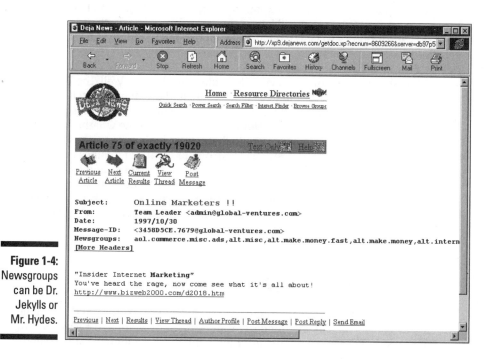

Figure 1-4:
Newsgroups
can be Dr.
Jekylls or
Mr. Hydes.

America Online and online services

Online services are the reason that so many computer users first got modems. Early modems were pokey things that ran at 300, 1200, or 2400 bits per second (bps), less than one-tenth the speed of the mighty 56 kilobits per second (a thousand bits per second, or Kbps) modems of today — let alone a cable modem or DSL connection at ten times that speed or more. But even with slow modems, a wondrous profusion of online services sprang up, each one meeting slightly different needs.

Now the world of online services has narrowed mostly to a single behemoth, America Online — which purchased its chief rival, CompuServe, several years ago — and several much smaller services. Recently topping 25 million users, America Online is far outpacing its closest rival, the Microsoft Network, and more users than all other online services combined. AOL is also the largest single gateway to e-mail, online chat, and the Web.

America Online and its remaining rivals are like a microcosm of the open Internet, with graphical presentations somewhat like Web pages, proprietary e-mail interfaces that can exchange text messages and files with almost anyone, and newsgroup-type areas for messages. Figure 1-5 shows the interface for America Online. Online services can be wonderful resources for people new to the Internet, offering services such as e-mail, free Web page hosting (that is, they'll let you put your Web page on their Web server for others to view), technical support, news, online shopping, and more.

What about using online services for online marketing? Well, the Web is a popular destination for online service users and all others as well, so you should focus your initial efforts on the Web — you reach the most people that way. Then research the major online services to see whether any of them have the kind of mix of people that you're looking for as customers. For example, CompuServe still has a strong presence of business-oriented users; with America Online, you reach more consumers at home and more Macintosh users. Barnes & Noble, for example, has an exclusive, multimillion-dollar arrangement with America Online to market and sell its books on that service. For more details on how to use online services for online marketing, see Chapter 12.

Online advertising

Online advertising is the extreme case of Internet marketing, in that online advertising is usually intended to produce an immediate and easily measurable result. In many ways, the Internet is the ideal medium for advertising, and in other ways, it's the worst place for ads.

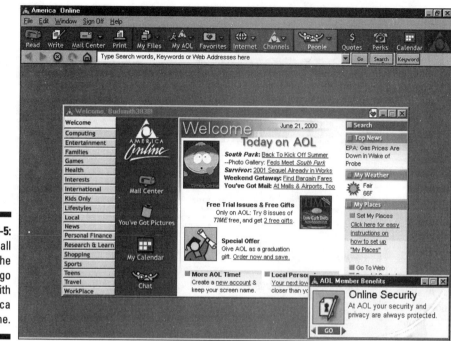

Figure 1-5:
People all
over the
world go
online with
America
Online.

There are two major kinds of Internet ads. One is banner ads, which are horizontal strips of advertising placed across the top or bottom of a Web page. Figure 1-6 shows a banner ad on AltaVista, one of our favorite sites. (One of the authors worked there until mid-2000.) The other major kind of Internet ad is everything else — larger ads, smaller ads, sponsorships, and anything else you can dream up.

The good news is that part of the impact of Internet ads, unlike any other kinds of ads, can be easily (if crudely) measured by how many people click the ad. A typical *click-through rate* on an Internet ad — the percentage of people who click the ad — is typically less than 1 percent. You can roughly measure the cost of an Internet ad campaign by taking the total cost of running the ads and dividing by the number of times that users clicked the ad, which yields the *cost per click*.

But wait, why "part of" the impact of Internet ads? Well, the cost per click captures only the actions of users who are so highly motivated by the ad that they stop what they're doing and click an ad that will take them somewhere else on the Internet. The part that's harder to measure is the impact on people who don't click, but later take some positive action because they've been influenced by the ad — just like newspaper and magazine advertising, TV, radio, bus benches, and just about every other kind of ad. This additional effect of Internet ads, sometimes referred to as "image advertising" or *branding*, is much harder to measure.

Figure 1-6:
AltaVista
doesn't ban
banners.

As an Internet marketer, you have to decide whether to promote your own ads, called *house ads*, within your own site and whether to allow others' ads on your site. You also have to decide when and how to advertise your products and services on other peoples' sites. Chapter 13 of this book is all about Internet advertising and should be a valuable resource, because the authors are among the few people who have worked on multimillion-dollar Internet advertising efforts and gone on to write about it.

Wireless access

Back when the authors were young, recording artist Thomas Dolby — now known by his full name, Thomas Dolby Robertson, and now CEO of Beatnik — released a record album called *The Golden Age of Wireless*. He was prescient but about 20 years early, because the golden age of wireless is now.

Strictly speaking, wireless access includes portable computers and even desktop computers that connect to the Internet without wires. But in common usage, wireless access refers to small-screen devices that can access the Internet, especially Palm handheld organizers and cell phones with WAP (Wireless Access Protocol) capability. Pocket PCs with screens between a portable computer and a Palm in size are threatening to become popular, too. (Yes, the authors each have at least one such device, so we know whereof we speak.)

What do these wireless devices have in common? A brief list:

- ✔ **Small screens.** A Palm system displays roughly 15 lines of about 40 characters each, less than one-fourth the text of a small laptop screen. A typical WAP phone displays about 4 lines of 12 characters each, far less than a Palm system.

- ✔ **Slow connections.** Most wireless devices have slow connections, but that's not a big problem because it takes so little data to fill up the screen. The slow part is the user trying to read a typical e-mail message or Web page off that little tiny screen.

- ✔ **High utility.** People tend to find their Palm devices and cell phones indispensable, taking them everywhere they go and trying to find new uses for them. The excitement level is much like the early days of PCs, with people interrupting meetings to beam new software from one Palm to another or look up a stock quote on a WAP phone.

- ✔ **Widespread use.** Cell phones are far more common than PCs and spreading fast. Palm devices are selling quickly and can easily be deployed throughout a company.

You may ask, like any good marketer, what's in it for you? For most marketing purposes, you probably don't need to do anything just yet. You should consider whether you can usefully and profitably deliver needed information to customers who use wireless access. It may not be cost effective to be the first on your block to jump into wireless information access, but it would be even more of a problem to not be ready to move when the time is right. Get the other elements of your Internet marketing strategy in place; then consider extending your domain to the wireless world.

Do You Need to Market on the Internet?

Because the Internet in general and the Web in particular have received so much hype, many companies have been swept up by a "gold rush" mentality, spurring them to get on the Internet and the Web quickly with the threat of otherwise missing out on the next big thing. The crash of technology stocks in early 2000 showed that too many investors had moved in to fast, with too much money, trying to make money from the Internet. If you're wary of technological flashes in the pan (and given the demise of the 8-track tape, CB radios, and CP/M computers, maybe you should be), you're excused for wondering whether you really need to market on the Internet.

In this book, we give you a lot of cautionary notes about how to avoid over-investing or foolishly investing in an online presence. A heavy investment in online marketing is not for everyone. However, we think that nearly all businesses need to have a clearly defined online strategy, including goals, methods to use in meeting those goals, and ways to measure success.

Though businesses vary tremendously in how many online customers they have — for example, most potential computer buyers have online access, but only a minority of all dog-food buyers do — the people who *are* online include most of the opinion-makers and trendsetters. Someone buying a can of soup made by your company may never see your Web site; but someone writing an article about trends in soup marketing is almost sure to try to look you up. (You do want your company to get mentioned in the press, right?) And increasingly, grocery-store managers who make decisions about what food items to stock are going to start their work by looking online, too. (And, of course, you want your company to be considered early in major buying decisions.)

So you need to market online. But just what is *marketing?* As we describe earlier in this chapter, it's the whole process of defining, promoting, and managing the sales of goods and services. The marketing cycle includes not only outbound communications such as advertising and public relations but also activities such as surveys, customer focus groups, demographic research, and so on that tell you what kinds of products to create and sell. This book shows you how to market your company, your products, and your services effectively using the Internet.

Marketing divides people up into groups called, strangely enough, *markets.* A market is a group of people who are conscious of themselves as a group and who communicate with one another on topics of shared interest that relate to your product. Gender and age groups are markets, as are people who share a profession, a nationality, or a specific role in a family — child, parent, grandparent. An important part of marketing on the Internet is knowing which markets you're trying to reach and where to find them online. This book helps you do just that.

Being online — especially having a decent-looking company Web site — is becoming as important as being in the phone book. If you want people to contact you at all, you'd better be listed. Elsewhere in this book, we explain the basics of creating a competent online presence cheaply, and we go into detail for people who want to go beyond simple *online presence* into proactive online marketing. But start by making sure that each product, service, or company that you're involved with has at least a basic, effective Internet marketing effort. The next section describes how to identify your target market as it exists on the Internet.

Finding Your Online Market

The online world has changed dramatically. More than half of U.S. households are now online, and most professional people in the United States have Internet access at work. (In general, the more purchasing power someone has, the more likely he or she is to be online.)

If you are doing marketing in the United States and you tell people that information they really want or need is available on your Web site, chances are that most of them can get to it if they want to. If you're selling goods and services to businesses, nearly all potential purchasers are likely to be online.

A great source for overall Internet data is CyberAtlas (see Figure 1-7), a service from Internet.com that's available at `cyberatlas.internet.com/`. CyberAtlas summarizes demographic and marketing data from dozens of sources into one convenient resource. For more in-depth info, just follow links from CyberAtlas to other services. Some of the information costs money, but you can learn a lot from the part that is provided free.

According to sources found on CyberAtlas and elsewhere, the population of the online world is different than the population of the United States or of the world as a whole. In deciding how much time, energy, and money to spend on your online marketing efforts, you really need to take some time to find out who's online and compare that to who you are trying to reach in your marketing efforts. Then you can size your online efforts to match your expected rewards.

Figure 1-7:
CyberAtlas
is a gold
mine for
finding
Internet
data.

Statistics are an attempt to capture a snapshot of current realities and can be accurate to within a few percentage points — or can be thoroughly biased, misrepresented, and misused. The statistics quoted here are the best freely available ones we could find. Projections are an attempt to *guesstimate* the future, and so are inherently unreliable unless you have Nostradamus on your payroll, or read tea leaves. We suggest that in your marketing planning for the online world, and indeed for all your marketing planning, you rely heavily on statistics and very lightly on projections. For a very entertaining look at the problems with projections, see the Robert X. Cringely column on the subject at `www.pbs.org/cringely/archive/dec397_main.html`.

The results from the surveys found on CyberAtlas and elsewhere are fascinating when you look at them from a marketer's point of view. In the next few sections, we describe some of these surveys' findings, which are consistent with other surveys and with our own experiences, as well as their implications for Internet marketing.

People like to talk about how fast the online world is changing, but the results from many surveys of the online world are actually becoming increasingly consistent from one survey period to the next. Though the number of Internet users is growing rapidly, with an additional 1 percent of the world's population gaining Internet access each year, the characteristics of the user population — for example, the percentage of males versus females, types of professions represented, and so on — now change little in the six months between surveys. You can make decisions about your Internet presence today with relatively good confidence that the Internet population, though larger, will still look much the same by the time you implement your decisions.

Internet user profile

What does it mean to be online? It means that you're almost certainly an e-mail user and almost as likely to be a Web user. According to the Find/SVP 1997 American Internet User Survey, about 90 percent of all people who were online at that time used the Web. Access to the Web has only improved in the succeeding years.

Following are implications of the prevalence of Web use and other conclusions that can be drawn from available surveys of the online and offline worlds.

> ✔ **More than 350 million people are online.** About 350 million people — just over 5 percent of the world's adult population — are online, according to the Computer Industry Almanac. TV and radio are far more pervasive. **Implication: The Internet has a large audience, but it is not the best way to reach a mass worldwide audience.**

✔ **The online world is still very American.** According to eTForecasts, the United States has 136 million Internet users, about 30 percent of all Internet users as of year-end 2000. Japan is next with 27 million, followed by Germany with 19 million — substantial, but far less than the United States. In addition to the United States, other English-speaking countries add another 5 percent or so of all Internet users. More important, the United States is the only major country that will have reached 50 percent Internet penetration by year-end 2000. **Implication: Online efforts that are focused first on the American market are more likely to get results.**

✔ **Europe and Asia will gradually catch up.** Again according to eTForecasts, Western Europe will surpass the United States in users and in Internet penetration in 2005. Asia will surpass both regions the same year in users, but not in Internet penetration of the population. **Implication: Be ready to make your efforts truly international over the next few years.**

✔ **The online world speaks English.** Almost all American online users speak English first; as do many online Europeans. Among Europeans, only about half think that having online information in their native language is important. (European and Asian computer users are commonly multilingual and are accustomed to using software in English or in a mix of English and local languages.) Among other languages, online users speak German, French, and Japanese (in order of popularity). **Implication: You can currently reach most of the online world with an English-only online presence.**

✔ **Online users are well off.** According to A.C. Nielsen, wired households — those in which at least one teen or adult uses the Internet — are larger, more affluent, and better educated than other households. However, as Net penetration grows, Internet households will gradually move closer to the mean. **Implication: Use the Web to reach people who are middle class and above (or even *rich*).**

✔ **Most users are ages 25–44.** Nearly a fifth of Web users are 18–24, much higher than their percentage in the population, and about one in five are between 45 and 64, less than their percentage in the population, according to Media Metrix. **Implication: Use the Web first to reach younger people.**

Some facts and implications are obvious and their effects on your marketing strategies are easy to figure out. However, other conclusions may take longer to grasp. For example, in the offline world, older people tend to be richer than younger ones; the fact that the Web has both a younger-than-average population and a richer-than-average population implies that it must have a very high percentage of people who are both young *and* rich. (Maybe that means you can think about marketing gold-plated skateboards on the Net? We doubt it.)

Working in the Online World

You picked up this book to help yourself do effective marketing work online. In this chapter, we provide an overview to help you get a handle on the online world, what the pieces are that make it up, who's in it, and how to start matching your marketing goals to it. Here are some lessons to carry forward as you use the rest of this book:

- **You have to be online.** No, not everyone is online, but the people who are online are young, well off, and influential. If you're not reaching them, you can be sure that your competitors are. You don't have to wrench your business up by the roots and replant it on the Internet; but if you ignore the online world, you do so only at your peril.

- **Start with the Web.** The Web is the big banana of the online world. Start your online efforts by planning now to create a Web site if you don't have one or to regularly update your site if you do.

- **Use other Internet services.** You have to be aware of Internet newsgroups to protect yourself from *flames* — harsh comments online — rumors, and worse; on the plus side, Internet newsgroups are a popular way for people to get product recommendations and URLs of interesting sites. E-mail is an important part of your Web and overall online strategies. Use the detailed information in this book to consider each Internet service separately and decide how best to use it.

- **Take a moderate approach.** Shakespeare's line from *Macbeth* applies to too many Web sites: "A tale told by an idiot, full of sound and fury, signifying nothing." Online users want easy-to-navigate, fast-loading, up-to-date Web sites that look good on a medium-sized screen. They want product and reference information and don't want to work hard to get it. You don't have to bet your company on a big, fancy online presence; just be competent, accurate, informative, and up-to-date.

The rest of this book shows you how to create an effective Internet marketing presence as quickly, easily, and cheaply as possible.

Chapter 2

Market Size Matters

In This Chapter

▶ Using Internet marketing resources
▶ Searching tips and tricks
▶ Finding your customers on the Net
▶ Figuring out what the competition is doing

*O*ne of the biggest challenges facing marketers is learning about target markets for products and services. How large a market may there be for a product or service? Is the market growing or shrinking? What are the people in the market like — in terms of income, affiliations, interests?

The Internet has revolutionized market research. Vast amounts of information are available for little or no cost. Research companies that used to charge a lot of money for basic information now must move up the food chain, digging out particularly hard-to-get data and analyzing it in a way that's valuable for each customer.

Competitive information used to be among the hardest kind of information to get. Now companies tell you a great deal about themselves on their Web sites. And their customers post complaints and kudos online, helping you learn their strengths and vulnerabilities — before your competitor does, if you're paying attention.

You're a step behind if you don't know how to get at the free and low-cost market information available on the Internet — and if you don't know how to use it appropriately. This chapter will get you where you need to go, fast.

See the *Internet Marketing For Dummies* Internet Directory in this book for pointers to market research sites such as Deep Canyon, Northern Light, and others.

Using Internet Marketing Resources

Using the Internet for marketing research can be very rewarding but also very frustrating. Rewarding because a lot of great data is out there. Frustrating because needed information can be hard to find: Either it's not out there, or it's so hard to track down that you can't find it in the amount of time that you have. This frustration is exacerbated because, in the search for the specific information you need, you're likely to find excellent, current, detailed information that's *almost* what you need — with no clues to help you take the one additional step needed for the exact information you just have to have.

The secret to solving this problem is found in the Nike slogan, "Just Do It." Diving into market research on the Net gets you the facts you need, to the extent that they're out there, and lets you know what facts you need to find or develop from other information sources.

You can use Internet resources to meet some of the following key marketing information needs:

- ✔ **Market definition and segmentation.** If you're involved in creating a new product, ask yourself: For what market is your product or service intended? For an existing product that has a market, ask yourself: Do other related markets that may be more profitable exist? Online resources can help you with the key marketing activities of defining and *segmenting* your market — that is, identifying groups of customers who may be interested in your product.

- ✔ **Market trends and demographics.** Is your target market growing? Shrinking? Do demographic trends support your marketing plans? Or do demographic trends undermine what you thought was a great idea?

- ✔ **Assessment of the competition.** What's the competition up to — both online and in the offline world? You can find out about both of these areas of activity online. For instance, competitors often let valuable information, such as features of upcoming products, leak out in online newsgroups.

- ✔ **Opportunities and *buzz.*** What new opportunities are coming up? Who's hot — or not? Figure 2-1 shows the news page for CNET's NEWS.COM, a leading resource for online technologynews, at www.news.com. The Internet, being the cutting edge place that it is, is full of information about what's on the horizon.

After you know where to look, you can fill much of your need for marketing information in all these areas online.

Use the Directory in this book as a starting point for creating your own list of top marketing resources.

Figure 2-1:
CNET's
NEWS.COM
has the
latest online
news.

After you find information sources for your industry, consider posting them on your Web site. Uh, why on earth would one hand such a tool to one's competition? Because it will really, really impress your customers as well as relevant press and analysts. People are used to looking to market leaders in an industry for critical industry information; if you provide that information, you position yourself as a market leader. (And if you give people an e-mail address to which they can send corrections and updates, you'll learn new info early — maybe even directly from your competitors!)

Though you may need only a modest online presence to match your offline competition's efforts, watch out for online-based competitors — either an established, well-known company that starts selling online or a new online-only venture. If you begin hearing back from your customers about new online-only competitors and you start losing sales to this new competition, your need to go online increases in a big way. To meet this kind of challenge, do everything in this book to bolster your online marketing presence and consider joining a new forum for online selling, the eCommerce forum at Tenagra. Sign up at `http://www.year2000.com/ecommerce`.

Goals and costs of online searches

The main cost of most online searches is your time.

So have a clear goal in mind at the beginning of an online search and keep your eyes on the prize. Figure out what you want to know and how long you plan to spend trying to find out. Then when that amount of time expires, stop and move on to a Plan B — which may be calling someone, sending e-mail to a knowledgeable source, or even hiring a consultant to investigate for you. Just don't allow yourself to spend hours searching for information, get distracted by the CoffeeCam Web site (`www.menet.umn.edu/coffeecam/`) that shows whether anyone has made coffee yet, and find yourself wondering two hours later why you went online in the first place.

The mantra: Know your goal, set a time limit, get in, get out. If you haven't found what you want, reassess how critical the information is — or if a similar approximation will work just as well.

Building up your bookmarks

In marketing, you can't afford to be the last one on your block to hear something — and being first gives you a big advantage over your competitors! As you search the Internet, build up a robust list of *bookmarks* (or *favorites,* as they're called in Internet Explorer) so that you can easily revisit valuable sites for new information. We suggest spending some time making your bookmarks list a valuable resource. Here are some tips:

- ✔ **Create subject folders.** Don't make your bookmarks list an unorganized catchpot for all your personal and business interests. Create subject folders for areas of interest — partners, the competition, demographics, marketing offline, marketing online, and more. Subject folders can make your future online searches much faster and more productive.

- ✔ **Create *frequency* folders.** Create folders for sites that you want to visit daily, weekly, monthly, and just occasionally. (Don't be afraid to put the same link in a subject folder and in a frequency folder.) With frequency folders, you can put your all-too-brief Web surfing time to the best use.

- ✔ **Prune early and often.** About a century ago, a candidate in a U.S. election used the irreverent catchphrase, "Vote often and early, for James Michael Curley." Although you're not really allowed to vote more than once per election, you *can* trim your bookmarks list frequently. Get rid of any links that you haven't used lately and are unlikely to need again in the near future. (If you need a link in the *far* future, you can find it by searching again.) The less deadwood in your bookmarks, the more you use them.

✔ **Share your bookmarks.** One way to elevate the level of discussion among your colleagues is to give them the opportunity to be as well informed as you are. Send your bookmarks to them as an e-mail attachment and then show them how to bring your bookmarks into their own bookmarks list. If you have people working for you or with you on a project team, sharing bookmarks is a great way to get everyone on the same (Web) page.

✔ **Know how to use your browser well.** Netscape Navigator and Internet Explorer each have their own tricks for searching, managing bookmarks, retrieving previously visited links, and more. (Because searching is so important when using the Web for online marketing, we give you some tips and tricks for searching using each browser later in this chapter.) Pick the browser you like and use it intensively.

There are several bookmarking sites that will help you manage your bookmarks. One of the best is Blink, at `www.blink.com/`.

Search tips and tricks

Ever watch a colleague working on his or her computer — and feel your jaw drop as you watch the person do something in a few keystrokes that takes you 2 to 3 minutes of mousing around? As a marketer, you should be that kind of expert when it comes to Internet searching. Here's a guided tour of how to use each of the two most popular browsers in search of key marketing information.

Internet Explorer shortcuts

Internet Explorer has a great number of cool features for marketing-related searches. This section describes just a few of them; for more, check out *Internet Explorer 5 For Windows For Dummies* (IDG Books Worldwide, Inc.). To make better use of Internet Explorer 5 for marketing searches, follow these steps:

1. **Click the grow box — the second button from the right in the upper-right corner of the browser window — to put your browser in full-screen mode.**

   Several of Explorer's features use the left 20 percent or so of the browser window area, so you need plenty of space to be able to see Web content at the same time.

2. **Click the Search button.**

   The Search strip appears along the browser's left edge.

3. **Click the Customize box.**

   The Customize Search Settings dialog box appears.

4. **Click the radio button, Use the Search Assistant for smart searching.**

   The Customize Search Settings dialog box changes to reflect customized search settings for Web pages, addresses, and other items, as shown in Figure 2-2.

5. **If you wish, click in the check boxes to choose which kinds of searches you want available and to customize the choices in each area.**

   We just use the default choices.

6. **If you wish, use the up and down arrow buttons to change the default provider in each area.**

   For instance, to change the default Web search provider, click your favorite to highlight it and then click the up arrow to move it to the top. We chose AltaVista, the most powerful search engine among the choices available, but you should use the search provider you feel most comfortable with.

7. **Click the Autosearch settings button.**

   The Customize Autosearch Settings dialog box appears.

8. **Choose a search provider from the pull-down list.**

   The search provider you enter here will be used to search from within the Address bar, saving you a step. We chose RealNames, which is specially constructed to find Web sites that match company names.

9. **Click OK to finalize your autosearch choices.**

   The Customize Autosearch Settings dialog box disappears.

10. **Click OK to finalize your search choices.**

    The Customize Search Settings dialog box disappears.

11. **Click the More button in the left search area.**

    Your Search area should look like the one in Figure 2-3.

12. **Try an address bar search: Type a search term in the Address bar and press the Enter key.**

    If you chose RealNames for your autosearch provider, you'll get either a list of choices or be taken straight to a specific page.

Figure 2-2:
Customize
your IE
search
settings for
fast and
efficient
searches.

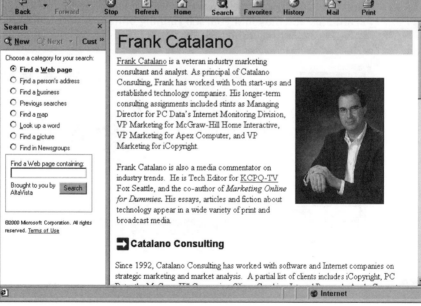

Figure 2-3:
You can
have the
best Search
box of
anyone you
know.

13. **Try a search bar search: Enter a term in the Find a Web page entry box and press the Enter key.**

    The results will appear in the search bar. An example showing the results of Steps 12 and 13 appears in Figure 2-4; we typed *gordon* in the Address bar, which caused the RealNames page shown in the figure to appear, and in the search bar, which then displayed relevant results.

All this is a lot of work but you have to do it only once, and you end up with a browser that is optimized for fast searching of Web pages, looking for people, searching in newsgroups (see Chapter 12), and more.

Netscape Navigator shortcuts

Netscape Navigator 4.7 (the most current released version at this writing) doesn't have the wide range of search customization options that Internet Explorer 5 does. The good news is that it uses the whole page for its built-in search, and you may prefer that to Internet Explorer's search-pane approach, as shown in Figure 2-4.

To learn more about Netscape Navigator, see *Netscape Communicator 4.5 For Dummies* (IDG Books Worldwide, Inc.). (Netscape Communicator includes the Netscape Navigator browser as well as e-mail and more.) If you really love searching, you may find yourself running both browsers simultaneously, just to use the most powerful features of each.

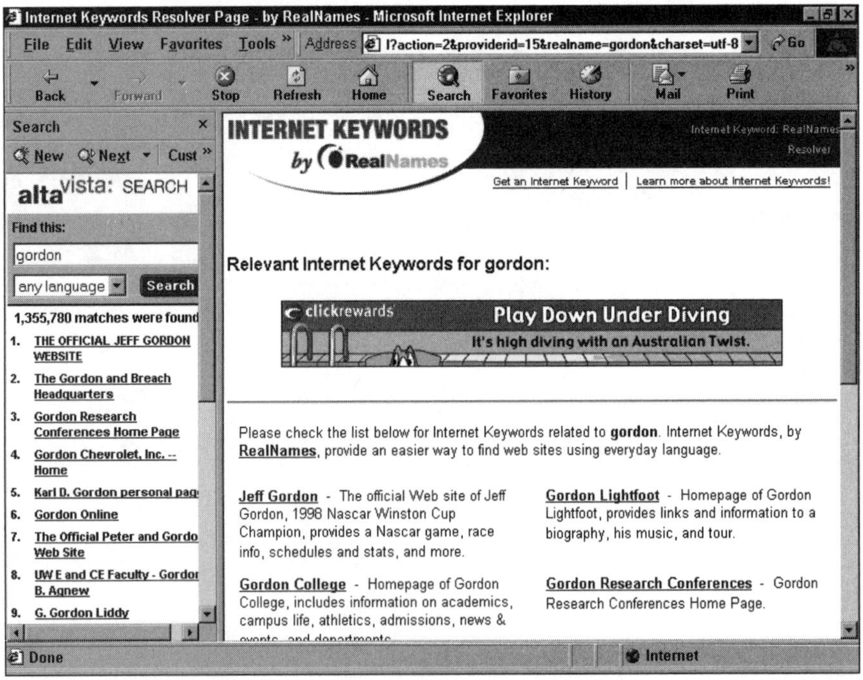

Figure 2-4: Use IE search features to untie Gordon knots.

To specify a default search engine for the Search button in Netscape Navigator 4.0 through 4.7, follow these steps:

1. **Click the Search button at the top of the screen.**

   The Search page appears.

2. **Choose the search engine that you want to use as your default from the choices in the window.**

   At this writing, the choices include Netscape, AltaVista, AskJeeves, Excite, GoTo.com, HotBot, LookSmart, Lycos, and Google.

3. **Click the check box, Keep <mychoice> as my search engine, where <mychoice> is the search engine you chose in Step 2.**

   The search engine you chose will now be the first choice whenever you click the Search button in Netscape Navigator. Figure 2-5 shows an example.

4. **To find people, click the People button at the top of your screen; for businesses, click the Yellow Pages button.**

You can download the latest version of either browser from the Web: www.microsoft.com for Internet Explorer and www.netscape.com for Netscape Navigator.

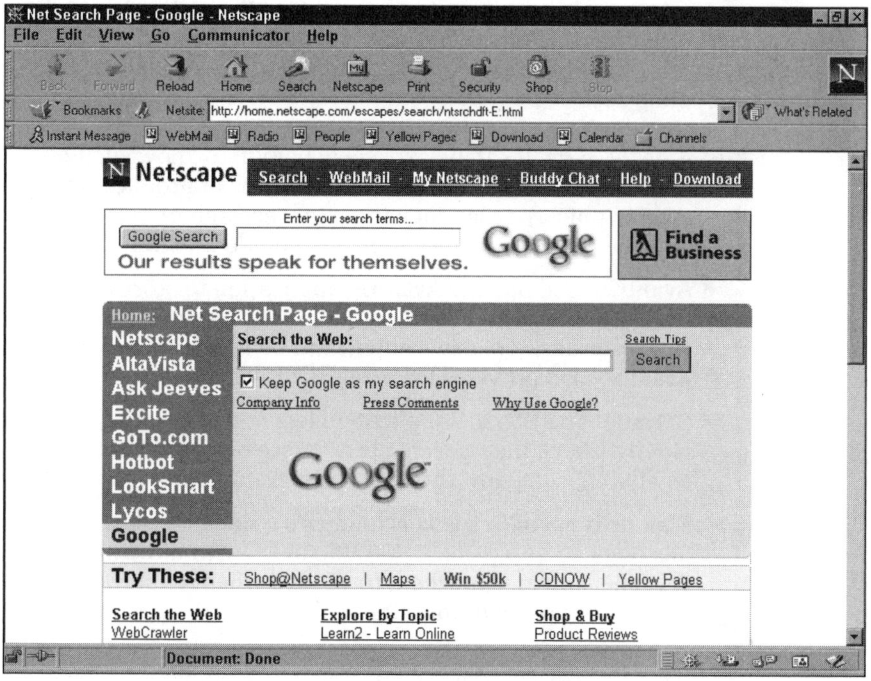

Figure 2-5: Navigator lets you get Google-eyed.

Which browser is better?

Internet Explorer and Netscape Navigator are both excellent browsers, each with their own advantages. Having used both over the years, we think that in the latest versions, Internet Explorer is a step ahead of Netscape Navigator, mainly because its search, bookmarks/favorites, history, and other capabilities are better integrated. Also, Microsoft came out with a solid 5.0 (and then a 5.5) version of Internet Explorer; Netscape skipped the number 5 and moved directly from Version 4.7 to its next release, Version 6.0. IE 5.5 is definitely better than Navigator 4.7; the jury is still out on Navigator 6.0. However, if you're already used to Netscape Navigator, stick with it and upgrade to Netscape Navigator 6.0 as soon as both it and you are ready.

Wireless Net access

Searching the Internet is a high-bandwidth activity, and it's best done with the fastest Internet connection and the biggest computer monitor you can get hold of. But you can use your wireless device to get a quick answer in between appointments or to really impress people you're meeting with (and that's all part of marketing, right?).

If you have a Pocket PC or other PC-like device with a wireless modem, you can use most or all of the tricks described previously for Internet Explorer and Netscape Navigator, and access all the sites in this book's Directory as well. If you have a Palm VII or other modem-equipped Palm device, here are a few cool applications you should download and install on your Palm for marketing use:

- ✔ **Amazon.com.** It can be extremely helpful to know what books are out there about a subject or what other kinds of products are available, or even to quickly order something for research or as a business gift. The Amazon.com Palm application lets you do that and more, fast.

- ✔ **AvantGo.** Use the free AvantGo application to store and view favorite Web sites on your Palm computer. Whenever you synchronize your Palm with your desktop, new content will be synchronized automatically. AvantGo also provides for wireless browsing.

- ✔ **E*trade.** The E*trade application lets you get stock quotes very conveniently. Check the relevant stock quote before meeting with people from any public company; then, offer congratulations — or condolences.

- ✔ **Etak traffic, Fodor's and Frommer's guides.** Getting from meeting to meeting can be a pain; Etak traffic helps with directions. Fodor's and Frommer's help with where to eat and where to stay. You can really impress people with this stuff.

- ✔ **Yahoo! People Search, USWest Dex, and the Palm address book.** Sometimes you need to reach someone, fast. Between Yahoo! People Search, USWest Dex business yellow pages, and the Palm address book that you so conscientiously maintain, you may be able to dial just the right person into your meeting, or call him or her from a cab on the way to or from the airport.

- ✔ **Weather.** The Weather Channel lets you know what to prepare for and can give you information on the one topic that's nearly always a safe way to start a conversation.

- ✔ **WSJ.com.** There's nothing more embarrassing than not knowing some critical piece of breaking news in your industry or technology area — especially if your hosts do know it. WSJ.com gives you a quick hit of up-to-the-minute business news.

You can and should use all these same sources to become well informed from your normal work desk before a meeting. But having wireless access to them is quite a bit more convenient, and far more impressive, than doing the same thing from your desktop.

Following the experts

As you search for information online, think about the process in relation to planning your own Internet presence. People with a strong Internet presence are, to a certain extent, experts. However, because the online world is still relatively new, even the experts make lots of mistakes! Here are some of the potential pitfalls to online marketing and how they relate to your own planning:

- ✔ **Hard-to-find Web sites.** The Internet has no secret search engines or places to go where all the cool people find sites easily. If you have trouble finding company or product information on the Web, lots of other people are having the same problem. Think about how you can make your own company and product information easy to find. Chapter 8 covers the details.

- ✔ **Slow-loading Web pages.** If you get frustrated waiting for someone's graphics-rich Web page to load, keep that in mind when you design your own Web site. If your site is too slow to load, people won't stick around to see it.

- ✔ **Missing information.** Often, people quickly find a site and then waste many minutes trying to find information that should be front and center. For instance, many companies don't give their real-world address or a main switchboard phone number for people who want more information. D'oh! Organize your site in such a way that it answers common informational needs, and at the very least provide numbers and addresses for more conventional methods of communication.

✔ **Unanswered criticism in newsgroups and mailing lists.** You can find some of the most amazingly harsh criticism of companies in their own company-sponsored e-mail lists and in newsgroups online — but what's even more amazing is that it often goes unanswered. Think about how to respond effectively and constructively to online criticism of your company or product. Chapters 11 and 12 discuss this issue in more depth.

✔ **Flame mail.** Many times, companies respond to criticism, whether harsh or gentle, with flame mail of their own. Think about how to get everyone who speaks for your company online to do so in a positive way. The old adage "fight fire with fire" definitely does *not* work online.

✔ **Unanswered registrations and e-mail.** Do you like it when you register at a Web site or send e-mail and never hear anything back? Visitors to your Web site won't like it if you do the same thing to them. Think about how to interact effectively with people who send you information and e-mail, and make sure that you respond to all e-mail messages and site registrations. Chapters 9 through 11 go into more detail on e-mail.

✔ **Privacy concerns.** Ever wonder what happens to that registration information you give online? So will people who register at your Web site. If they don't have a feeling of trust, they often enter false information. Think about how much information you ask people to give you online and how to tell them what you plan to do with it. And see Chapter 8 for more on privacy.

Sizing Up a Market

As we mention at the beginning of the chapter, the biggest challenge in marketing may be identifying prospective customers for your existing and proposed products and services. To us, this is the key skill in marketing: Marketers typically don't build, sell, or physically deliver products, but we do make sure that the product is the right thing for one or more groups of customers, and we do size the target group to help build the financial model for a line of business or a company. We think this is the most important activity in the entire life cycle of a company and the products and services that support it.

Identifying customer characteristics

The first step in sizing up a market is identifying your ideal customer: the type of person who would be most likely to buy your product or service. For now, set aside the wide range of people who might buy your product, and concentrate on the ideal customer. You should brainstorm with others inside and outside your company to identify this person. The first things you might look for are not strictly Internet-related:

✔ Is this person more likely to be male or female — or do you have that rarity, a truly gender-neutral product?

✔ What age group is your ideal customer? Beware if the answer to this question is always "the same age as me."

✔ What is the profession of your ideal customer? This is a crucial question, because it's relatively easy to reach people by their profession.

✔ Where does your ideal customer live? Pick one country. (In most cases, additional countries are separate marketing targets.)

✔ How much money does your ideal customer make? How much education does he or she have? Higher income and higher educational levels are related factors; consider income and education together and come up with a combined target that makes sense for both factors.

✔ What kinds of media does this person consume? Leave out the Internet for now; think about newspaper reading, magazine subscriptions, and TV and radio choices of your target customer. (Take your best shot initially; you can always fine-tune this later.)

✔ Can you guesstimate anything about your ideal customer's personality? Among the people of the same gender, age, profession, and media usage as your other ideal customers, what are the personal characteristics that differentiate people who will be quick to buy your product or service from the rest? "Smarter" or "better read" are likely to be promising answers; "plays more video games" or "more likely to visit porn sites" are generally not. But be honest, at this step and throughout the exercise.

You can do a lot of fun things here to brainstorm: Ask questions of all your colleagues, call people, role-play, free-associate, and so on. Include your non-marketing co-workers; they no doubt have valuable information you need.

Beware of the tendency to be inclusive — "boys and girls will both love my product, and after all, adults are like grown-up kids, so let's include them, too." You're trying to identify your *ideal* customer, not *every possible* customer.

The trick is to create the easiest initial problem for yourself: how to sell to the person who is most likely to love your product or service and to be quick to buy it. After you solve that problem, you can figure out how to reach people who are nearly ideal (one difference from your ideal customer), a bit less ideal (two differences), and so on.

Customer characteristics and the Internet

Notice that we don't mention the Internet once in the previous section. (We can't keep that up, or we'll have to change the name of this book to *Bud and Frank's Random Musings*, and that probably wouldn't sell as well.)

So after you've identified the real-world habits of your ideal customer, consider his or her Internet habits as well. Include the following:

- ✔ Is this person likely to have Internet access at work? At home? Low- or high-speed (DSL, cable modem, ISDN, satellite) connectivity? If you know the home country and income level of your target customer, you can get a pretty good fix on that customer's likely level of connectivity using the resources in this book's Directory.

- ✔ Is this person's professional group heavily online?

- ✔ What kind of Web sites is this person likely to visit for professional use? For personal use?

- ✔ What automated e-mail lists, discussion groups, chat rooms, and Usenet newsgroups might your ideal customer be part of?

- ✔ Is your target customer more or less likely to click a Web banner ad than most people? How about clicking a link embedded in an e-mail newsletter?

Don't get discouraged if the answers to the preceding questions lead you to believe that you can reach only a small number of your prospective customers over the Web. You need only a few. Product and service success these days is tremendously dependent on "buzz," and there's no better way to get buzz these days than through positive customer comments posted on the Internet. The small percentage of your potential customers who can be reached through any one Web site or e-mail newsletter will have a large impact on the rest.

Sizing up the competition

The Internet may be the best tool ever for sizing up the competition. You should take a 360-degree look at each of your competitors through the prism of the Internet before undertaking any serious product development or marketing effort.

Internet competitive research is so easy that you can even consider a broader range of potential competitors when you're doing your research. You want to start out, of course, with your direct competitors: those who offer a product or service that is most nearly identical to yours.

After you've looked at direct competitors, though, you can broaden your search to include less direct competition — a new, affordably priced wine, for instance, may find itself competing for mindshare with a high-end, imported beer. And you can include "psychographic competition" (yes, we just made that up) — any product or service that is targeted at the same core customers as your offering.

In looking at a competitive set, include all your direct competitors, a couple of less-direct competitors, and a couple of "psychographic competitors" (now we really like that term), including one big-budget offering and one small, scrappy newcomer or niche product. By doing so, your thinking will cover a wide range of options on how to proceed.

Here are just a few of the many ways you can use the Internet to size up your competition:

✔ **Web-based product and company information.** The Web is the first place most people go to learn basic information about competitive products and companies. Figure 2-6 shows the products page for Autodesk, a company with dozens of products, as an example of how a big company offers product information. Start your search with information on the Web and then use the contact information on a company's Web site to follow up by phone and to have more information mailed to you.

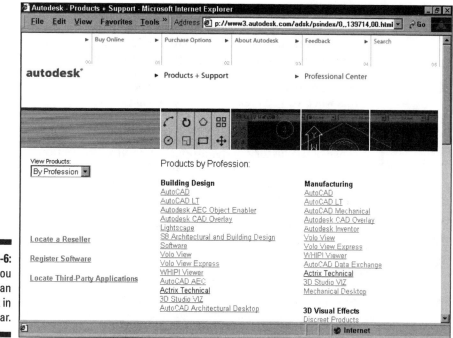

Figure 2-6:
Maybe you can use an Autodesk in your car.

✔ **Web presence.** The quickest test of a company's or product group's competence these days is to check out its Web site. One of the authors (Bud) considered working for a big company that was launching a new product to knock a smaller company out of a coveted, mid-priced market. The big company had a single Web page — with a black background and tiny type — for the "killer" product, whereas the smaller company had hundreds of pages of product information, user commentary, add-on products, and more. Bud did not take that job.

✔ **Web mentions.** How many Web sites mention the competing product or service? This is a quick, rough gauge of the competitor's impact — and a good place for you to go looking for potential customers.

✔ **E-mail lists.** Is there a newsletter or e-mail list for competing products and services? If so, subscribe! You'll learn a tremendous amount of inside information and get a good read of customers' attitudes. (See Chapter 11.)

✔ **Discussion groups, newsgroups, and chat.** Use dejanews (`www.dejanews.com`) and other search engines (see the Directory in this book) to find mentions of competing products, services, and companies. Can you connect the dots between what you know about the competition, what you can see of their Web presence, and how people "talk" about them online? (See Chapter 12.)

✔ **Internet advertising.** Net ads can be annoying when you don't need them, but it can also be very hard to find a particular ad that you badly want to see for competitive purposes. Any time you see such an ad, make a copy of the screen right away (see the Tip that follows) and then click the ad and make a copy of the page you end up at as well. Doing this will give you ideas — usually of what not to do — for your own offering. (See Chapter 13.)

✔ **Internet PR.** Use the press releases on a company's Web site to get a sense of the history of the product or service in question and of the company as a whole. This is a valuable source of information and another quick gauge of overall marketing competence. (See Chapter 14.)

To make a copy of the current screen on a Windows-based PC, just press the Print Screen button to copy the current screen image to the Windows Clipboard. Then open the Windows Paint application (by choosing Start⇨ Programs⇨Accessories⇨Paint) and paste the screen grab into Paint. You can then save it or print it from within Paint.

The good news is that you can learn a tremendous amount by doing all this; the bad news is that no one else is going to want to read 20 or more pages of your notes. Summarize the result in a convenient chart, as described in the next chapter.

Chapter 3

Your Internet Marketing Plan

. . . .

. . . .

*W*e're reminded of an old saying from the days when computers were first being used to automate business processes — no, not "If it ain't broke, don't fix it." The saying is "Computerizing a bad process doesn't make it a good process." The upshot of this cliché was that you often had to fix your existing business processes before computerizing them or you would just end up with an expensive mess.

The same holds true of your Internet marketing efforts. If you have a poor or incomplete marketing effort in the physical world, you end up with a poor or incomplete marketing effort on the Internet.

Does this mean that you can't do anything on the Internet until you fix every conceivable problem in your existing marketing effort? Not at all. But it does mean that you should keep your Internet marketing effort modest until you have your overall marketing effort operating effectively. Remember, unless you're starting an Internet-based business, many or most of your customers are not on the Internet. For most businesses, Internet marketing is the tail; the rest of your marketing effort is the dog. The dog should wag the tail, not the tail wag the dog.

So to mount an effective Internet marketing effort, you start with modest goals; meet those; add more ambitious goals; meet those; and so on. At each step in your online marketing effort, think of marketing resources you wish you had in the offline world, such as white papers, data sheets, press releases, Q & A (Question and Answer) documents, and others. By building your Internet marketing presence gradually, you give yourself the opportunity to budget for and develop traditional and Internet deliverables together and reinforce one with the other.

This chapter tells you how to plan your overall Internet marketing effort so that it succeeds the first time out. However, whereas planning is vital for the longer term, the "just do it" philosophy (also known as "ready, fire, aim") has a long and honored role on the Internet as well.

If you're really in a hurry to get something up on the Net, use Chapter 4 to start researching and securing your domain name, and Chapter 5 to create an initial Web site. This way, you'll cover your, uh, *derrière* until you can complete and implement the more thorough planning process described in this chapter.

Assessing Your Overall Marketing Effort

The first step in creating an effective Internet marketing presence is to quickly assess your overall marketing effort. Nearly every traditional marketing resource you have can be used to help make people aware of your Internet marketing effort, and almost every marketing document, ad, white paper or other resource you have or create can be *repurposed* — modified and reformatted, but with the content left basically intact — for use on the Internet. So, knowing where you stand in the offline world is vital to going online effectively.

You need to look at your current marketing effort for your company and for each part of what you sell — the products and services that are the reason for your company's existence. Then you can best decide how you want to represent yourself online.

What's your role?

If you're part of a small company or organization, you may be responsible for the whole enchilada: the company's strategy, products, services, public relations, and online presence. But in a medium-size or large company, you may be responsible for part of the picture: a division of the company, or a specific product or service.

Unless you have all the levers in your own hands, you need to work with others to create an effective Internet marketing presence and mesh it smoothly into the overall marketing efforts of the rest of the company. And even if you own only part of the picture, and even if some of the decisions we discuss here are likely to be made by others, go through all the steps in this chapter so that you can understand all the different roles and perspectives.

Assessing your current company-level marketing efforts

To effectively market your company, you need to understand its strengths so that you can use them in marketing, and its weaknesses so that you can help alleviate them through new product development, partnerships, and other efforts. Start the process of better understanding your company by asking yourself some questions:

- ✔ **What does your company sell?** List all the products and services that your company sells. (If you work for a really big company and you're taking only a small part of it online, restrict your answers to your division or product group.) Then come up with one short phrase that describes the majority of your product and service sales. Typical answers may be auto tires, computer software, or forestry services. That phrase tells you where to best direct your initial online marketing effort.

- ✔ **Who are your customers?** List the major groups of customers that you have. Your customers may include home-based professionals, home-makers, middle managers, or golfers. If you know your customers well, you already have a mental image of each type of customer, or even know one or more representatives of each type. Match up your major customer groups with the information about the demographics of the online world in Chapter 1 to identify those among your customers who are most likely to be on the Internet in large numbers.

- ✔ **What differentiates your company from other companies?** For instance, don't say you're "fast" unless your company is the fastest in some measurable way, or at least close and working on getting to Number 1. And don't say you're "customer-oriented" unless you have the customer feedback or customer service awards to prove that you are among the most customer-oriented companies in your area of business. "Largest" is good — but largest in what market? Use the information in Chapter 2 to help you do a search of your competition online to identify your own advantages. With any luck, you end up with one or two differentiators for which you have good, solid backing.

Don't be surprised if you can't come up with much that makes your company stand out from the crowd; many companies, at certain points in their existence, don't really have strong qualities that differentiate them from the competition. But if you don't have even one at this point, it's a warning signal that you're vulnerable to competitors who do differentiate — and when they do, it will be at your expense. If your company is FredCo, they'll tell customers they're "faster than FredCo," "more customer-oriented than FredCo" and, eventually, "larger than FredCo." Start thinking now about what differentiating qualities you want to develop.

A good example of the importance of differentiation is a company both of this book's authors have done work for (one as a consultant, the other as a seven-year employee): Apple Computer. Shortly after it was founded, Apple had the best-selling personal computer, the Apple II. When it lost that distinction to the IBM PC, Apple moved on to selling the easiest-to-use personal computer, the Macintosh. But when Microsoft Windows helped the PC close the ease-of-use gap, the Macintosh differentiation eroded. Lately the company has taken to selling the fastest personal computers — with its G3 series — and the most stylish, with the iMac. This new differentiation seems to be attracting some big-spending, high-end customers and helping the company return to profitability — though the jury is still out on the ultimate fate of the company.

Also assess your existing company marketing efforts. Gather together your logo, some stationery, any company-level press kits you have, catalogs, press releases, print ads, TV and radio commercials, annual reports, speeches by company officials, any Web pages you already have, and so on. Consider how you can use the text, graphics, and even audio and video clips from these resources in your Internet presence. Figure 3-1 shows the home page of a multimedia company that uses several of these elements.

Figure 3-1: Virage pushes all the media buttons.

Making it so

One common mistake at this point in the marketing process is to come up with differentiators for your company and products that you'd *like* to be true rather than ones that *are* true. So if you come up with an adjective that describes how you'd *like* to be able to present your company or products, think about how you can "make it so." If you want to claim to be the "friendliest," identify training programs and practices that you can put in place to make your company the best at customer service; for instance, auto repair companies and others talk about the checklists their personnel use to make sure that they do a complete job. Or investigate ways to improve your product to make it the fastest or easiest to use;

look at the practices of competitors who claim these differentiators now, and figure out how to meet and then beat them.

Changing what your company is doing to make its products more marketable is where marketing becomes part of a company's overall business strategy and is part of why marketing is so important to companies (and why so many company CEOs come from the marketing side of the company). In taking the time to think through these issues and make needed changes in products and services, you're making it possible to better market those same products and services in the offline world and on the Internet as well.

 If your company's image really does need a makeover, your online efforts can be a key part of that change. Consider hiring an experienced consultant to help make a concerted push in this direction. Just don't try to make over your company's image only in the online world; until that overall company image makeover gathers steam, your online presence should reflect the image your company has today.

Internet marketing at the company level

Many people who look for your business on the Internet are primarily interested in finding out where you're located, what business your company is in, how many employees you have, how much money you make (revenues), and how much you keep (profits). Having a competent, basic online presence at this company level is very important.

Company marketing, whether online or offline, is somewhat vague and amorphous. Think of those "image" advertising campaigns that you often see on TV for large companies in areas such as financial services or computing services. These ads don't sell you anything, and you may not even ever buy anything directly from the company. They just lay the groundwork for the company's more targeted marketing efforts.

The job of company-level marketing is to communicate the key attributes of your company and create a base of recognition with the customer for your more targeted, product-based marketing efforts. Such efforts also help market your company to potential investors. Figure 3-2 shows the home page of Superscape, a medium-sized company with a good understanding of how to market its company and products online.

Assessing current product marketing efforts

Your products can be physical things that people buy, or services, or some mix of the two. You may have packaged one or more services in a very product-like way by standardizing what gets done, rates, duration, and so on. If you haven't already done this, consider doing so. By packaging services in a product-like way, you make it easier for people who visit you online to compare your offerings to those of other companies.

In this book, we generally use the word "products" to refer to products, services, and mixed product/service packages. If there's a concern or an idea that's specific to services, we point that out. In general, just think of your products as whatever the specific things are that people buy from you.

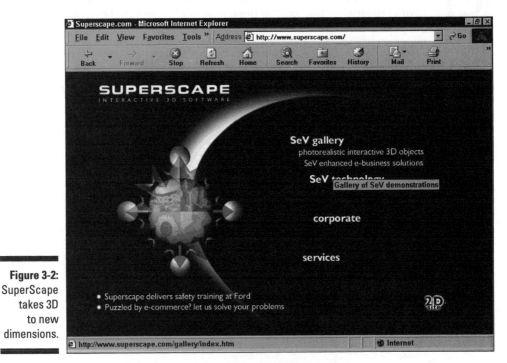

Figure 3-2:
SuperScape takes 3D to new dimensions.

Now think about what differentiates each of your products or each service that you market as a product. If you think your product is the best for its purpose, decide what "best" means for your kind of product. List ways to back up your claim to be the best if it's challenged. For instance, your product may be made of higher-quality materials, created by more experienced people, or used by customers who themselves have a reputation for doing good work. If your product is the cheapest, define the term more exactly as lowest purchase price, lowest cost of ownership, or some other aspect of low cost.

To gather evidence for your claims, use the Web and other online resources described in this book. The *Internet Marketing For Dummies* Internet Directory section of this book includes listings of not only Web sites but also discussion groups and other online resources that have valuable marketing and product information.

Wrack your brain for product differentiators and work to back them up; undifferentiated products are not only vulnerable to competition, they're hard to make much profit from. Figure 3-3 shows a Web page for a product that doesn't mention competitors directly but instead shows off its "different"iation.

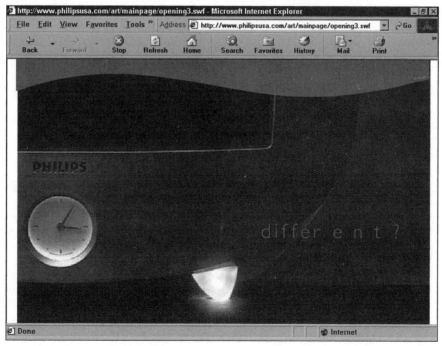

Figure 3-3:
And now for
something
completely
differen-
tiated.

Start your online product marketing effort by assessing the existing marketing materials you have for the product, but don't feel too limited by them: You're more likely to have success in remaking the image of a product online than in remaking the image of a company. A company's image usually reflects some realities about the company's history, current practices, and executive staff that are hard to change. Product images are more susceptible to "spin," as long as they're based on identifiable product realities.

Consider how to change your product's current image online. For example, you may be able to better emphasize the technical advantages of your product to the online audience than you've been able to manage offline. In marketing a lawnmower on the Internet, you can include detailed photographs and explanations of what "makes" your lawnmower so special more easily than in a typical print advertisement. If your online effort works, you can then consider how to change your offline marketing efforts.

Marketing your product on the Net

You can do a tremendous amount with product marketing on the Internet — everything from putting up a single, simple Web page to an entire Web site with accompanying efforts on e-mail, in discussion groups, on online services, and more. You can also decide whether to sell all or just a selection of your company's products online — see *Selling Online For Dummies,* by Leslie Lundquist (IDG Books Worldwide, Inc.), for details.

You can also address the fuzzy line between products and services online, as we discuss in the "Assessing current product marketing efforts" section, earlier in this chapter. Figure 3-4 shows an example of a Web site hosting service marketed as a product online — all in a single Web banner ad.

Net marketing for the sole proprietorship

What if you're pretty much a one-person band — an independent consultant, author, freelancer, or other lone wolf? Do you need an online presence? If you size the effort carefully, the answer may well be *yes.*

If you're like most people working independently today, you're probably already using online resources for communications, for developing a feeling of community with others doing similar work, and for research. If not, your first order of business is to get online. The easiest way to do this is by getting an account with an Internet service provider (ISP) such as America Online (the easiest as well as a good marketing venue for you to keep an eye on) or EarthLink, another popular ISP. Then consider getting a domain name for your business and a customized e-mail account, as described in Chapter 4.

For a small business, an online-first marketing effort may make sense for you. As an independent, most of your marketing efforts so far have probably been informal, person-to-person efforts. You probably have at least some of the basics, such as business cards, stationery, and a fax number; but mass mailings, Yellow Pages advertising, and other small-business marketing tools are probably more than you need, considering their cost.

If this is your situation, a modest online presence makes perfect sense. A small Web site describing you and listing some of your accomplishments serves as a seemingly external validator of your success and technical savvy. Unless an unusually small number of your current and potential customers or clients is online, consider creating a simplified and scaled-down but professional-looking version of the business Web presence site described in detail in Chapter 5, and use other low-key online marketing efforts described in this book.

Is your traditional marketing sufficient?

As you look at your company and product marketing materials, you may notice that some marketing pieces you'd like to have are missing. This is normal; just about everyone can use a brand new or updated data sheet, marketing plan, Q & A, white paper, or what have you.

If you find that your overall marketing effort is lacking — if you can't identify strong company and product differentiators and see those reflected in a reasonable number of marketing materials for each of the audiences you need to reach, then you have a bigger problem than an online marketing effort alone can solve. The best way to jump-start online marketing is by borrowing logos, layouts, ad copy, and other resources from your existing marketing materials — if those are missing, the online marketing effort becomes much more expensive and difficult.

If this case sounds familiar, you need to create an overall marketing plan now. *Marketing For Dummies,* by Alexander Hiam (IDG Books Worldwide, Inc.), can be a real help. Then decide on either a physical reality-first or an online-first plan. If few of your customers are online, create a limited online presence to cover yourself while you build up your traditional marketing portfolio. But if many of your actual or prospective customers are online, consider developing a reasonably strong online marketing presence first and then extending it to print, broadcast, and other media. In either case, working on your online marketing can be a catalyst for creating a strong overall marketing effort.

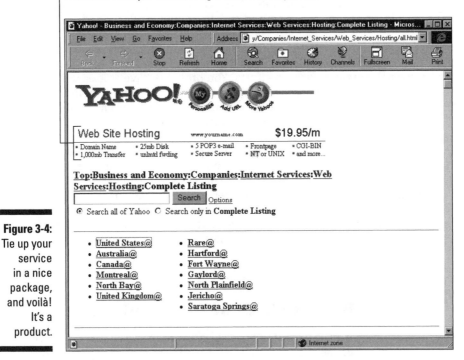

A consise example of marketing a sevice like a product

Figure 3-4:
Tie up your
service
in a nice
package,
and voilà!
It's a
product.

Matching Your Customer Base to the Online Community

You've looked at your existing marketing effort, probably finding a few holes in the process, and, we hope, getting some new ideas about what your company's image is, how each of its products and services should be marketed, and what traditional marketing resources you need to develop. You're also probably pretty excited about creating or improving your presence on the Internet. Good, because now it's time for your first reality check.

The reality check is simply this: How many of your current and potential customers can be reached via the Internet? Use Chapter 1 to get a good idea about the big picture of who's online and discover how to research how many of your customers are online already. Unless your customer base includes groups that are online in high numbers, consider creating a modest initial online presence and then improving your traditional and Internet marketing efforts in tandem.

You need to carefully research your customer base — which can mean anything from simply asking all your own contacts in your industry to commissioning a formal study — to find out how many of your customers use the Internet. Ask your customers what they expect from you online and whether they are frustrated or disappointed with your lack of an online presence. Ask them what Web and other online resources they find useful and how they use them. Don't be surprised if what they want isn't "gee-whiz" multimedia stuff but rather solid information about your company and industry that they can use in their work.

Here are some of the products and services that definitely require a strong Internet presence to adequately reach their customer base:

- ✔ **Computer products.** Absolutely anything having to do with computers must be represented on the Internet. Computer users and computer professionals want and expect to find computer-related products and services online.

- ✔ **Educational products.** Almost anything having to do with education is a good subject for an online effort. Not only is a large proportion of students online but so are many of their parents. Students and parents both are receptive to college, university, and private school recruitment, educational CD-ROMs, books, tapes, you name it. Figure 3-5 shows an online site for education products.

- ✔ **Products marketed strongly to professionals.** Computer and educational professionals are the strongest professional presence online but are followed closely by other kinds of professionals. And although people often surf the Web aimlessly at work, they feel good about surfing sites that contain information or products helpful to them in their work.

- ✔ **Any product with a high-tech edge to it.** Having the latest high technology in your products is an important way to create highly differentiated (read: highly profitable) products, and many people strongly associate high technology with the Internet. You need a forceful online presence to support your claim to be on the technical cutting edge, and to reach customers who are receptive to these kinds of claims.

Match up your customer profile against who's online not only for your company as a whole but also for individual products and services. You may find that some are better candidates than others for early development of your Internet presence.

You may have less need to market on the Internet if your customers are of lower income, aren't American, work outdoors, are craftspeople, or are otherwise unlikely to own or use computers. If you ask around, whether formally or informally, about which of your customers are on the Internet and get little response, you can probably build your online presence more slowly.

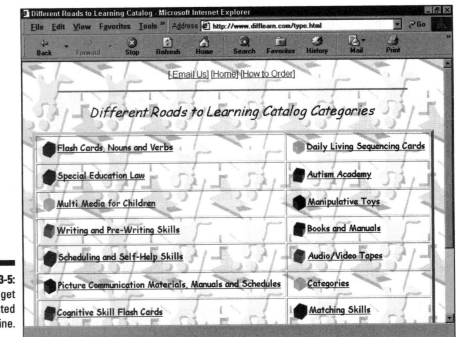

Figure 3-5:
Time to get
educated
online.

What if my customer base is typically not wired?

Maybe comparing your customer base to the online community described in Chapter 1 shows that not many of your customers are online, leading you to think that you don't need to do any marketing on the Internet at all. However, we can present three strong arguments against doing nothing.

Well, first

First, remember that almost any business has potential and current customers on the Internet, and that press, analysts, investors, and other influencers are online heavily. This reality argues for at least some online presence. The tricky point here, though, is that you aren't likely to impress these people with an Internet presence that's disproportionately large compared to your size in the physical world. What they do need to see is an up-to-date, simple, up-to-date, competent, up-to-date, complete, Internet presence. Did we mention that these people will think poorly of you if you don't keep your Internet presence up-to-date?

What about handhelds?

The handheld device market is like the World Wide Web was in the mid-'90s: everyone's talking about it but only a few million people so far are doing it. And those few million people are split among multiple platforms: the Palm OS, the Symbian handheld platform popular in Europe, the Pocket PC platform, and Wireless Application Protocol (WAP)-enabled cellular phones. Developing content for viewing on these platforms is hard because of the wide range of different development targets and the tiny size of the screens. For most businesses, the best idea is to market to the personal computer audience first and then size the handheld market as it applies to your business.

And second

The second reason you need at least a basic online presence — no matter what business you're in — is that the current limitations on who's heavily wired are unlikely to last. As your existing and potential customers get wired, you don't want their first cyberspace experience to be that of getting a bad impression of you from your hard-to-find, out-of-date, or even completely missing Web site. Get your feet wet on the Internet today so that you can be ready to dive in fully tomorrow.

And finally, third

The third reason you need some Internet presence is the unpredictability of marketing in general and Internet marketing in particular. Many companies have failed in their Internet objectives, whereas others have succeeded beyond their wildest dreams, and quite a bit of unpredictability remains as to who will and who won't do well. Keeping your initial effort modest reduces the risk of failure, but getting some presence online quickly improves the odds that you can build it into a big success.

What if my business is local?

How much should you invest in your online presence if you operate only in a limited geographic area? Internet users have access to a growing number of local sites or services such as MapQuest (www.mapquest.com) that pinpoint local resources. However, locally based Internet sites face heavy competition from the Yellow Pages, local newspapers, and word of mouth. Local businesses may have difficulty deciding how much effort to put into a new, globe-circling medium that can reach tens of millions of people, 99.99 percent of whom are guaranteed not to be within driving distance of your store.

However, if you're in an area with high Internet usage, consider charging ahead. Size your effort to match a realistic estimate of the number of visits you're going to get from people who are locals and therefore potential customers. And take extra steps to publicize your online presence in local media and in Web sites, discussion groups, and so on that have a strong local flavor. Figure 3-6 shows a Web page from Sidewalk, CitySearch's Web service for local information. Services like this are increasing quickly in impact. CitySearch is local — and global.

To find an initial list of local resources, go to www.yahoo.com and click the Regional link to find resources in U.S. states, cities, and foreign countries.

What if my business is global?

If your business is outside the United States or has customers sprinkled around a continent or the entire globe, don't believe the hype: Study your local situation carefully before charging ahead. For instance, several Spanish-language sites have geared up to go after the Latin American market, only to find too few actual people in Latin America spending much time on the Internet. There's a happy ending in this case because the sites found a large and receptive audience among Spanish-speaking U.S. users. But a lot of time and money would have been saved if these sites had been better planned from the beginning. Don't make the same mistake yourself.

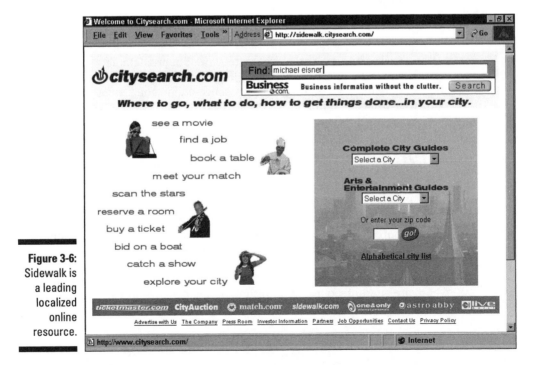

Figure 3-6:
Sidewalk is a leading localized online resource.

The other special consideration for most non-U.S.-centric businesses is the language barrier. You may have several languages among your customers, but how many sites can you afford to build for each? Again, study the situation. You may find that one or two languages are spoken at least part of the time by your otherwise highly polyglot clientele. Consider translating key content into multiple languages but keeping your main site monolingual or bilingual.

Assessing Your Competitors' Net Work

A key step in deciding on how big an Internet marketing effort you want to mount is to assess the online presence of your competitors. You have no doubt already encountered your competitors' online presence in several ways: visiting their Web sites, seeing their press releases, business cards, and other traditional marketing materials with pointers to their online presence, and hearing from your customers and colleagues what they've seen your competitors doing on the Internet. (If none of your direct competitors has an online presence, look at similar businesses that operate in a slightly different geographic area or business area.) Also take a look at the Net marketing presence of suppliers and customers, any industry or trade groups that your company is part of, and others who you work with. Use the categories in Yahoo! (www.yahoo.com) to find larger and more established industry segments; for newer and smaller industry areas, use a fast, wide-ranging search engine such as AltaVista (www.altavista.com).

Creating a comparison chart

Looking around and gathering impressions is very valuable, but the thing that's really going to help you is to compare and contrast the Internet efforts of your most direct competitors with your own. Doing so is not as hard as it sounds; all you need to do is make a simple chart briefly describing key aspects of your competitors' online presence.

The best way to create such a chart is to restrict it to quantitative aspects: questions that can be answered by a yes or no, a number, or a short, factual phrase. Stay away from qualitative judgments, such as "lousy" or "slow" or "beautiful," for now. Making objective decisions is most easily done when they are based on objective facts, and working through your findings with others is much easier if you initially stay away from value judgments and stick to "just the facts, ma'am," as Jack Webb used to say on "Dragnet." An example of this kind of chart is shown in Figure 3-7.

FEATURES	MAP CENTRAL	MAPS BY THE BEACH	OUTDOOR CLUB'S MAP NOOK
Web site	No	Yes	Yes- page on Outdoor Club's site
Active in newsgroups?	No	No	Yes (Outdoor Club, occasionally Map Nook)
Online mail list	No	Yes	Yes- for Outdoor Club, not Map Nook
Online service forums	CompuServe forum	No	AOL area for Outdoor Club
Web URL	x	www.beachmaps.com	www.outdoorclub.com/ mapnook
Number of Web pages	x	12	Dozens for Outdoor Club, one for Map Nook

Figure 3-7:
Map out a competitive comparison.

Here's one way to create such a chart. Take a large piece of paper and create four columns — a narrower one for features of the online presence, and three wide ones for your top three competitors. (You may want to add more later, but start with three to help you focus.) Then create rows for key aspects of their online presence. The first few rows should be simple ones that you can fill out with check marks for yes, *X*s for no, or a number or short phrase. Examples include Web site (yes/no), active in discussion groups (yes/no), has customer automated e-mail list for customers to subscribe to (yes/no), online service area (yes/no).

The most important part of your online presence, and the most expensive part to develop, will almost certainly be your Web site. So go into some detail on your competitors' Web sites. Create rows for different aspects of the Web site: Web URL, number of pages (estimate if the site is large), e-mail address for feedback, sales locations listed, online selling, uses graphics, uses multimedia, has advertising.

Don't get caught up in an arms race to have the biggest, most expensive Internet marketing presence. Chapters 5–7 discuss creating an appropriate Web presence for your company and its products and services.

Now create a new row and, for each competitor, list the major areas of that competitors' Web site. Areas may include About the Company, Products, News, Technical Support, and Feedback. If you're feeling energetic, put the number of Web pages in each area in parentheses after the area name.

Finally, create one more row for what you've been itching to write down this whole time: your opinions, or more formally, your *qualitative observations*. Note one or two plusses and one or two minuses that stick out for each competitor — things such as whether the site has complete descriptions of products, fast- or slow-loading pages, well-written text, and most vital of all, whether the site is up-to-date. Note whether a site has major categories missing or present compared to the others. You can also note whether the site is ugly or attractive — but don't be surprised if others disagree with this or any other qualitative assessment that you make. Don't feel that you have to write a lot about every competing Web site; if a site is competent but not spectacular, you may have nothing to say here.

If you are really concerned only about a specific product, you may still find performing the company-by-company comparison described in the previous few paragraphs very valuable; the company online presence often forms the base for the product online presence. You can easily use the same exercise we describe in the previous few paragraphs for each product you want to market. Create categories that reflect the features and appropriate marketing resources for the kind of product you're interested in; then assess each competitor in those categories. You may find, as we have in the past, that some products have an entire site, e-mail contacts, mailing lists, and more, whereas a head-to-head competitor has only a single page and no contact information. Guess who's going to impress — and keep — customers more?

After you're done, step back and take a look at the overall chart. Think about changing the comparative points for clarity or adding one or two competitors for completeness. Consider recopying your chart on a clean sheet of paper or recreating it in a word processor or spreadsheet program for neatness. Show it to a few colleagues and see whether they understand it.

Using your completed chart

At the end of this exercise, you probably have some bad news and some good news. The most likely bad news is that at least one of your competitors is doing much more on the Internet than you are. If you're anything like us, seeing just how much your competitors are doing on the Internet can make you feel very nervous. As you consider the cost and effort to match or exceed your competitors' efforts in the online realm, you may find yourself in need of a stiff drink, a walk in the park, or the rest of the day off.

The likely good news is that the analysis you just did to create your chart gives you a tremendous amount of information and many good ideas for your own online presence. The areas (discussion groups, e-mail, and so on) of the Internet marketing universe that your competitors do (or don't) use, the size of their Web site, the areas they cover, and the overall impression their online presence gives are invaluable touchstones for you to use in planning your own effort. A chart like this is also a great motivator for getting your colleagues to understand the importance of creating a presence on the Internet and getting management to approve the money and personnel you need to make it happen.

Sizing up your Net-only competition

Take time to search the Web for Web-based competitors — competitors that complete most or all of the sales cycle online. If you're a local plumbing company, this is not such a big concern; no one can fix a leaky sink over the Web (although several Web-only companies now can recommend and hire plumbers on a customer's behalf). But if you're a retailer, wholesaler, or consultant, you need to know just how much your current customers can accomplish without ever leaving their keyboard. Figure 3-8 shows the Web site of Amazon.com, the Web-based superstore that has posed a significant challenge to retail bookstores everywhere without ever opening a storefront of its own.

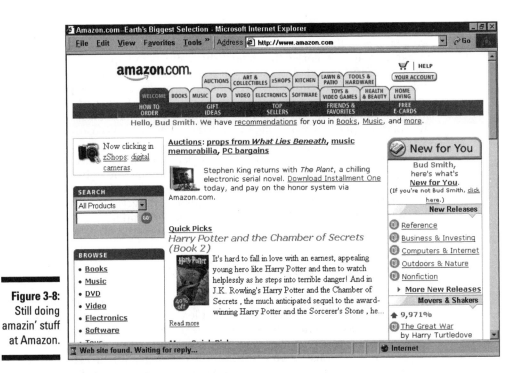

Figure 3-8:
Still doing
amazin' stuff
at Amazon.

One way to find online sales sites is to search for keywords associated with online sales. One good keyword is the word *order*. If you use the Boolean operator + to combine the category you're interested in with the word *order*, you're likely to find Web pages for online sales. For instance, if you use the search engines described in Chapter 2 to search for "books + order," you're likely to get a link to the order page of Amazon.com.

If you have significant online-based competition, people can browse, buy, and specify delivery options online, all without actually going anywhere and all without giving you a second thought, or any chance for the business. Such competition will only grow in the years to come. Consider separately investigating and evaluating Web-based competitors. You may decide to launch an Internet sales effort yourself.

Sizing Your Internet Marketing Effort

If you've worked your way from the start of the chapter to this point, you've assessed your overall marketing effort, matched your customer base against who's online, and analyzed what your competitors are doing online. This work, combined with the ongoing Internet hype we're all subjected to, may induce a certain degree of panic on your part.

Take a deep breath and relax. It's still early in the Internet game, and only a small fraction of American commerce — let alone commerce in other countries — actually occurs on the Internet.

It's too late to get in on the first round of Internet mania that has gripped the world's media over the last decade. You can, however, have the advantage of being able to benefit from the lessons learned as fortunes were made and, just as often, lost in the initial bubble of online enthusiasm. You may well be better off launching a sustainable and steadily growing Internet presence now than if you had gone through the booms and busts that have occurred to date.

So now it's time to size the initial online presence that you want to achieve — the base from which you build in the years to come. Grab the comparison chart you made in the previous section — if it's a bit out-of-date, you may want to visit those sites again, or perhaps do another search for any other competitors. Remember that your competitors are the benchmark against which your customers, the trade press, and your management and shareholders or other investors measure you. Then make an initial decision as to where you want to be on the continuum of online innovation:

- ✔ **Innovator.** Maybe you want to be an innovator online. This means that, compared to your competitors, your online presence is larger, more expensive, and has more gee-whiz features. As an innovator, some of your online efforts are expensive failures; others succeed so well as to get you noticed outside your industry and your traditional markets. You're the first in your segment to introduce selling over the Internet, and you work to increase your online sales even if they aren't initially very profitable. You spend significant amounts of money in the offline world to advertise your online presence, and you try to partner with other leaders.

- ✔ **Fast follower.** One smart way to play the innovation game is to be a *fast follower*. This means that you watch your competitors' efforts for good ideas and adopt them while avoiding expensive mistakes by letting others make them instead of you. If you do this right, you spend less on Internet marketing than your most aggressive competitors and, unlike them, every dollar you spend counts. You keep a healthy balance between your Internet-based and traditional marketing efforts.

- ✔ **Competitor.** Another reasonable approach is to create an online presence that is in the middle of the pack. You may occasionally do something innovative, but in most areas, you wait for solid evidence of success or failure before adding new directions to your online effort. Your expenditures are low; their impact high. Your traditional marketing efforts take priority over your Internet efforts.

✔ **Conservative.** You may well decide that your business needs are best met by having a minimal Internet presence for now, letting competitors take the lead and instead spending your marketing money in other areas. As an example, Figure 3-9 shows the single Web page that Cosmo Software, a former division of Silicon Graphics Inc., initially put up for Cosmo Worlds, a 3D authoring package. It simply announced the product's presence. (Subsequently, the site was greatly expanded.) Or you may not spend much on marketing at all, preferring to focus your efforts into other areas of your business. In this scenario, you spend very little online.

Your position on this continuum of online innovation may or may not be tied to how innovative you are in other areas of your business. You don't necessarily need to be a top-flight technical innovator with your products to take a leadership position in your online presence. Do avoid causing confusion among your online visitors, though. If your overall company culture and marketing efforts typically take a conservative approach, don't suddenly go wild in your online marketing approach. If you do decide to be innovative, do it in a lower-key way, with a classy overall design and without getting in customers' face too much in the look or content of your site. Lead in the useful content and features of your site rather than in the use of advanced Internet technologies or whizzy design features.

What if they're not online?

Throughout this book, we advise a conservative approach to building your online presence, mostly because we've seen so many overdone Web sites that went up with incredible speed, enthusiasm, and expense and then quickly turned into liabilities because of poor initial design and infrequently updated content.

Another reason for a conservative approach is that getting going from a standing start takes time. If one or more of your competitors already have a complete, competent online presence — or, worse (for you), an exciting, innovative, technically excellent Web site and solid use of other Internet services — and you have little or no presence online, you need all the time and money you can muster just to catch up.

On the other hand, if your investigation of the competition reveals that your competitors are not online or that they have limited or poorly executed online presences, you may want to roll the dice and make a stronger initial effort — one that clearly *beats,* not just meets, the competition. Though the biggest bubble of Internet hype occurred a few years ago, people continue to be fascinated by the ever burgeoning online world. If you can make a concerted effort that results in online leadership, you benefit twice: once by the positive impression you make and again by the additional impression you make when you trumpet your Internet leadership in the offline world.

Don't bet the farm (or the company) on this kind of effort; your competitors can always surprise you with a sudden online makeover while you're working on your own, and the positive marketing impact you make with your Internet marketing effort still takes time and work to translate into sales. But business is often about taking some chances, and the opportunity for Internet leadership within your business segment may be a chance worth taking.

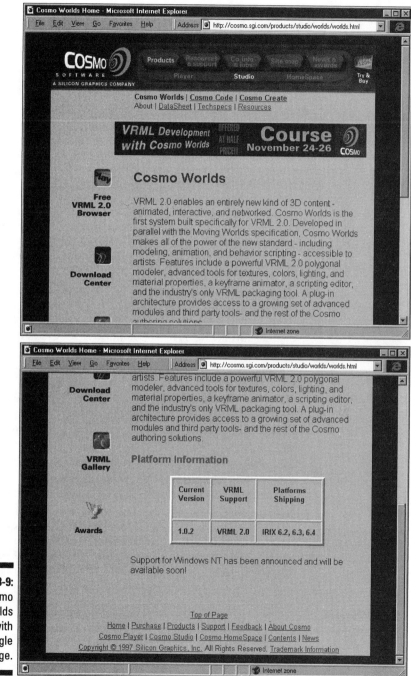

Figure 3-9:
Cosmo
Worlds
started with
a single
Web page.

Creating a Written Plan

Before investing the time and money to create and maintain your online presence, you need to create at least a brief written plan. Companies vary in how much they depend on such plans. Your company may require you to submit a highly structured, well-researched plan to justify your project to senior management before you can spend a single dollar. Or you may be encouraged to just "throw something up on the Internet and see what sticks." If possible, take a middle course and write a relatively brief plan that covers at least the following elements:

- ✔ **Marketing assessment.** Quickly describe your current marketing goals and resources and the state of your current Internet marketing effort relative to how many of your current and potential customers are on the Internet. Include any feedback you have received about your current Internet presence. This stuff should be lying around your office if you already went through the "Assessing Your Overall Marketing Effort" section in this chapter.

- ✔ **Competitive assessment.** One problem businesspeople have in working with the Internet is that they are often thinking about profit and loss while the Internet types are talking about hits per day and other technical measurements. A brief competitive assessment translates the online issues into terms that businesspeople can understand, such as who's ahead and who's behind. If you have already worked through the section "Assessing Your Competitors' Net Work" in this chapter and created the comparison chart suggested there, you're in business; if not, now's your chance to do so.

- ✔ **Goals.** Specify your goals for your initial online effort, framing them in terms of your customers' needs and competitive comparisons as much as possible. Use concrete terms such as the names of the major sections you plan to develop for your Web site, the specific online service forums you plan to monitor, any newsgroups you plan to create, and so on.

- ✔ **Resources.** Even if you are considering doing most or all of the work in-house, get bids from outsiders so that you can get a reality check on your internal estimates. Wherever you are using internal resources, make sure to consider what other work will be deferred or not done while employees are busy working on the company Internet presence. In many cases, you are best off planning to use external resources.

- ✔ **Budget.** List the budget figures you have developed, or create a budget now. Specify that Internet marketing is a crucial enabling factor for your company's sales and relate the proposed Web investment and the number of people it is intended to reach to the rest of your company's marketing efforts. If about 10 percent of your target audience is reachable via the Internet, for instance, you can build toward having about 10 percent of your total marketing budget devoted to the Internet effort. If you need to get into more detail about defending your budget, see *Marketing For Dummies,* by Alexander Hiam (IDG Books Worldwide, Inc.).

✓ **Time frame.** Specify a time frame for completing your initial online effort. Allow more time than you at first think necessary; the more work you expect to do in-house, the more generous you need to be with your schedule. Stage the effort to allow control by setting several smaller deadlines, rather than just one big one, and allow time for testing before you take the online resources you create public. Consider using a chart developed in a word processing or spreadsheet program, or specialized project planning software such as Microsoft Project, to make deadlines and progress visible.

✓ **Maintenance.** Your online effort doesn't end just because you finish the design and load the pages up to your Web server. As part of your plan, specify what your Internet presence requires in terms of ongoing maintenance and updates, including: responding to e-mail that arrives at your Web site; updating Web site content; monitoring discussion groups and online service forums; managing and responding to questions on an automated electronic e-mail list (such as LISTSERV, if you have an e-mail list); and more. Don't be surprised if maintenance of your online presence ends up taking longer than you expected — if you don't prepare, it probably gets done poorly or not at all.

✓ **Next steps.** If someone in your organization is pushing for a much bigger online presence, and that someone wants it fast, he or she may be disappointed when seeing your carefully staged, conservative plan. (In fact, if no one who sees your plan is disappointed in it, it may well be overambitious.) Here's where you can mollify any critics by pointing out what you can do in the future, after you've completed, deployed, and proven the value of your initial online efforts. (Don't be too blue-sky here either, though; you may be called to account for what you write here someday.)

As you work on the plan, continue gathering information. Keep an eye out for changes in competitive efforts and in customer requests for an online presence. If your online presence is successful, you may receive a great deal of e-mail from potential and current customers — all of whom expect an answer. A smallish company or medium-sized product group may find itself receiving enough e-mail to require a full-time person just to respond to it. See Chapters 9 and 10 for information on how to manage the flow of e-mail, and don't put an e-mail address on your Web site until you're ready to respond to the messages you get.

After you create a plan, you have every right to be proud of yourself. You've done a lot of work and set the tone for your company's online presence for years to come. But you still have a few concerns to address:

Who owns your online presence?

The answer: marketing. The computer people may be responsible for running the server and providing you with reports — and you need them on your side, and there's no reason to alienate anyone involved in the overall online effort. But at the end of the day, the marketing department needs to be responsible for the look, feel, content, or other aspects of your online presence. Also, as we recommend throughout this book, you should consider outsourcing tasks such as running your Web server anyway; it's much easier to control and reduce costs, and to add and remove services, through an outside vendor than through people in your company.

If your company, division, or product group already has an online presence through the efforts of other departments besides marketing, then you may have to work with the other departments for now (and slowly bring them around to letting marketing call the shots). This has to be backed up by money, of course, so start planning now how to have marketing pay most of the bills.

Even with marketing running the overall show, others in your company are part of your online presence whether you like it or not. Every e-mail message sent by an employee and (especially) every discussion group comment made by an employee using a company e-mail account are also marketing messages from your company. See Chapters 9–11 for information on how to get everyone on the same page to support — or at least not undermine — your company online marketing messages.

✓ **Justifying the cost.** Even the senior manager who was initially most enthusiastic about going online may wince when she sees the budget. Marketing expenditures are always hard to justify; after all, they're expenses that don't immediately or measurably increase sales or decrease expenses. You'll be pressured to cut the budget or to do more internally and less with outside resources. Use the competitive assessment to defend the need for your online presence; if someone wants to cut expenditures, show exactly where your online presence suffers if you do so. To support using outside resources, point out that using experienced, accountable outsiders reduces risk.

✓ **Riskiness.** As the old saying goes, "making predictions is dangerous, especially when they concern the future." Your plan is likely to be more optimistic and have more risk in it than you realize. An online development effort is somewhere between a major documentation effort and a software development effort in terms of the difficulty of predicting completion dates and the possibility of abject failure. (Robert Brooks claimed in *The Mythical Man-Month* that half — yes, half — of all major software projects fail. It's not that they come in late or go over budget — that's almost routine — but that they simply fail. The more complex your Web site, the more like a software project it is.)

✔ **"But you said."** A problem that your plan may cause is a phenomenon we call, "But you said," after something that kids like to say to parents. The online efforts that you propose in this plan will likely be taken as firm promises rather than reasonable projections. If you try to modify your goals during the project, people may be disappointed and upset and question your character, integrity, and maybe even ancestry. Use some qualifiers in the plan, such as "expect to," "as resources allow," and "as competitive comparisons indicate," to help manage this problem if it occurs.

When you complete your initial plan, don't show it to anyone. (If a group has worked on it, keep it within the group for a day or two.) Get a good night's sleep and then take another look at the plan. Trim it back. Adjust the plan so that it contains only the core elements needed to meet your customer and competitive goals. Delete or defer everything that's not critical to scoring an early success in the online world. Doing this reduces the amount of money you're asking for, greatly increases your chances of success, and thus increases the odds that management will trust you with more money later to expand your online presence as needed.

Creating an online marketing plan makes more sense if it's done while referring to an overall marketing plan. However, you may not have one, or your overall marketing plan may be out-of-date. If you need to have all your ducks in a row before proceeding, create or revise the overall marketing plan first; if it's more important to get going on your online presence, create or revise the overall marketing plan after the online marketing plan is done.

Implementing Your Internet Marketing Plan

If you've done most or all of the steps we suggest in this chapter to this point, congratulations! You're much better prepared to succeed online than many others who've just rushed in, spending time or money without a clear plan or goals.

The rest of this book shows you the nuts and bolts you need to implement each part of your online marketing plan — designing and building your business Web site, using e-mail and automated e-mail lists, and more. Use this book and, if needed, other resources that focus on each element of your online presence.

Should you start an Internet-based business?

In your planning process, or at the end when you show your plans to others who haven't worked on them, you may be asked whether selling online will be a part of your project. This is the wave of the future, but it's not really a marketing issue, even though one could say that online selling is best built on a base of successful online marketing. The *mindshare* (meaning, basically, awareness) that you build with your online marketing effort can be converted into *market share* for your online sales work.

Plan your online sales effort as a separate business with income, expenses, and (you hope) a profit. See *Selling Online For Dummies,* by Leslie Lundquist (IDG Books Worldwide, Inc.), to get started with online sales.

If you're working with others to implement your online marketing presence, ask them regularly for progress reports and for demonstrations of work in progress. (The squeaky wheel gets the grease, and the colleague or customer who's asking about a project regularly is the one who gets more time and effort devoted to it.) Return the favor for them: Track your own and others' progress to quickly identify any elements that are exceeding the time or money allotted to them.

As you implement your Internet marketing plan, keep a record of departures you make from it. You may find that the Web site, for instance, needs to be larger than expected; or the first time you actually see the prototype running on a Web browser, you may decide that the look needs revamping, thereby adding expense. You may also decide to cut back elsewhere to stay within budget. Keep a brief record of decisions you make, the reasons for them, and their impact on your schedule and budget. Such a record helps a great deal when you assess the overall success of your project and when you plan to revise your Internet marketing presence later. (The only thing constant in cyberspace is change!)

Chapter 4

Mastering Your Domain

. . . .

. . . .

*T*his chapter is about the one piece of the Internet marketing puzzle that may affect your online presence more than anything else. It can be as memorable as `www.dummies.com` or as forgettable as `gold.website.net/users2/webhosting/nybusiness/`. This thing is your *domain name*.

Your domain name is the set of letters in the middle of your Web site's URL, and also (usually) the letters after the "@" symbol in your company-issued e-mail address. For instance, if you work at Sayonara Company, your Web site URL is likely to be `www.sayonara.com`, and your e-mail address is likely to be `yourname@sayonara.com`. In this case, `sayonara.com` is your company's domain name.

People use your domain name to reach you on various Internet services such as e-mail, ftp, and the Web, all described briefly in Chapter 1. A domain name is your identifier in cyberspace — kind of a cross between a company name, a business address, and a CB radio handle, if you're old enough to remember Citizens Band radio.

Getting the right domain name is extremely important. The good news: You can register any available domain name quickly and for a small fee, as we describe later in this chapter. The bad news: Someone else may beat you to your ideal domain name, as we also explain later in this chapter.

If you're working in a company, or thinking of starting a company, that doesn't have a domain name yet, cancel your appointments, take your phone off the hook, and read this chapter right away. The Internet marketing presence that you save may be your own. If your company or other organization already has a domain name, read this chapter anyway — you may need to change your domain name, (including your e-mail addresses and Web URL,) to a better one, add a secondary domain name for people who misspell your company name, or establish a new domain name for a product or service that you're working on. Thousands of new domain names are established every day. Time is of the essence.

But along with choosing a domain name, you may want to take a few extra minutes to think about who should provide the online access needed for your online marketing efforts. Do you want to stick with your current Internet access provider, or should you switch to someone better able to handle domain name registration, Web hosting, and more? The next section gives you the inside scoop.

Choosing an ISP for Online Marketing

You probably already have Internet access in one form or another. You may use an Internet service provider (ISP), such as EarthLink, or an online service such as America Online. (The difference is that online services provide a lot of proprietary content that you can't access any other way, and a fair amount of hand-holding; ISPs provide a basic package of software and services but little content of their own.)

Choosing an Internet service provider (ISP) or online service for online *access* is quite a bit different than choosing one for online *marketing*. All you need for Web surfing and Usenet newsgroup access is a reliable connection to the Internet. If your ISP gets sold or goes out of business, you can just change to another one.

However, for online marketing, your needs are much greater. You need to choose a business that can do some or all of the following:

✔ **Register your domain name.** If you want to register your domain name yourself, see "Discovering How Domain Names Work," later in this chapter. If you want your ISP to do it for you, pick an ISP that you can trust to do it right.

If you register your domain name through an ISP or online service, make absolutely sure that you end up as the legal owner of the domain name. Some unscrupulous ISPs (or "free" domain name services) register "your" domain name to themselves and then charge you whatever they can get for full ownership later, putting you at a real disadvantage in regard to this important piece of virtual real estate.

✔ **Receive and forward your e-mail.** You need an ISP or online service that can quickly and reliably receive and send your e-mail. (Your ISP receives all e-mail sent to you and then routes it to you.) Occasional mis-routings are inevitable, but regular blackouts, crashes, virus incidents, and wholesale losses of mail aren't.

✔ **Support you on the road.** When you and others in your company travel, you need access to local access numbers in as many places as possible to keep costs down.

✔ **Provide you access to Usenet newsgroups.** Your ISP must provide you access to all the thousands of newsgroups on the Internet. For more on Usenet newsgroup access, see Chapter 12.

✔ **Host your Web site.** Your ISP needs to be able to host your Web site at reasonable rates. Carefully compare basic charges for business Web sites, per-hit (or data transfer) charges for the number of visitors that you get to your Web site, and disk-space charges for storing the content of your Web site. Some providers hide high charges in these rates. You may also want to consider putting your Web site on a separate, specialized hosting service other than your ISP; we describe hosting services in the next chapter.

✔ **Give you support.** Although you can't expect your ISP to manage your online presence for you, you really need to be able to get someone on the phone to help you upgrade your online presence or troubleshoot problems.

✔ **Stay in business.** Given all the things you may be depending on your ISP for, the most important thing is that your ISP stays in business. With more than 4,000 ISPs in the United States alone and with ISPs dropping like flies — or merging like rabbits — turnover is a fact of life. The death throes of a failing ISP during its final months may include downtime, billing problems, sudden fee increases, and more. Pick a large national ISP or accept an increased risk of problems or outright disappearance of your ISP.

Your best choice for online marketing may well be a *standalone ISP*. (Technically, online services such as America Online and CompuServe are ISPs, too, given that they provide Internet service to people. By standalone ISP, we mean an ISP that's not also an online service.) If you're reasonably comfortable with the Internet and you're willing to search for one of the top standalone ISPs, a standalone ISP may be the right choice for you.

To find an ISP for online marketing, look for a major, nationwide provider that has been in the business long enough to get write-ups in major magazines. Search for those reviews online and compare carefully.

One excellent review from *CNET* can be found at `www.cnet.com/internet/ 0-3762-7-2518426`. The *Internet Marketing For Dummies* Internet Directory in this book contains pointers to even more information.

For online marketing, you also want an ISP that is technically savvy and thoroughly up-to-date. Among other things, an ISP should support a broad range of Internet applications and services, not just the Web and e-mail; if you can't even get access to Internet Relay Chat (IRC), you sure can't use it for marketing. (Chat is described in some detail in Chapter 12.)

According to *PC Magazine,* its readers' favorite ISPs include America Online, AT&T Worldnet, CompuServe, EarthLink, and MSN Internet access. Good choices for business include EarthLink (which recently merged with MindSpring), GTE Internet Solutions, and Netcom. The home page for EarthLink is shown in Figure 4-1.

Now (that is, before you start your online marketing effort) is the time to switch to an ISP that can keep up with your Internet marketing needs, including your Web site. With all the competition out there, you should be able to lock in good rates for a package of services that meets your needs.

Though your ISP can be your best choice for hosting your Web site, a specialized Web-hosting provider may be a good choice as well. Consider investigating Web-hosting services if you expect to get a lot of visitors — hundreds a week or more — to your Web site and if you need multiple e-mail addresses for your domain.

Figure 4-1: EarthLink is well regarded as a business ISP.

What about free ISPs?

There's something alluring about the word "free," which is why many marketers use (and overuse) it. However, "free" may not be quite as good a word when it comes to the ISP you're considering for your business.

Several ISPs have offered free Internet service, trading advertising targeted at you for your free Internet access. Unfortunately, there hasn't been enough advertising to go around. As a result, some free ISPs began to shut down in the second half of 2000, among them early high fliers WorldSpy.com and FreeWWWeb.com.

Between them, they claimed nearly 1 million subscribers.

Subscribers to WorldSpy and FreeWWWeb had the opportunity to switch to another free ISP, Juno. But it meant that these subscribers had to give up their original e-mail addresses — essentially, their online identities.

If you have to use a free ISP, use it for Web surfing and for a "backup" account when you can't use your primary ISP. But it's probably a bad idea to use it as your primary business ISP. You may get what you pay for.

Discovering How Domain Names Work

Few businesspeople understand how domain names work. But understanding how domain names work is like being able to read a map of cyberspace — and with this knowledge, you can put your business, product, or service at a prominent spot on that map.

You're probably familiar with domain names of your regular e-mail correspondents and of Web sites that you frequently visit. But what if you're trying to find a company marketing site on the Web and you're not quite sure of the domain name? Of course, as we point out in Chapter 2, you can search using appropriate keywords. But even better, the right domain name can make a business much easier to find on the Web. A well-chosen domain name can further facilitate marketing communication by making your Web site address and your marketing e-mail address (maybe something like `sales@yourproductsite.com`) much easier for people to remember.

Take a quick look at the Web URL in Figure 4-2 — which is the address of a personal Web page on the GeoCities Web site — and find the domain name in it. The URL has three parts:

> ✔ **Internet protocol name.** Each Internet service has its own special code, or *protocol,* for deciphering its messages. The World Wide Web uses *HyperText Transfer Protocol,* or HTTP, usually seen on the Web as `http`. (In English, acronyms are usually in capital letters, but UNIX people — the

originators of the Internet and many other important things in computing — tend to avoid them.) A colon and a double slash are used as separators, so the Internet protocol name always appears within a URL like this: `http://`.

In recent versions of Microsoft Internet Explorer and Netscape Navigator, you don't have to type in the protocol name to reach a Web site. For example, to reach the . . .*For Dummies* Web site, you can simply enter **www.dummies.com** in the Address or Location text box.

✔ **Domain name.** The domain name identifies a particular Web site. The part of the domain name that you need to be most concerned about is the period and three-letter code at the end — `.com`, `.edu`, `.org`, and so on, called the top-level domain (TLD) — and the group of letters just before the last period in the domain name, which in Figure 4-2 is `geocities`, called the second-level domain.

✔ **Subdirectory and filename.** The subdirectory and filename simply identify the particular file that the user wants. (If no specific filename is used, the Web server usually looks for a file named `index.htm` or `index.html` as the default.) If you've ever used MS-DOS or UNIX, you're very familiar with this kind of pathname and filename; on Windows and the Macintosh, folders play the role of subdirectories, and the three-letter extension at the end of the filename is more or less hidden.

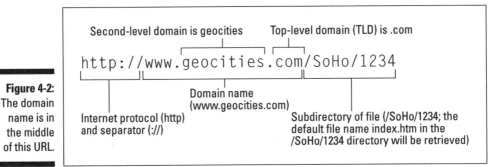

Figure 4-2:
The domain name is in the middle of this URL.

Second-level domain is geocities Top-level domain (TLD) is .com

`http://www.geocities.com/SoHo/1234`

Internet protocol (http) and separator (://)

Domain name (www.geocities.com)

Subdirectory of file (/SoHo/1234; the default file name index.htm in the /SoHo/1234 directory will be retrieved)

Breaking down domain names

The original role of a domain name is as a shared name for a group of machines connected to the Internet. Every machine on the Internet has a specific identifying number called an *IP address,* but people have trouble remembering long numbers. So machines can be assigned names as well; the names and the numbers that go with them are stored on an Internet server called a Domain Name Server, or DNS — initials you may recognize from setting up programs that access the Internet.

Domain names allow an organization to take over for itself the job of naming all of its machines that are connected to the Internet. After an organization receives a domain name of its own, it can also assign any name it wants that's at a lower level within that domain. For instance, an organization with the domain name `mybiz.com` can call machines that it owns `fred.mybiz.com`, `bigserver.mybiz.com`, and so on.

The confusing thing about domain names is that they're read backward, not forward, with the three-letter top-level domain, or TLD (such as `.com`) at the right end, the second-level domain just before it, and so on, as shown in Figure 4-2. Only a few top-level domains are currently in use as this is written, and they can show you a great deal about what kind of organization or company you're dealing with, as shown in Table 4-1.

Table 4-1	Top-Level Domains (TLDs)
Top-level domain	*Meaning*
`.com`	Commercial organizations, businesses
`.net`	Originally reserved for organizations responsible for supporting the Internet and considered prestigious; now used by businesses as well
`.edu`	Educational institutions (four-year colleges and universities only)
`.org`	Nonprofit organizations
`.gov`	U.S. government agencies (nonmilitary)
`.mil`	U.S. government military agencies
`.int`	International organizations formed by treaty or as part of the Internet database infrastructure
`.uk`, `.ca`, and so on	Country codes determined by an ISO standards committee

Network Solutions, the leading vendor of domain name registration services, has relaxed the rules that once separated the use of `.com`, `.net`, and `.org`. However, old habits die hard: `.com` is still the most desirable top-level domain for businesses; `.net` is widely considered acceptable for business use; and `.org` is still strongly associated with nonprofits (or just unknown to some users) and should be avoided, unless you're considering turning your business into a charitable institution (as some dot-coms unwittingly did before they went out of business).

As far as online marketing is concerned, the most important part of a domain name is the second-level domain. The second-level domain is the middle part of a typical Web URL — for example, the `computerz` component of `www.computerz.com`. The second-level domain that you choose needs to represent your company and organization as well as possible within a few constraints:

> ✔ **No special characters.** Your domain name can contain only letters, numbers, and the dash character.
>
> ✔ **Not too long.** Your second-level domain should be only 22 characters long. For example, the second-level domain name for the House of Natural Sound (`houseofnaturalsound`) is 19 characters.
>
> ✔ **Not already registered.** This part is tough. The combination of your second-level and top-level domains, such as `smallinc.com`, `bigcollege.edu`, or `nonprofit.org`, has to be new (not already registered). If it is already registered, you either have to induce the current nameholder to give it up or come up with a new name. (More on this later in this chapter.)

The number of allowable characters in a domain name has recently been expanded to 63(!). However, domain names this long are hard to remember, and people aren't used to them and so they may think such a domain name to be strange. Try to stay under the old 22-character limit.

The Network Solutions online domain name registration service (described at the end of this chapter) checks any domain name you enter to make sure that it fits the rules in the preceding list.

The second-level domain of your choice, combined with the appropriate top-level domain, is what you register for your use on the Internet. Below the second-level domain, you can do anything you want. For instance, many people use the third-level domain `www.` to indicate a Web site — but this is just a common practice and is not required. Some organizations use third-level domains to indicate departments within the organization; for instance, when Bud Smith worked on the QuickTime VR team at Apple, the team's domain name was `www.qtvr.apple.com`. However, this use of third-level and fourth-level domains is fading because people have trouble remembering multilevel domain names. His department eventually started using `www.quicktimevr.com` instead.

Some domain names are set up so that you don't have to type **www.** in front of the domain name to reach the site. Savvy Web users try this a lot — and get irritated when it doesn't work. As soon as you get your Web site set up, make sure that you can reach it with or without the `www.` in front of the domain name.

AltaVista's troubles

By developing the original AltaVista search engine, Digital Equipment Corp. (DEC) made an effort to show that it "gets it" on the Net — but the service didn't have the right domain name. In order to use AltaVista, users had to go to altavista.digital.com. Most people looking for the search engine didn't think of the .digital part. Eventually, Compaq acquired DEC and paid the owner of the name www.altavista.com $3 million to give it to Compaq. (The original AltaVista Technology Web page is shown in Figure 4-3.) Now AltaVista is a Web search engine and portal site valued at more than $3 billion, so the $3 million wasn't such a bad investment.

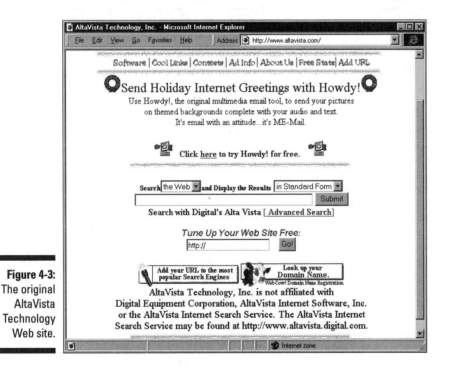

Figure 4-3: The original AltaVista Technology Web site.

The competition for domain names

According to Network Solutions, the leading company for registering domain names, more than 10 million domain names have been registered. The suffix .com is by far the most common top-level domain. Table 4-2 shows top-level domain registrations as reported by Network Solutions through mid-2000, when total Network Solutions–registered names reached the 10 million mark. As you can see from Table 4-2, nearly 80 percent — 7.7 million out of the total 10 million — of domain-name registrations have been for the .com top-level domain. The use of .net, however, is becoming much more popular than it used to be.

Table 4-2	Total Top-Level Domains (TLDs) through Mid-2000	
Top-level domain	*Approx. registrations*	*Percentage*
.com	7,700,000	77%
.net	1,500,000	15%
.org	800,000	8%
.edu, .gov, .mil		< 1%
Total	10,000,000	100%

If you're part of a government agency or the military, please check out the policies that apply to your agency before registering a domain name. We don't want to get blamed for someone's online tax return getting sent to the wrong e-mail address.

If you want your domain name to make it clear that your organization is located outside the United States, you should use the appropriate country designation in your top-level domain (TLD) name. To see country designations, look online at www.iana.org/cctld/cctld-whois.htm.

Because the .com domain is so widely used, many organizations that aren't really companies register and use the .com version of their domain name as well as the more appropriate version — country-specific or .edu, .org, or whatever. If your domain name ends in something besides .com and you need to reach many of the noncyber-savvy, you should consider registering the .com version as well.

A great deal of competition exists for desirable domain names. A land rush is going on for prime spots in cyberspace, and you can't risk not staking your claim.

Why domain names are so important

A business consultant once said that the three keys to starting a business are location, location, and location. Your domain name is the location on the

Internet to which all your e-mail and Web traffic comes. You are likely to print it on business cards, stationery, and advertising, as well as hastily tell it to inquiring people in the elevator.

Typically, when people use the Internet, they're trying to get information quickly. If they've heard of your company in the offline world, they are likely to try to guess your Web URL and enter it in their browsers. If you have the URL that they expect — www.[*a reasonable version of your company name*].com — they may find it on the first or second try. If not, you have problems.

Having failed to find you quickly, Web surfers — also known as your customers, investors, prospects, news reporters, industry analysts, and others — can do several things. More often than not, they just go surf somewhere else. Or they may try using a search engine to find you. But even if their search is successful (and especially if it's not), you've inconvenienced and annoyed someone important to you by not having the "right" domain name.

In many cases, figuring out a good domain name is easy: Your company name translates into an easy-to-guess second-level domain, the domain name that you want (your desired second-level domain and the appropriate top-level domain, such as .com) is available, and you're in business. Other times, identifying the appropriate unused domain name is much more difficult, especially if only one name is really a good fit and that name's taken.

The benefits of the right domain name are significant. With the right domain name, every time you advertise your company name or communicate it in any way, you effectively communicate your online location as well.

For one marketer's aggressive strategies for reserving domain names, see the article, *The Smart Marketer's Strategy for Reserving Domain Names,* by Andy Bourland, at www.clickz.com/archives/112897.html.

Tuvalu for you?

The small Pacific island nation of Tuvalu has the top-level domain .tv, short for Tuvalu. An American company called dotTV (www.tv), seeing the potential value in new URLs ending in .tv, has licensed the top-level domain from the country for tens of millions of dollars. The company has had great success in reselling these domain names to media companies such as NBC, Sony, and others who want a .tv name, and this success means that people are likely to hear about these names and find them an easy-to-remember and credible alternative to the much more common .com suffix. Consider staying away, though, from other top-level domains such as .md — the suffix of the former Soviet republic of Moldavia — until they become popular enough to catch on widely.

Possible new domain names

As this book is being written, a proposal to add new top-level domains (TLDs) to the existing set is being actively pursued by various parties on the Web. Proposed additional top-level domains include .news for news organizations, .shop for online retailers, and more. For details of the proposal, see the Internet Corporation for Assigned Names and Numbers Web site at www.icann.org. This site includes pointers to valuable information about the current domain name system as well as the proposed changes.

Although the proposals are highly controversial and their implementation has already been held up for several years, some additions to the existing set of top-level domains may very well be made. What's unknown, however, is whether any new domains will be widely accepted and used. Keep careful track of possible changes to the set of available domains and consider moving quickly to register any appropriate new domain names that become available as a result of these proposals.

Choosing Your Domain Name(s)

With a little thought as to how people use domain names, you can understand why registering the domain name(s) that you need is so important. Consider registering the following kinds of domain names:

- ✔ **Ideal company domain name.** Figure out the ideal domain name for your organization, as we describe in the following section, and register it if it's still available.

- ✔ **One or two close alternates.** If reasonable alternate domain names for your company — names that people may try — are available, consider registering them, too. You can then set up your Web server to automatically redirect people who type in the alternate name to your main Web site.

Is my business too small?

You may think your business is too small to need to register a domain name. Surprise! About two-thirds of domain name registrations go to companies with 1–4 employees. And about 20 percent go to consumers.

Table 4-3 shows domain name registrations through Network Solutions by company size for the month of April 2000. These statistics are similar to other months in the same time frame. As you can see, small businesses lead the way.

Among the top business types registering domain names are attorneys, real estate and insurance agents, and doctors as well as computer businesses and consultants. The rush is on. If you have a small business, now is the time to reserve your domain name.

✔ **Product and service domain names.** If you sell products or services that have gained wide awareness — anything a substantial number of current or future Web surfers may find interesting — register the domain name that's the best fit for each one soon, before someone else does. Do the same for products under development.

Table 4-3	Domain Name Registrations by Company Size
Business size	*Percentage of registrations*
1–4 employees	67%
5–9 employees	5%
10–19 employees	3%
20–49 employees	3%
50–99 employees	1%
100–249 employees	1%
250 or more employees	<1%
Consumers	20%

Domain name follies

Your domain name is not a chance to rename your company something different online than in the offline world. (If you don't like your company name, change it — and consider what domain names are available as part of the company renaming process.) Neither is it a chance to be cute, funny, interesting, intriguing, or anything else except *easy to guess.*

The ideal domain name is the domain name that a savvy Internet user who knows your company's name would guess first when trying to find your company on the Web. It's simply the closest translation that you can make of your company's name into a single word with no spaces, commas, periods, or other punctuation.

As we mention earlier in this chapter, the only characters allowed in a domain name are letters, numbers, and dashes. However, we suggest avoiding the dash — remembering whether a domain name has a dash in it and where the dash goes can be difficult, and may cause potential visitors to miss your site. Stick to letters and numbers whenever possible.

For some examples, Table 4-4 lists 14 top American companies, the best domain names for them, alternates that would probably be worth registering, and their actual domain names.

Table 4-4	Domain Names of Top American Companies		
Company name	Ideal domain	Alternates to name	Actual domain registered
BankAmerica	bankamerica.com	bankofamerica.com	bank-america.com, bofa.com
Chase Manhattan	chase.com		chase.com
Citicorp	citicorp.com		citicorp.com
Coca-Cola	cocacola.com	coke.com	cocacola.com, coke.com
Du Pont de Nemours	dupont.com		dupont.com
Exxon	exxon.com		exxon.com
Ford Motor Company	ford.com		ford.com
General Electric	ge.com	generalelectric.com	ge.com
General Motors	gm.com	generalmotors.com	gm.com
IBM	ibm.com		ibm.com
Intel	intel.com		intel.com
Merck	merck.com		merck.com
Procter & Gamble	procter&gamble.com	proctergamble.com, pg.com	proctergamble.com, pg.com
Wal-Mart Stores	walmart.com	wal-mart.com	wal-mart.com

Looking at Table 4-4, you may think, "Well, those companies are all big and they no doubt have lots of lawyers working on getting the right domain names and rights." In fact, one of the most profitable companies in the world, General Motors, was too slow to register the domain name generalmotors.com. This hesitation left the field wide open, and another group took the Web Uniform Resource Locator (URL) www.generalmotors.com.

Figure 4-4 shows what you got, until recently, when you tried to reach General Motors by typing in **www.generalmotors.com** in your Web browser. In 1999, General Motors finally got control of its own most logical domain name.

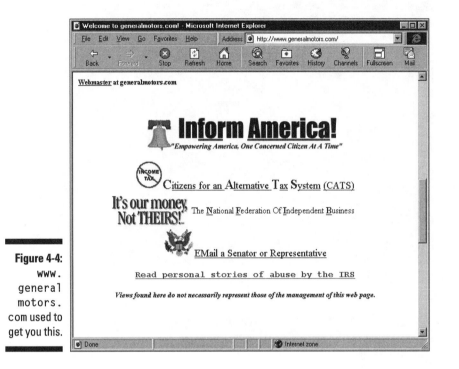

Figure 4-4: www. general motors. com used to get you this.

Government agencies aren't immune to domain name confusion, either. The URL www.dod.com gets you a sound company; www.whitehouse.com gets you a porn site that claims more than a million hits a day — sad, but an example of good marketing practice. (To reach the White House's Web page, use www.whitehouse.gov.)

The U.S. Navy, however, has gotten hip to the scene; the URL www.navy.com gets you to a recruiting-oriented Web site, shown in Figure 4-5, and www.navy.mil (the proper URL for the Navy under the usual domain name rules) gets you the official Web site of the Navy, shown in Figure 4-6. (The recruiting site even features both a Flash-animated and a plain HTML version.) The Navy's approach shows perfect pitch in terms of how to handle Web users: Newer users who are more likely to know only the .com designation get recruited to join up (with a pointer to the official Web site on the home page of the recruiting site); those in the know, who are more likely to try the .mil designation, get the official Web page.

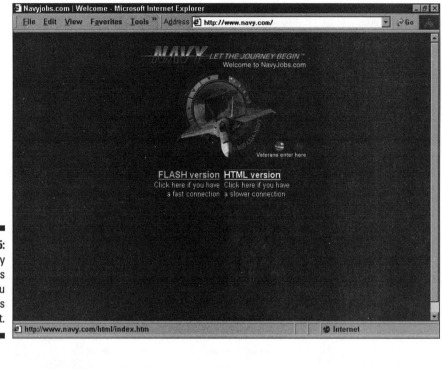

Figure 4-5:
The Navy
wants
all you
.commies
to ship out.

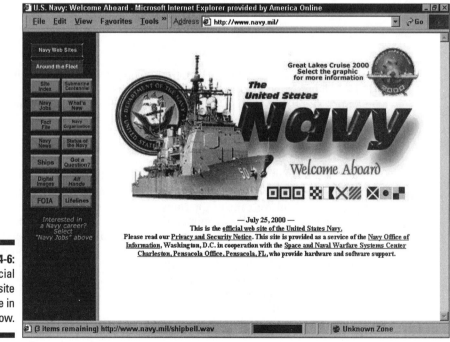

Figure 4-6:
The official
.military site
for those in
the know.

Good and bad domain names

You can see from the examples in the previous section how to pick the best domain name for your company: Find the word or short phrase, with no spaces or other punctuation, that best represents your company name. You simply translate your company name into a domain name. (The test of whether you have the right domain name is: Can someone who knows your company and regularly uses the Web guess your company's domain name on the first try?)

Not all companies come as close to the ideal domain names as most of the companies shown back in Table 4-4. Also, many companies' names are difficult to render into a domain name. To see some examples relevant to your own business, search the directories in Yahoo! (www.yahoo.com) for businesses in your category and see how well or poorly they've done in registering good domain names. You can also check other search engines for relevant examples.

For instance, looking up "Home Theater" in Yahoo! and elsewhere, you can see some interesting examples of good and not-so-good domain names:

- ✔ **Active Buyer's Guide: Home Theater Systems.** URL: www.hometheatersystems.activebuyersguide.com. More and more companies with long names are trying this brave solution: If you have a long company name, just make the whole thing into a domain name. It makes sense to keep your domain names under the old 22-character name length limit. Active Buyer's Guide has pushed this to the edge with a long second-level domain name (activebuyersguide, 17 characters) plus a long third-level domain name (hometheatersystems, 18 characters). Memorable? Only somewhat. Accurate? Very much so.

- ✔ **Ambiophonics.** URL: www.ambiophonics.org. This nonprofit group promotes realistic music reproduction. The domain name is easy to remember except for the .org part. This group should also register ambiophonics.com — it's available, at this writing — and create a Web page at www.ambiophonics.com that automatically redirects the user to the correct Web page at www.ambiophonics.org.

- ✔ **Audio Design Associates.** URL: www.ada-usa.com. This manufacturer has worked around the fact that its obvious domain name choice, ada.com, was taken by adding a geographic identifier, -usa. This solution is a decent one, but unfortunately no one is likely to guess the URL when searching for the company on the Web. Also, the dash is easy to forget. The company should have gotten audiodesign.com instead, if it was still available, or adausa.com if not.

- ✔ **Big Matt's Home Theater and Audio Page.** URL: www.msu.edu/user/churches. Big Matt has received more than 175,000 hits on his audiophile Web page in four years, and he has an ad running on his home page to help make money. But Big Matt has not taken the time to get a good domain name. Who knows how many users have missed out on his advice because they couldn't find his site — or didn't take it seriously when they saw the university-based URL in their search results page?

✔ **Performance Imaging.** URL: www.performanceimaging.com or www.hdtvsystems.com. Many companies use a URL that refers to the *type* of product they make rather than their company name. We think the company name should be the first and foremost choice. In this case, Performance Imaging registered www.performanceimaging.com as well, which is good, but the company hasn't updated www.hdtvsystems.com to make it point to the new site. See Figure 4-7 to check out the "dead" Web page at www.hdtvsystems.com.

Though we picked one very narrow category for these examples, any group of organizations is likely to have a similar range of easy-to-guess and hard-to-guess domain names. Just make sure that yours is in the easy-to-guess group!

Choosing a company domain name

Now is the time to choose your own domain name (or, if you already have one and you don't like it, to choose a new one). With new top-level domains such as .shop likely to be added, and with millions of new domain names being registered every year, there's no time like the present to get registered. Follow these steps to choose a domain name:

1. **Sit down with a piece of paper or a blank document in your word processor and list all the possible domain names that fit your organization.**

   Start with .com as the ending (top-level domain, or TLD for short) for your domain name if it's for a company. Also consider .net (which is rapidly becoming a popular "backup" to .com) and any new top-level domains such as .shop. If you're part of a nonprofit, educational, government, or military organization, or you're in a country outside the United States, use the appropriate TLD (.org, .edu, .gov, .mil, or .uk, for example). Because the .com ending is so much better known, you may want to consider registering your nonprofit (.org) or other organization domain name with .com at the end as well.

2. **Ask several friends and colleagues who use the Web what domain name they think your company should use.**

   Most people encounter domains as part of Web addresses (URLs), so ask some of them what Web address they think you should have. Experienced Web users try to guess Web addresses without consciously thinking about it, so you may want to even ask a few people to sit down in front of their browsers and try typing in the right URL for your company. Just hope your friends don't type in something like **www.<yourcompany>sucks.com**!

3. **Shorten your list to a few favorite candidates.**

   Include alternates that aren't the best choice but that some people may try — for instance, a name with your company's acronym should be kept as an alternate if people usually think of your company by its full name.

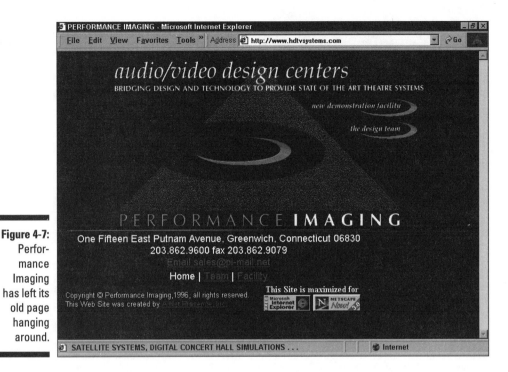

Figure 4-7:
Performance Imaging has left its old page hanging around.

4. **Go to the home page of the Network Solutions Web site to find out whether the domain name that you want is taken.**

   Fire up your Web browser and go to www.networksolutions.com. The Network Solutions home page is shown in Figure 4-8.

5. **Enter the first domain name that you want to check; for instance, as a domain name for this book, we may try** imfd.com.

6. **Press Enter.**

   The Network Solutions domain name checker service tells you whether someone already has your domain name. If it's still available, you see the message, "Congratulations! yourdomain.com is available." If it's taken, you see the message "Sorry, yourdomain.com is not available," and you see a list of possible alternatives such as similar names ending in .net or .org. You also get a link to NameFetcher, a useful service for generating similar names that may be available.

7. **Click the check box next to any domain names that you might want to use; then click Continue.**

   Names you choose will be kept on a list on the Web page as you proceed. Put a check mark next to all the domain names you want to keep. Even if your first choice is available, check the others in case you want to register them as alternates.

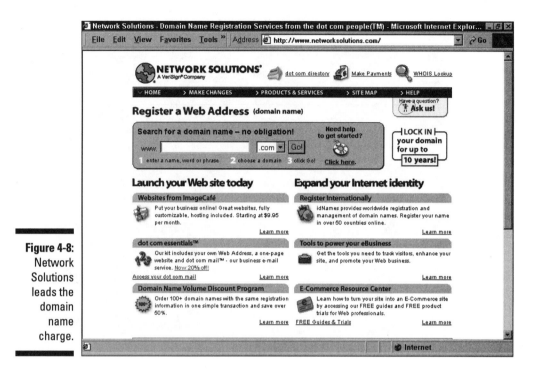

Figure 4-8:
Network
Solutions
leads the
domain
name
charge.

8. **If your top choice or top few choices are taken, try the Whois service at** www.networksolutions.com/cgi-bin/whois/whois **to see who registered them before you.**

   Follow up with the domain name holders and see whether any of them are willing to part with their domain name for a reasonable price or even for free.

9. **For the choices you like that are taken, try entering the domain name as a URL in your Web browser — add www. at the beginning and then the domain name — to see whether the domain name is in active use.**

   If it's not in use, it may be easier to negotiate getting the domain name for yourself.

10. **After you have compiled a list of choices that you like, print the list.**

    Choose File⇨Print to print the Web page. Consult your colleagues and financial advisors — quickly, before the name gets taken — then come back to the Network Solutions Web site to register the name, as described later in this chapter.

Should you make your product name a domain?

One interesting dilemma is whether you should make your product name a domain name. We don't think that you should use your main product's name as the domain name for the whole company unless the product is much more well known than the company (in which case, you may want to change your company name to match it!).

However, you may want to consider registering key product names as domain names in addition to your company name. You may eventually want to have a Web site dedicated to a product, or automatically reference people who enter your product name as a URL to your main company site. (For instance, if you enter `www.kleenex.com`, you'll automatically be redirected to the Web site of Kimberly-Clark Corporation, the makers of Kleenex.)

There are defensive reasons for registering your major product names as domain names as well. If you don't register your product names, your competitors may; other sites desperate for traffic, such as porn sites, may even have a go at it (as with the sad example of whitehouse.com noted earlier in this chapter). And if you are trying to trademark your product names, registration is even more important. Someone else who wants to use the same name could use your failure to register the name as evidence that you were never serious about protecting the name in the first place.

If your first choice or a strong alternate is available, you're ready to take the next step and claim your domain name. If all the reasonable choices for your business are taken, consider using a variant on the name of your business. For example instead of `abcplumbing` (which is taken as we write this), consider `abcplumbers` or `abcp` (which are not). If you're really stuck, try inserting a dash — `abc-plumbing`, for instance. California Plumbing could use `calplumb`, `calplumbing`, `californiaplumbing`, or other variants.

You can also contact the current holder of the domain that you want to use and see whether the folks who own it are willing to give up their rights to it. If the domain name is not in active use, they may be willing to let you have it.

Many domain names are held by domain-name brokers, speculators who reserve domain names that they don't need in hopes of selling them to a high bidder later. (Yes, this practice is common, and no, it's not a crime.) If such a person holds your domain name, you may have to pay him or her to get the rights to "your" name, or consider another name.

You can also consider suing the current holder of a domain name for rights to it. If you have a strong trademark claim to the name and the current holder doesn't, then you may be able to win — but suing is often a long, expensive, and uncertain venture. Threatening to sue a domain-name broker for this reason may drive the price down — or, if the broker believes your claim is weak or is just stubborn, it may drive the price up instead.

If the domain name holder is actively using the domain name for a Web page, you may want to ask the holder for a link from its Web page to yours — just as the Navy's job site and official site link to each other. One of the authors once did this when the short version of his product's name was in use by a consultant — and the consultant, not wanting to anger the product group and fearing legal action, put up the link that same day.

If your business is small and your desire to be accessible on the Internet is large, you may even consider changing your business name to one that translates well to an available domain name. ABC Tools may become LA Tools (domain name `latools.com`) or Toys Aren't Us (`toysarentus.com`). (Just kidding on the last one; you don't want anyone suing you.)

After all your efforts, you may just be stuck and end up having to use a less desirable name. If so, go ahead and get the less desirable name registered — before someone else takes that one, too! — and take steps to make reaching your Web site by a link or by a search engine easy, as we describe in Chapter 5.

Starting out in a subdirectory

As you get your virtual feet wet in cyberspace, you may decide to go ahead and start out with a Web site that's in a subdirectory of someone else's domain. Here are a few dos and don'ts:

✔ **Don't use an America Online (AOL) domain.** AOL is the leading online service, and you may find having AOL host your initial Web site tempting. If you do choose AOL and don't pay extra for your own domain name, you end up with a URL like `www.members.aol.com/yourbiz`. This kind of URL is an instant mark against you in your online marketing efforts. AOL has had many well-publicized problems and has somewhat of a bad name in cyberspace. No sense in associating yourself with someone else's problems.

✔ **Do use an ISP.** Many users consider independent ISPs to be cooler than big online services such as America Online and CompuServe, so start out with an independent ISP. EarthLink is one ISP that offers Web-hosting services. With EarthLink, your Web URL would look like this: `www.earthlink.com/yourbiz`.

✔ **Don't publicize a subdirectory URL too widely.** If you do put your Web site in a subdirectory of someone else's site, don't publicize your URL too widely; you'll just be publicizing the fact that you haven't gotten your Web presence just right yet. Also, you're just making life more difficult for yourself later on when you do get your own domain name and need to publicize it.

✔ **Do get your own domain quickly.** Most ISPs help you quickly move your Web site to your own domain name and even register the domain name for you for a small fee. Then you can publicize your Web site freely.

A tale of one domain name

Even the Internet-savvy get burned when it comes to registering the ideal domain name. One of the authors, Frank Catalano, thought he would have no trouble getting `catalano.com` in January 1996, long before the dot-com boom. Unfortunately, `catalano.com` was taken in December 1995 — by an international deli in Ohio.

Frank's solution? Rather than go with a hard-to-remember but shorter alternative, such as `catconsulting.com` (which his colleagues noted made him sound like a veterinarian), he opted for using the full company name, `catalanoconsulting.com`. In addition, he registered another domain that a potential client might use to find him, `frankcatalano.com`, and pointed both new domains to the same Web site.

Total investment was less than $100 per year for the two domains, and so far, none of his clients has received a pepperoni rather than marketing counsel. Also, you can find this book's Directory, in clickable form, on the `catalanoconsulting.com` Web site.

What if you're local?

For a local or regional business, the trouble with the World Wide Web is the "World" part. Your Internet presence is held up to the same standard as the big boys, and your domain name must be available everywhere.

No one looking for a place to eat lunch cares whether there's a Sandy's Sandwich Shop in Connecticut and a different business with the same name in California. But desirable domain names for such a business, such as `www.sandys.com` and so on, are available only once. You can't have two businesses with the same domain name on the Web, no matter how unlikely these two businesses are to compete for customers in the real world.

A variety of ways exist, none of which is very appealing, to make your domain name localized. (Your customers expect to find you as `www.yourbiz.com` on the Web, and anything different from that is a hassle for them.) In non-U.S. countries, using the country name at the end of the URL is a good bet and meets customer expectations. But the best name for your business ending in your country's top-level domain may be taken, too!

A good approach is to work the name of your city, state, province, or region into your domain name. A sandwich shop in New Haven, Connecticut, can be `www.sandysnewhaven.com` to set it apart from its California cousin. You'll have to repeatedly tell your customers about your domain name, though, for them to have any chance of remembering it.

Another technique is to rename your business to something that's not already taken online. A law firm, for instance, might take the opportunity to add good old Skivers to the name of the practice, if that makes for a unique domain name. But you have to carefully weigh such an option against the value of the name your business already has.

Someday, someone will invent a way for people to have a locally based view of the Internet when shopping for goods and services, but we've never heard even a good proposal for how to handle this. For now, locally oriented businesses will just need to be creative — and be ready to get a dollar's worth of mileage out of a dime — when setting up their presence on the Internet.

Registering Your Domain Name (s)

After you identify an available domain name that you want, you need to register it. You can register the domain name yourself or have someone you hire register it for you. Each approach has its own benefits and hazards.

Registering your domain name yourself

The first approach to registering a domain name is to do it yourself. The good news is that you can register the domain name by filling out a form on the Network Solutions Web site at www.networksolutions.com. The cost is as little as $35 a year.

There are other registration services, but at this writing, Network Solutions is the biggest and, we believe, the best. Some competing services are out-and-out rip-offs, whereas some are valid businesses. But none gives you the same peace of mind as Network Solutions.

Before proceeding, if you want to get a site up right away, you will want to get Domain Name Server (DNS) information from your ISP or Web-hosting provider. However, you do not have to have this information to register a name.

To decide what URL(s) you want to register, and to research their availability, see the preceding section on choosing a domain name. Then follow these steps to register your domain name:

1. **Open a Web browser and go to the Network Solutions Web site at**
   www.networksolutions.com.

   The Network Solutions home page appears.

2. **Enter the domain name in the text entry box; then choose a domain —
   such as `.com` or `.net` — from the pull-down menu.**

   If you want to register a name using more than one top-level domain —
   such as `wewinyoulose.com` and `wewinyoulose.net` — just choose one
   on the home page; you'll be given the opportunity to register the others
   at the same time.

3. **After you have the domain name and top-level domain right, click the
   Go button.**

   The Web Address Search Results Web page appears, as shown in Figure 4-9.

4. **Click to check the check box for each name that you want to register now.**

   You're getting ready to make a financial commitment here, so pay
   attention.

5. **Click Continue.**

   The Registration Options Web page appears.

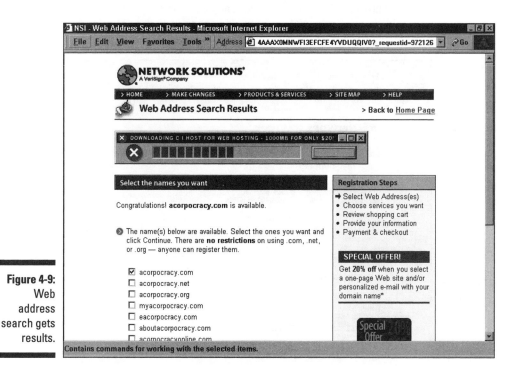

Figure 4-9:
Web
address
search gets
results.

6. **Choose an option: Register the Web Address only; register the Web Address and get a one-page Web site; or get all the above plus one or more personalized e-mail addresses; then, click Continue for the option you choose.**

   Choose the option that best suits your needs. You can always upgrade from a simpler option later, though doing so may make the total cost higher. The key thing is to get your domain name reserved.

7. **Specify whether you already have Domain Name Server (DNS) information or not; then click Continue for the option you choose.**

   If you have DNS information, be ready to provide it. If not, Network Solutions will give you information to provide to your Web-hosting service.

   After you click Continue, the My Shopping Cart page appears, as shown in Figure 4-10.

8. **Click the Refresh button to make sure that the page is up-to-date.**

   Review the page. If everything is as you wish, click the Continue button. If you have DNS information, be ready to provide it. If not, Network Solutions will give you information to provide to your Web-hosting service.

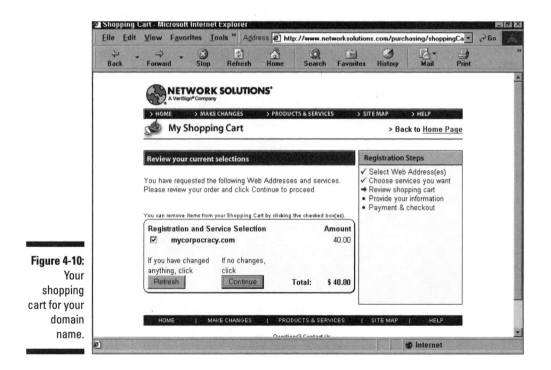

Figure 4-10:
Your
shopping
cart for your
domain
name.

9. **Choose the appropriate radio button to register as an individual or a business; then Click the Sign Up button to sign up as a new customer.**

   The New Customer Registration page appears.

10. **Fill in the form with your information; then click the Continue button.**

    The Order Verification & Processing page appears. Watch out — you complete your transaction in the next step.

11. **(This is the step in which your credit card is charged!) Enter your credit card information; then click to check the check box and consent to the service agreement.**

    Specify Yes or No to receive or not receive e-mail about new services and then click Submit to complete the transaction. Unlike similar Web-based shopping services, you do not get one more chance to review your order; clicking Submit completes the transaction. Your order information appears.

12. **The Thank You page appears, as shown in Figure 4-11.**

    Print it as verification. You're done!

NSI - Register a Web Address - Microsoft Internet Explorer

File   Edit   View   Favorites   Tools   »   Address 🔲 https://www.networksolutions.com/purchasing/21.jhtml;$ ▼ 🔗 Go

Back   Forward   Stop   Refresh   Home   Search   Favorites   History   Mail   Print

> HOME   > MAKE CHANGES   > PRODUCTS & SERVICES   > SITE MAP   > HELP

Thank You   > Back to Home Page

Click Here for a Free Demo   **Track-It!** from Blue Ocean Software   Sponsored by: CLICK HERE

Thank you for doing business with Network Solutions!	Congratulations! You're Done!
You will receive an e-mail confirming registration of your Web Address(es) in approximately 24 hours.	— PRINT THIS PAGE AS A RECORD OF YOUR TRANSACTION — YOU WILL NEED YOUR ACCOUNT NUMBER AND PASSWORD TO ACCESS YOUR ACCOUNT
Contact Network Solutions	**Account Holder:** BudCo
To contact Network Solutions:	**Account Number:**
Contact Us via e-mail	**Password:**
	Vendor Password:
Customer Service: 1 888 642-9675 International: +1 703 742-0914	mycorpocracy.com (one year) ├LOCK IN┤ your domain for up to 10 years! Total : $ 40.00

🔒 💠 Internet

Figure 4-11:
You're king of the World (Wide Web)!

Having an ISP or Web-hosting service register your domain name for you

If you don't want to register your domain name yourself through Network Solutions, as described in the previous section, you can get someone else to do it for you. Major ISPs and Web-hosting services offer domain-name registration as part of their range of services.

Reputable companies charge about $100 for registering your domain name, depending on what other services they include. A good Internet partner can have you up and running with a basic Web site very quickly and for just a few hundred dollars.

You can use a combination of methods to find a good ISP or Web-hosting service. First, make a clear, understandable list of your wants and needs, such as fast connections, e-mail services, Web consulting help, and so on. Pass it around among colleagues to make sure that you all agree on your goals.

Then look around. Talk to other businesspeople about their experiences. Check with people in your own industry, if they'll share the information. Use resources such as those found on ZDNet, as described earlier in this chapter, to identify promising resources.

Then, talk to several potential providers. Watch out for some of the following possible pitfalls:

- ✔ **Overcharging you.** Some ISPs charge you a high monthly fee, such as $100 a month, for a package of Internet services that includes your own domain name. Shop around for a reasonable price, and try to pay a low one-time setup fee for your domain name and monthly fees for the rest of the service.

- ✔ **Ripping off your name.** Some unscrupulous Web-hosting services or ISPs have registered customers' domain names to *themselves,* not the customer. The ISP can then charge you to get your own domain name back if you ever quit using its Web-hosting service. Check the contract you sign with the ISP to make absolutely sure that you own the exclusive rights to your domain name.

- ✔ **Insufficient backup.** Your ISP or Web-hosting service should have backup hosting of your site using a different Internet connection in a different location than the main Web-hosting computer. That way, if a problem with the main host computer arises, support for your site can continue at the backup location while the problem at the main hosting site is resolved.

✔ **Using subdirectories.** Some ISPs or Web-hosting services with limited technical capabilities host your Web site in a subdirectory of your own domain, as happened for a while to one of the authors (Frank Catalano). His URL was `www.catalanoconsulting.com/catalano,` thereby not making use of the effort spent registering the domain name in the first place. Get an ISP who can give you your Web page in a domain with no subdirectory. (Incidentally, Frank's Web site now happily pops up at `www.catalanoconsulting.com.`)

✔ **Going out of business.** You really don't want your ISP or Web-hosting service to go out of business; for the online marketer, it's like being a cowboy and having your horse shot out from under you, as you some-times see in old westerns. Try to ensure that your ISP will be around for a long time. (We discuss some of the general considerations of choosing an ISP in greater depth in the "Choosing an ISP" section, earlier in this chapter.)

✔ **Confusing legal language.** You need to be able to clearly understand the terms of any contract that you sign regarding ISP and hosting services. In particular, make sure that the contract clearly states that you own your domain name and that you can transfer it to another ISP or Web-hosting service at any time.

Do all you can to avoid these potential problems. If you screen out potential service providers who can't reassure you on these issues, those who are left may well be a good choice for you.

Part II
Marketing on the World Wide Web

The 5th Wave   By Rich Tennant

"You know, it dawned on me last night why we aren't getting any hits on our Web site."

In this part . . .

World Wide Web hype has reached such dizzying levels that it obscures the fact that the Web is perhaps the single most important new marketing tool since the advent of television. In this part, we cut through the technical jargon and show you exactly how to create an easy-to-find, effective Web presence, whether you're doing all the work yourself or working with others.

Chapter 5

Planning a Business Web Site

. . . .

. . . .

A marketing-oriented business Web site is the meat and potatoes of the online marketing world: not too exciting, but satisfying and sustaining. By creating and maintaining a straightforward business Web site, you can easily provide customers, press, and analysts with vital information about your company and products. If the initial effort is successful, your site can lay the groundwork for a larger online marketing effort, possibly including online sales.

You've probably seen a lot of advanced Web technology used in high-profile Web sites — technologies such as Java, Dynamic HTML, and immersive 3D worlds. These innovations are all good, if used properly, but they have little place in a marketing-oriented business Web site. You can create a basic business Web site without too much planning. You can even begin construction of the site while you're also beginning the planning process. The idea here is to get off your duff and jump-start your online presence by getting a competent representation of your company up and running — fast.

In this chapter, we describe how to create your initial site yourself or working with a few colleagues or consultants.

Although some companies and consultants advertise that they will create a basic business Web site for you for as little as $500, many of these ads are teasers designed to get you to pick up the phone and begin a process that results in big expenditures. Although you can and should use consultants for larger Web efforts, creating and publishing the initial site yourself is sensible. After you get some hands-on experience, you can know what you're paying for when you hire a Web-design firm to expand your Web site later. If you do hire help for the initial Web site effort, use this chapter to do as much of the work as you can on your own, and to double-check the outsiders' advice so that you can make sure that you're getting your money's worth.

Guiding Principles for Business Sites

A basic business Web site is like a simple, glossy brochure that briefly describes your company and products. It reassures people that you're a competent player who will be around for a while and from whom they can buy with confidence. Your Web site also lets users move easily from picking up basic information to more active steps such as calling you, writing you, or sending you e-mail. But watch this last option, because it can byte you (excuse the pun); you can receive so much e-mail that you have trouble responding to all of it. See Chapter 10 for details.

Here are the underlying principles that should guide your effort to create a basic business Web site:

- ✔ **Harmlessness.** The first words of the doctor's Hippocratic Oath are "First, do no harm," and this dictum should be honored by people doing marketing as well. Misspellings, poor grammar, and errors in your site's text harm your company's image of competence. Web pages with large graphics that download slowly, or with advanced technologies that not everyone can use, irritate potential customers. Allowing people to send you e-mail that goes unanswered can cause lost sales. Be cautious and avoid problems.

- ✔ **Fast construction.** Your initial Web site effort should proceed quickly from initial idea to a live site. If you can do all the work yourself and don't need anyone's approval, you may get it all done in two weeks. If you need to discuss certain aspects of your site in advance and you need approval of the final product at the end, you may need a month or two to complete the site. Keep the project time as short as possible.

- ✔ **Cheap.** A basic Web site can be created by in-house personnel, with perhaps some outside help on the look and feel, and published on a Web server by an Internet service provider (ISP) or Web-hosting service for very little cost. Expect to spend a few person-weeks on creating the site, possibly a couple of thousand dollars to a consultant for graphics and navigation help, and somewhere around $50 a month for an ISP to maintain the site on its server.

- ✔ **Effective.** Any marketing effort needs to support moving a prospective customer along the sales cycle. A basic Web site helps potential customers consider you as a possible supplier and encourages them to contact you in order to go further. (It gets press, analysts, and investors to take you seriously, as well.)

- ✔ **Widely usable.** A basic Web site needs to be usable by anyone with an Internet connection and a Web browser; it should not contain any advanced Web technology that isn't supported by almost every available browser. That means no frames, no Java, no Dynamic HTML. This kind of simplicity makes your Web site easier to design and use.

✔ **Fits in on the Net.** Because of its origins among academics and scientists, the Internet has certain standards and practices that you ignore at your peril. (Until early in the 1990s, any commercial use of the Internet was forbidden, and even now, some resistance to online commerce remains.) Respect the history of the medium by avoiding hype, overstatement, alarming layouts and graphics, and so on. A conservative approach will serve you well until you develop a good feel for where you can have some fun without seeming like a gate-crasher at a fancy party.

Specifying Your Site Content

A basic business Web site is not something you advertise or market heavily. The site is there for people to find when they're looking for information on the Web. Therefore its contents should be simple and spare, attractive but not exuberant. In baseball terms, the idea is that it's early in the game, and you want to start things on a positive note by hitting a solid single for your team.

A basic Web site fulfills the first marketing-related function that any Web site must fulfill, that of a validator. "Valid" means "worthy," and a Web site functions as a validator by showing that you're worth doing business with. Validators do much of their work on a subconscious level, so the absence of key validators makes people feel uncomfortable, in ways that they find difficult to define but that operate very effectively in steering them clear of you. The powerful role of validators is why, as we mention in the previous section, making your Web site free of errors, technical barriers, and other irritants is important. (Would you send out salespeople who were poorly groomed, ignorant of your products, and unable to speak the same language as your customers? Similar considerations apply to your Web site.)

A basic Web site needs to meet fundamental information needs, but not much more than that. In fact, putting in more information than is strictly necessary is more likely to make your site difficult to navigate than to make it more useful. Avoid piling on a lot of content until you can also devote some time and energy to making your Web site easy to navigate.

If some of your planned material seems like a good idea but not strictly necessary, drop it (or, better yet, put it on a list for later). Your final list of contents will vary depending on your company, your industry, and the available information resources you have at hand that can readily be repurposed for the Web. But most sites include the following:

✔ **Contact information.** This information is really, really important, and many sites — even big ones that cost big bucks to create and maintain — either don't include it at all or bury it. Provide your company name, address, main phone number, and fax number. (Don't include your e-mail address until after you read Chapter 10.) Make your contact information easily accessible, one link away from your home page. Figure 5-1 shows contact information displayed on a relevant Web site.

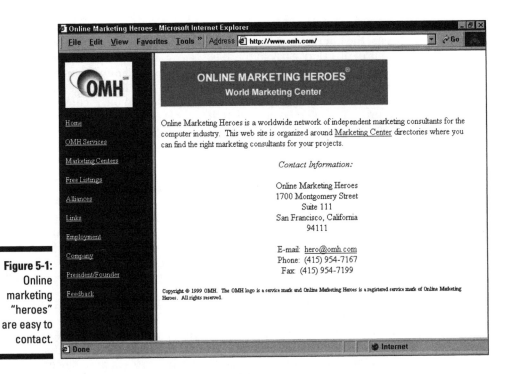

Figure 5-1:
Online
marketing
"heroes"
are easy to
contact.

✔ **Where you do business.** If your geographic range is limited, make this fact clear up front. Be subtle and positive. On your home page or contact information page, include a phrase like "San Francisco's leading supplier of electrical services to business" or "Western Europe's most innovative maker of eyeglass holders." Help people who don't need to spend time on your Web site find that fact out quickly and in a positive context so that they leave happy, rather than angry.

✔ **Key people.** A brief list of key people, with a paragraph or so of descriptive information about each, can go far to make people comfortable with your company. (Some companies are reluctant to include this kind of information because they're afraid of attracting executive recruiters, but the benefits to your site's visitors outweigh this risk.) Don't include spouse-hobbies-and-kids stuff — just name, title, and a brief professional biography.

✔ **Key customers.** Though some companies are reluctant to include it for fear of attracting competitors, a list of key customers is a very strong validator of your success. List the customers' names and a sentence or two about how they use your product. (Take the time to ask your customers whether they mind this inclusion and whether they want you to include a link to their Web sites.) But don't include this kind of list until your customer list is at least a little bit impressive.

✔ **Products and services.** Include simple, brief descriptions of your products and services. You can also link to more detailed information, but put the simple descriptions in one place and make them easy to access; that way, prospects can scan the descriptions quickly to decide whether to explore your site further.

✔ **Price.** Include specific price information if you can. Price can vary by sales channel, by geography, by options, or by many other factors, so including specific prices can be difficult, but at least find some way to communicate the rough price range of your product. Describing the price paid in a few specific instances does nicely. People hate to "turn off" customers, which may happen when you indicate your pricing structure, but encouraging people who can't afford your product to contact you (by not letting them know your price range) is not in anyone's interest.

The "where to buy" crisis

Putting even seemingly innocuous information on the Web can have serious offline consequences. Consider "Where to buy" information. One Web site managed by one of the authors (Bud) included links to all the service companies from which customers could get consulting and customization services for a software product. The links worked very well and sent a lot of traffic to the partners. But, over time, two problems developed:

✔ **Too much demand.** Several dozen new companies entered the market, worldwide, in a one-year period. These companies sent e-mail to the overloaded Webmaster e-mail account requesting a link. When that e-mail address got backlogged, their links were slow to appear on the site. Angry e-mail messages (which fell into the e-mail black hole), then phone calls, then personal visits to the company's offices and to its trade show appearances ensued. This problem was easier to remedy — by catching up on the link backlog — than was the dilemma described next.

✔ **Repeated requests from the biggest service company for special placement, a larger entry, or other premier status on the Web site.** The company deserved this favored status; it had at least double the staff and client volume of any competing company. But special treatment for one company would have opened a big can of worms in terms of fairness, proportional representation, and so on.

The solution to this problem was to enter into a series of newsworthy arrangements with the leading service company that got it prominent mention in the news section of the Web site, leading to some well-deserved new business for it. The company still wanted more prominent coverage in the service providers list but was at least somewhat satisfied by what it got. Of course, all these special efforts that generated news irritated the other service companies . . . .

✔ **Where and how to buy.** Tell people who visit your Web site where and how to buy your products and services. You would think that this kind of information was a national security secret from the way it's hidden or absent on all too many Web sites. If you have several sales channels, list each of them, along with a brief description of each channel that highlights its unique advantages. One excellent method is to set up an interactive area of a Web page that lets people enter their locations and then receive information about nearby sales outlets. If this feature involves too much work to handle right now, consider getting and publicizing a toll-free number as a stand-in until you can design and implement an interactive Web capability.

✔ **Company, product, and service validators.** This is where you put information that validates specific products and services, employees, or the company as a whole. List positive descriptions of your company, people, products, and services from any reputable source, including analyst reports, the general press, the trade press, and individual customers from well-known companies or other organizations. Include any awards you've won. Like your company Web site itself, these validators let people know that your company is worth doing business with.

✔ **Company news.** People visit your Web site when they hear about your company in connection with offline events such as trade shows, product launches, and even that pesky lawsuit that just keeps moving upward toward the Supreme Court. You look clueless if you don't list a few basics: trade-show appearances, product launches, press releases, article mentions of your company, and so on. (Oh, you don't do many press releases? Now's the time to start! Read Chapter 14.) Figure 5-2 shows the news section of a well-designed Web site. Construct this section after you've cut your teeth on the others and then put some real time and energy into getting it right.

✔ **Industry news.** This is optional, but important. One great way to position your company as an industry leader is to put industry news on your site. The goals of such an area include educating your customers about your industry, validating your place in the industry, and getting repeat visitors by creating a "must-see" area for customers, analysts, and press. (You think your competitors won't be annoyed when everyone in your industry goes to your site for news? Especially when they find themselves doing it, too!) Don't hold up your site launch in order to get this in, but seriously consider creating such an area as soon as you can.

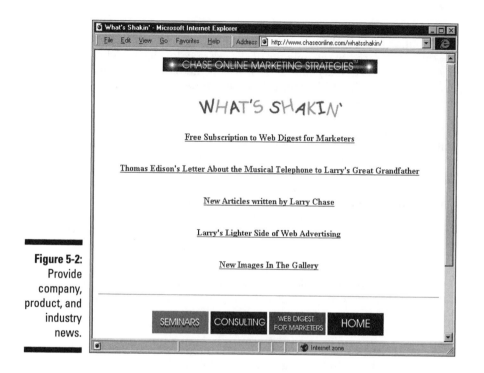

Figure 5-2:
Provide
company,
product, and
industry
news.

Creating a Look and Feel for Your Site

Most marketing pros are good with words — either in writing, public speaking, or both — and can create vivid pictures in listeners' minds. However, like many other people, most marketing pros lack graphic-design skills.

Graphic design is the art of using visual elements to create a pleasing impression in the viewer's mind, and it's an important element in Web-site design — to some of your Web site visitors, the most important element of all.

Graphic design for the Web is a specialized art. Users view a company Web page in different-sized windows, using different-sized screens, with different color capabilities, in all sorts of lighting conditions. Some users have custom settings to override the designer's choice of font, size, and text colors. Large graphics may make a page look strikingly attractive, yet take such a long time to download that they annoy and drive away users.

Using color correctly on the Web is an art in and of itself. Colors and color combinations that look attractive on one computer can look awful on another. In fact, out of the millions of shades of color that a higher-end computer system can display, only 216 "browser-safe" colors exist that work well across most people's Web setups. If you use other colors, your site is likely to look awful to at least some of your visitors.

All these complexities and opportunities for error add up to a simple rule: Unless you have graphic-design experience and know, or are willing to learn, the details of Web-specific design, you need help in designing the look and feel of your site. Here are a few possible sources of help:

- **Existing resources.** Your company may already have a "look" based on its logo and printed pieces, such as annual reports. Consider adapting this look for the Web, giving people who are familiar with your company in an offline context a comfortable feeling when they encounter your firm online.

- **Other well-designed sites.** Stealing the designs of other sites just isn't kosher. Looking at other sites, finding ones you like, and using the same *principles* as they do, however, is fine. (You are also free to avoid the practices of the sites that irritate you!)

- **Online advice.** Many sources of online advice on all aspects of Web page creation, including graphics, are available. Two good places to start are the World Wide Web Consortium at `w3.org` and HotWired's design advice site at `www.webmonkey.com`. Other places include online magazines such as Web Review (`www.webreview.com`).

- **CD-ROM resources.** CD-ROMs with "clip art" — professionally designed, noncopyrighted graphics optimized for online use — are available. You can pick up a few thousand buttons, backgrounds, icons, and other graphical elements for under $100 in many cases. With a little time and a good CD-ROM art collection, it's amazing what an average schmoe can do.

- **Printed advice.** Many good books and articles describe how to create and deploy online graphics. Visit online bookstores such as Amazon.com (`www.amazon.com`) and Barnes and Noble (`www.barnesandnoble.com`).

One resource that's always available, and an especially good idea when creating your first site, is outside help. Consider hiring a graphic designer to assist with the look of your Web site. Graphic designers who advertise on the Web are likely to have designed several sites they can refer you to as examples of their work. An example of one designer's Web presence is shown in Figure 5-3. If you need help finding a designer, one company that specializes in finding suitable professionals is Paladin (`www.paladinstaff.com`).

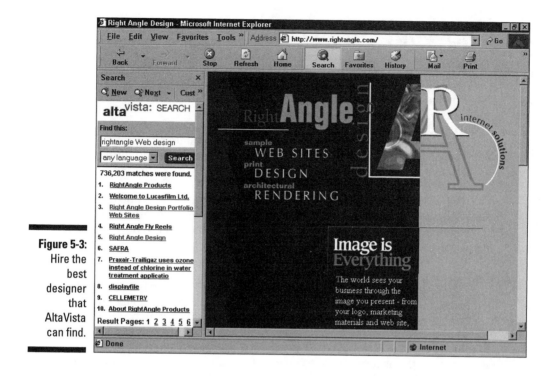

Hiring a graphic designer is different from hiring a Web-design company. A Web-design company will construct your entire site for you; a graphic designer will just work on the look. For a basic site, which you want to do quickly and cheaply while learning as much as possible yourself, a graphic designer is preferable. You can get him or her involved early in the game, late, or even after your initial site is up.

Tell the designer who your expected visitors are, share any existing design elements that you have, and then let the designer work. Unlike a Web design company, a graphic designer will need clear instructions on everything else about the site, including content and navigation. Expect to get a couple of alternatives and a quote for updating your site to include the design. (The designer may even offer to update your printed materials as well, improving consistency.)

At the end of the job, you should own the designer's work. This arrangement is called *work for hire* and is looked down upon by top professionals doing large jobs but is a fact of life for smaller jobs and for designers who haven't yet made a name for themselves. Avoid complicated licensing arrangements in which the designer retains rights to the design.

Having Your Site Done for You

Although it's a good idea to create your initial site yourself, you may simply feel that you don't have the time or the expertise to do so. If that's the case, you'll need to get outside help.

The good news is that many individual consultants and consulting companies have sprung up to help companies create and maintain their Web sites. The bad news is that there are many, many ways to go wrong in hiring a Web consultant.

But wait, there's more bad news! Having a consultant do your Web site will probably save only a small amount of your time. A Web site is such an important reflection of your business that you should expect to be heavily involved with the project from start to finish.

The important steps in working with an outside consultant are setting up the consulting engagement, managing the work, and following through when the work is done. Although these steps are the same for any consulting work or any general project, there are some specifics for a Web project that may surprise you.

Many of these steps apply to managing an internal Web project as well. Check them out even if you're doing the work yourself.

Getting engaged

A consulting project is often referred to as an "engagement," and starting one might require more forethought than some marriages! Here are some simple rules that will help you get good results from a Web consultant.

- ✓ **Find a site that has the elements you need.** Spend some time surfing Web sites, both inside and outside your own industry, to find a site that has most of the pieces you need. A clean and attractive front page, easy-to-find contact info, simple navigation, and brief, clear product descriptions are some of the elements you may be looking for. Figure 5-4 shows a site map of a business site with these elements.

- ✓ **Decide how many pages you want in your site.** Remember those sites you surfed in the previous step? See what the major areas are in some sites you like and count how many pages are in each area. Come up with a rough estimate of the number of pages in your site. *Hint:* The lower the number, the lower the cost and the greater the odds that your project will be a success.

✔ **Find several local consultants.** Even in this wired age, being able to meet with your consultant in person is a real benefit — especially for your initial project. Look at local business sites that you like and find out who created them. Talk to friends and colleagues to find consultants in your local area who have done good work. Check the Yellow Pages or specialized small business Web sites such as Onvia (`www.onvia.com`) and Office.com (`www.office.com`) for any local listings. Ask about pricing.

✔ **Set a budget.** Now that you have some idea of what you want and what other sites have cost in your local area, set an upper limit for your budget. Make sure that the figure you come up with is in line with the benefits you expect to get from your site. As a test, consider the impact that spending the same amount of money on radio advertising might have for you.

✔ **Interview consultants.** Talk to the consultants you identified in Step 4. (It really helps to talk to more than one, so don't rush this stage.) Get their ideas of what they think you need. Tell them what you're looking for and get a ballpark estimate as to time frame and budget.

✔ **Choose a consultant.** Make an initial choice as to your consultant. Don't throw away the others' business cards until your first choice has shown you some good initial results!

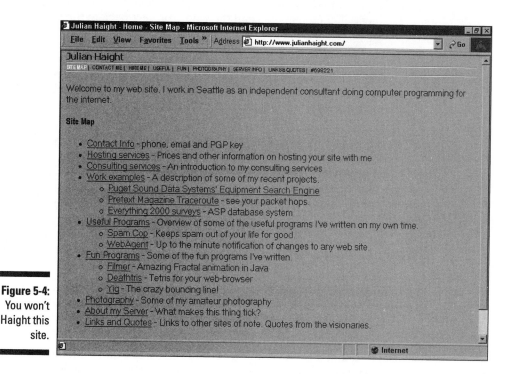

Figure 5-4:
You won't
Haight this
site.

Picking someone you believe you can trust is the most important part here. You can always have your Web site made larger or flashier later, but the initial site simply needs to look good, be complete within a limited initial scope, and be delivered on time and on budget.

Make sure that you understand before engaging a firm whether the consultancy considers itself primarily a Web-programming company, a Web-design company, or a balance of both. Some Web-site consultants are excellent at creating the technical infrastructure of a site and making it work well but aren't adept at doing the graphics and copywriting. Others are excellent at look-and-feel but have little understanding of good Web-site navigation or making things work "under the hood." The ideal consulting firm is one with a good grasp of both — or one that admits what its expertise isn't, allowing you to hire a freelancer to fill the gap.

Projecting your management style

Project management for Web sites has a lot in common with other projects, but there are a few Web-specific techniques you should be aware of in addition to your usual tactics. The main problem with a Web project is that people react strongly to the look of a Web site — and if you wait until the end, some influential person could send the whole project back to the starting gate. So clear up process hurdles early on to avoid hassle later.

- ✔ **Identify approvers.** Before you start, identify everyone who will need to okay the site before it can go live and be publicized. This should be a short list — and the people on the list should be shown progress at every major step.

- ✔ **Image is everything!** People are likely to react first and foremost to the look of your Web site — the way background colors, images, navigation elements, and layout work together. Get a mockup early on, and have all your approvers look at it and, when it's acceptable, initial it. Better still, get two or three mockups that you can live with, and let the approvers choose a single candidate with which to go forward to the next step.

- ✔ **Make a first impression.** Have your consultant create a working version of the first page of your Web site. At this point, get everyone's final okay on the basic look of the site. Figure 5-5 shows the first page of a Web site we like.

  It's common for the first page of a Web site to get 20–25 percent of all the page views for the site, so it's important to get it right. Also, if the first page meets with everyone's approval, the rest of the site is likely to receive only minor comments.

- ✔ **Get a skeleton crew.** Next, fill out the site by creating a dummy page for each and every page on the site. Each dummy page should have the agreed-upon look and feel for the site plus a one-paragraph description of what will be on that specific page. You can use the skeleton to test overall navigation. Have people review the dummy pages, too; this should be the last chance for "shouldn't we have a page about our company history?" type of comments.

✔ **Fill in the blanks.** Now fill in the content of each page. (This task can often be spread among several people, who can "borrow" content from your business plan and any brochures or other marketing materials you have.) If your site has several sections (news, products, and so on), each written by several people, make sure that each content section has a content "lead" who is responsible for ensuring that the writing style and tone match across all of that section's pages.

✔ **Time for the test tube, baby.** After the site's dummy pages are filled in, set aside some time to test it. Have one person read through all the pages to make sure that they're consistent in how they present your company and its products. Then do a "soft launch" — put the site up on the Web, but don't publicize the fact that it's there until everyone who needs to approve of the site has had a chance to do so.

✔ **Go, go, go!** After the site's up and you're happy with it, get the word out. Put the URL on business cards, stationery, advertisements, and more. Ask for feedback from people you know and from site visitors as well.

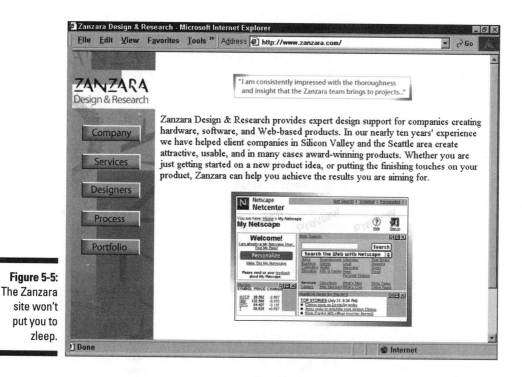

Figure 5-5:
The Zanzara site won't put you to zleep.

The important part about this process is that it has many checkpoints, so it's hard for the project to get too far off-track without your knowing about it — and having a chance to fix the problem.

Beating the wrap-up

Plan now for future updating of your Web site. The basic structure you've created should last for a long time. Work with your consultant now to identify procedures for the following important tasks:

- ✔ **Updating content.** You should be able to do this without the consultant's help, unless you want him or her involved as a checkpoint. Specify how content within a page will be updated.

- ✔ **Adding pages.** Identify likely areas in which you may want to add a new page; the product area will need to be extended, for instance, if you launch a new product. Figure out how long it should take to add a page from initial idea to launch, and who needs to be involved.

- ✔ **Revising the whole site.** At some point, you'll want to revise the whole site. Figure out what might trigger that, and set up regular meetings with your consultant — say, quarterly — to identify needed changes and to start the next major overhaul.

Don't be afraid to tell your consultant that you may get other people involved for some or all of the work ahead; it's very common for your first consultants to play a lesser role, or even to have no role at all, going forward. Do let your consultant know about any expectations that weren't met, as well as the things you were happy about, and whether he or she can expect a good reference from you for future clients.

A caution about copyright

It's easy to get wrapped up in the gorgeous graphics and clean navigation that a Web-site consultant develops for you. But take a deep breath and — before making the new site live — ask the consultant the difficult question, "You do have the right to use all those design elements, right?"

A few inexperienced, rushed, or simply unscrupulous Web-site consultants have been known to copy graphic elements they like from existing Web sites and re-use them in sites they're creating, without permission. That can violate the copyright of whoever created or owns the original site — and cause legal problems for you later.

In one case, a pioneering automotive Web site found that another car site was eerily similar — largely because most of the other site's design, graphics, and even text was identical to the pioneer's own. Lawyers quickly got involved.

Play it safe. Make sure that you get assurance from your Web consulting firm, in writing, that all its design elements and text are either original or properly licensed.

Chapter 6

Creating a Basic Web Site

• •

• •

Marketing touches so many parts of what a company does that marketers are constantly juggling whether to do things themselves, get someone else to do things for them — or just let certain things go undone. When a company makes this kind of decision, it's called a "make vs. buy" decision; when you make this kind of choice yourself, it's just another part of doing your job.

But how do you decide how to get started on your Web site? Never fear, . . .*For Dummies* is here! This chapter is intended specifically to get you over the hump. Drawing on the experience and insight we've accumulated over several decades in old and new media — enough to get us into some really interesting arguments — we show you how to pick a target and do useful Web work yourself, or manage a colleague or contractor doing the work. This chapter helps you become a Web marketing "insider," fast.

Deciding Whether to Do It Yourself

Internet marketing adds a new dimension to the classic marketer's dilemma — should I do it myself or have someone else do it? There still aren't as many people with appropriate Internet marketing skills as there are with more traditional skills such as copy writing for print, script writing for broadcast, art and illustration for print, production for broadcast, and so on.

This is really a sticky wicket, to borrow a term from the ancient and confusing sport of cricket, because it makes both sides of the "make vs. buy" decision harder. Because the Internet is so new, it's unlikely that you have all the needed skills yourself — so it's unlikely that you can "make" the whole thing yourself.

But, again because the Internet is so new, going out to "buy" Web development services is hard as well. Costs, time frames, and desirable outcomes for Internet marketing tasks are not as well established as for print or broadcast counterparts. This makes it harder to hire and effectively manage outsiders to do the work.

The sheer range of possibilities for what can be done in Internet marketing is so mind-boggling as to make you want to consider giving up before you start. Luckily, deciding what role you should take in creating a Web site for your company, product, or service is not an all-or-nothing decision. Actually, a number of related tasks are involved, from setting goals for the Web site to writing the actual HTML code to giving final approval, and it's rare that one person does them all.

No matter what your target, in order to make the right decisions, you need to understand the major steps involved in creating a Web site, know what kinds of people usually are involved, and pull it all together into a plan.

The best thing is for you to be responsible for ensuring that things get done but not necessarily do them all yourself. Manage the whole process and make sure that the results are satisfactory. Plug in other people — even people above you in the organization — to get the work done, but take charge of keeping it on track.

One of the most useful things to do in planning your Web site is to check other sites as a source of ideas for what needs to be included. One useful directory of small but useful sites is the list of companies invested in by Softbank Venture Capital, shown in Figure 6-1. You'll find the list of these sites in the Portfolio section of the Softbank Venture Capital site at www.sbvc.com.

If you look at a number of small but professional-looking, sites, you'll get a pretty good idea of the major topics you need to cover in the first or second version of your own site. You'll also begin to get an idea of what kind of graphical designs for a site look professional and which ones look amateurish. Also view sites of some of your competitors to further flesh out your "To Do" list.

The same basic decision-making considerations apply whether you are creating a whole new Web site or just adding a new area to an existing site. In this chapter, we talk about "creating a site" with the understanding that you may just be creating one area within a larger overall site — or that you may even be creating an intranet site or a Web-based business.

Figure 6-1:
Many
Softbank
companies'
sites are
good small
sites.

Steps to creating a site

It's very easy to just jump into creating a Web site yourself or hiring someone else to do it for you, without a full understanding of all that's needed to make the project a success. In Chapter 5, we describe the project plan you need to follow to create a site. Now, here are the details. Follow these steps to create a basic marketing-oriented Web site:

1. **Set your goals, budget, and target launch date.**

   Set your goals and determine what the budget is going to be. Then decide your deadline. Walk before you run — if this is your first cut at a site, for instance, then try to make it as good as the sites of a couple of your competitors, but not necessarily better than any site ever done. Make sure to get approval of your goals, budget, and time frame from anyone who can force you to go back to the drawing board if he or she doesn't like the site. (See Step 9, "Final approval," in this list.)

2. **Sketch out the initial site structure.**

   This is the part where you save the project from disaster. Sketch out the major pieces of the site and how they relate to each other. What are the major "buckets" you're going to put content in? For a product or service site, for instance, you need a product description, how to buy information, and any awards, press mentions, or positive customer comments you've received.

3. Create a detailed page mockup.

Here's something you may want help with. You need to create a detailed mockup of the look and layout of one or two pages in your site — usually the home page and one interior page. Get approval on these! Having needed approvers physically sign final mockups helps to avoid confusion and finger-pointing later in the project.

4. Create Web pages and navigation.

Again, get help here if you're not an expert. You need to create, or have someone create, the actual HTML files, placeholders for graphics (or the graphics files themselves), and navigation to link them all together. One of the authors (Smith) likes to have a consultant create a bunch of blank pages with the right "look" and navigation so that he can then focus on getting the copy and final graphics right on each page. Sites that have site maps are good models to look at to see what's in a site. Figure 6-2 shows a site map for a medium-sized site.

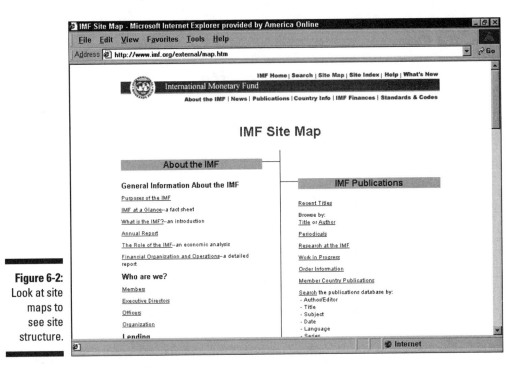

Figure 6-2: Look at site maps to see site structure.

5. Write copy.

If you try to combine the copywriting and navigation issues, you're likely to fail miserably. That's because it's hard to know what to write until you have the site structure figured out. After you know where your pages go in relation to each other, write a draft of the copy for each page. And follow the Web writer's version of the old acronym, KISS: Keep It Short and Sweet.

6. Create graphics.

No matter how much you want or need to do an entire Web site yourself, you will probably need some help here. There is no quicker way to make a site look amateurish than to skimp on graphics. If you really need to save money, create the entire site — links and everything — and then bring in a graphics person, when everything else is nearly done, to make the site look good. That way, you aren't paying a graphics expert to do interface design, copy writing, and so on. (You'd be surprised how often the graphics expert ends up doing almost everything.)

7. Combine pieces into pages.

You need someone expert in HTML to pull text and graphics together within the overall "look" of the site specified by your page mockups and site design.

8. Test.

Give yourself several days after the site is "finished" to test, copyedit, and proofread it. If you run out of testing time before launch, at least try all the links before launch. Then give the site a thorough going-over just after launch, including trying all the links (again) and proofreading all the text. Quickly fix all mistakes.

9. Get final approvals.

Early in the process, identify all the people who could make you take the site down if they don't like it. (This can be a surprisingly broad circle of people, including not only your co-workers but also members of your board of directors, investors, and even opinionated outsiders.) Then, make sure that each such person — or that person's boss — approves the site before launch.

10. Launch.

Launch means either: copying a new site over an existing site, thereby updating it; or letting the world know about your new site after it's built. For a new site, consider doing a "soft launch," which is turning the site on at its real URL but not publicizing it until you've had a few days to make sure that it's right. But for any type of launch, make sure that at some point soon after you turn on the site, you do let everyone know about it. (See Chapter 8 for more.)

11. Celebrate and get ready for next time.

Near the end of your site-building adventure, you'll find people coming up with good ideas that you don't have time to implement before launch. Collect these ideas and then save them in three categories: quick fixes, major fixes, and next-time fixes. Quick fixes are minor things that you'll fix right away; major fixes are larger problems that will require serious work and re-testing; and next-time fixes, whether major or minor, will wait until the next time you overhaul the site.

There are also a few useful things you can do after launch. One is to hold a post-mortem meeting: Gather together everyone involved, thank them, ask them what went right and wrong, and ask them about their ideas for future revisions of the site.

Another useful step is to put a survey on your site and see what people think. You can do this yourself, as part of the site, or use an outside service.

Who does the work?

Many different people are involved in the creation of most company Web sites, even simple ones. You may get someone to "do your Web site for you," but even then, people in your company will end up doing an awful lot of the needed work. Even the most expert outside consultants will still need people in your company to give direction, provide existing graphics and text documents to be adapted for use in the site, give approvals along the way, and, of course, write the final check.

The most important thing is for someone in your company to take responsibility for the successful creation and launch of the site. This person can be called the project manager, the Web site guru, or even the DRI ("Directly Responsible Individual"). One person is needed who can stand up and say "the buck stops here" for the Web project.

Here's a list of some of the roles that need to be filled to create a smallish, but serious, business Web site.

 ✔ **Sponsor.** Someone in senior management needs to be the project sponsor. This person must approve the project goals, budget, and time frame and is mainly responsible for project signoff just before launch. This person must also face down any other senior people who try to force big changes on you late in the project. Do not wait until the end of the project to try to obtain a sponsor.

 ✔ **Project manager.** This is the person responsible for the budget, schedule, and goals of the Web site. The project management role can be a relatively narrow one, in which the project manager basically coordinates the project within strict parameters set by others, or a broad one, with considerable decision-making responsibility. (Frequently, project management for a Web site is seen as a narrow role at first but ends up broadening as the project proceeds.)

✔ **Site designer.** This person lays out the different structure and navigation of the Web site. It's possible for project managers to do this by themselves or to coordinate closely with someone else to do it. The site design must support the goals of the site or the project won't be very successful.

✔ **Writer.** The writer or writing team creates or edits all the text in the Web site. Don't just cut and paste text from disparate sources without having one person or group review and edit it or the site will seem like Frankenstein's monster — a bunch of unrelated pieces sewn together.

✔ **Graphic designer.** The graphic designer creates the overall "look" of the site and also creates graphical elements such as buttons, headings, and others. Having a good graphic designer involved is often the key factor in ending up with a professional-looking site.

✔ **HTML expert.** The HTML expert takes the site designer's layout, the writer's text, and the artist's graphics and actually puts them together into Web pages. This role is extremely important — and it's important that this person not be expected to do all the other jobs as well.

✔ **Programmer (if needed).** A programmer handles more complex tasks, and simple sites usually don't need one — except if you have a form for people to fill out, in which case a programmer will help send the data coming from the form into a database. Try to avoid having programming in your first cut at a site; if you do have programming involved, start it early and manage it as a separate, high-priority project.

✔ **Interaction designer (advanced sites).** An interaction designer (sometimes also called an "information architect" or "usability specialist") tests your site to make sure that people can accomplish needed tasks with it. It's amazing how often an interaction designer finds that it's difficult or impossible to complete simple tasks using your lovingly created site.

For smaller sites, several roles can be combined. One of the authors (Bud) was both site designer and writer for the Zanzara site, shown in Figure 6-3; Frank has been both project manager and writer on another site. Often, the HTML expert also handles simple programming tasks. (If so, make sure that the programming tasks get their own plans and deadlines and then watch them carefully.) When roles are combined, it's very important to be clear up front about who's doing what, or you'll find that crucial work doesn't get done.

If you have to coordinate the efforts of a lot of different departments, each with a section of the Web site, it sometimes helps to push responsibility down to each individual Web site section. Name a *content lead* for each distinct section of the Web site to make sure that all the writing, graphics, and other elements from that department get pulled together in a timely manner. The content leads may have other responsibilities for the overall site — writer, site designer — but knowing who is responsible for coordinating each Web site section makes it easier for you to collect all the bucks from the right different people.

Putting it all together

The questions of who does what, and when, are the critical questions for managing a project such as creating your own Web site. To show how you can sum up these questions, we've created Table 6-1. It combines "who" — the various roles, across the top of the page — and "what," which are the tasks listed down the left side. If you fill in "when," you have a pretty good start on understanding what needs to be done to create a Web site.

You can use the table "as is," or use it as a guide to creating your own. You may have different roles and different tasks for your specific project, but the overall picture is likely to be similar to Table 6-1. To download a spreadsheet that contains the contents of Table 6-1, visit the *Internet Marketing For Dummies* Web site at www.catalanoconsulting.com/imfd.

Table 6-2 is a filled-in example showing how you may use Table 6-1. Each date shown is the end date. Notice that the total elapsed time is about two months. This amount of time is high for a small site with 12–15 pages and 3–4 people working together, but about right for a larger site with 20–30 pages and a full team of 6–8 people.

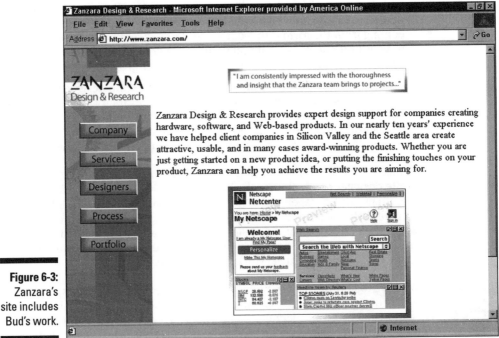

Figure 6-3:
Zanzara's site includes Bud's work.

Table 6-1   **Just Fill In Names and Dates to Create a Plan**

	Sponsor:	*Project Manager:*	*Site designer:*	*Writer:*	*Graphic designer:*	*HTML expert:*	*Programmer:*
Goals & Budget							
Structure							
Mockup							
Navigation							
Text							
Graphics							
HTML							
Test							
Approvals							
Launch							
Celebration							

Table 6-2   **Example Project Plan**

	Sponsor: SUSAN	Project Mgr. (approves): FRED	Site designer: TRACY	Writer: XIAN	Graphic designer: CHRISTA	HTML expert: DEAN	Programmer: XXXX
Goals & Budget	1/15	1/15					
Structure		1/22	1/22				
Mockup		1/29			1/29		
Navigation		1/29	1/29				
Text		2/12		2/12			
Graphics		2/12			2/12		
HTML		2/19				2/19	
Test		2/26	2/26	2/26	2/26	2/26	
Approvals	3/05	3/05					
Launch		3/12					
Celebration		3/16					

Creating a Web Page

One of the great things about the Web that has contributed so much to its popularity is that just about anyone can create a Web page. Web pages are set up using a simple language called HyperText Markup Language, or HTML.

Here's a simple example of HTML. If you type the following in HTML:

```
HTML makes it easy to specify <b>bold</b> and
             <it>italics</it>.
```

It appears as follows when you view it in your Web browser:

```
HTML makes it easy to specify bold and italics.
```

The characters surrounded by angle brackets are called *tags,* and they tell your browser how to display text or perform other special functions. A tag with a slash in front of it, such as </b> to end bold text, is called an *end tag.* It tells the browser to stop following the matching command that came before, such as <b> to begin bold text.

Not only is HTML fairly simple, at least to get started with, but also you don't even have to use HTML to create a Web page. A number of free and inexpensive tools exist that make creating a Web page as easy as creating a word processing document. (It's still good to understand some basics of HTML, as described in the preceding paragraphs, so that you understand what the tool is doing for you.)

Plug alert: A number of easy ways to create Web pages are described in *Creating Web Pages For Dummies,* 5th Edition, by Bud Smith and Arthur Bebak — yes, the same Bud Smith who is co-author of the book you're reading right now. If you really want to create your own Web page, this bestselling book is a great way to do it. And now back to our regularly scheduled marketing book.

Actually, the main barrier to creating professional-looking Web pages isn't HTML knowledge. It's having the graphics sense needed to make a page look good. Just as learning how to use a word processing program doesn't make you a good writer, knowing how to use HTML (or a Web page creation tool) doesn't make you a good Web page designer, either.

Should you do it?

So now that you know you *can* create your own Web page; the question is, do you *want* to? There are three reasons you might want to create a Web page yourself:

1. So that you can learn to create your own Web site.

2. So that you can learn to create specific Web pages that you hand off to someone else, who makes them look good and adds them to the site.

3. So that you can learn something about the process of creating a Web page to manage a Web site project better.

Learning to create your entire Web site yourself is not really practical unless you have graphics sense and are willing to devote several months to learning. It is practical, though — and a good idea — to learn enough to be able to create single Web pages and to better manage a Web site project. In that spirit, consider trying the following hands-on project.

How to do it

This section tells you how to create a simple Web page using a very popular program, Allaire HomeSite. The steps describe how to download a free trial version of HomeSite and use it to create your own Web page.

Because Web sites change all the time, and Web tools change almost as often, it's possible that some of the details of the following steps will change after this book is published. If the steps don't seem to be working for you, check the *Internet Marketing For Dummies* Web site at www.catalanoconsulting. com/imfd for an update.

To create your own Web page, follow these steps:

1. **Download the evaluation version of Allaire HomeSite from the Allaire Web site at** www.allaire.com; **then Install HomeSite.**

   Use the instructions on the site to complete this process. Look for the Downloads tab on the front page; then fill out the requested information to register and reach the Downloads page. Ignore the information about Jrun Server; you don't need it to complete these steps.

2. **Find a graphic that you can use in your Web page.**

   The graphic can be a photograph, a logo, or a background graphic — anything that relates to your business. Save the graphic as a .GIF graphic (if it's computer generated with relatively few colors), as a .JPG image (if it's a photograph or other image with hundreds of colors), or as a Windows bitmap (.BMP) file (if you don't have the ability to save a .GIF or a .JPG from your graphics program).

   Right-click any graphic on a Web page to save it to your hard disk. (But don't republish it to the world without permission.)

3. **Using a word processor, write some text that you can use in your Web page.**

   For instance, you can write a paragraph describing your company history and a paragraph or bulleted list describing your products and services.

Don't spend much time on formatting the text; you will probably have to redo the formatting in HomeSite.

4. **Also using a word processor, write a brief description of Web sites that you use in your work, in paragraph or bulleted list form.**

Just name the site and briefly describe its value.

5. **Start HomeSite.**

6. **Copy and paste the text from your word processor into HomeSite.**

Figure 6-4 shows work in progress on a Web page.

7. **Use the text-entry and text-formatting commands in HomeSite to create a first-level header with your business name; a second-level header, About the Company; a paragraph of text describing your company; a second-level header, Our Products and Services (drop one or the other if you don't offer both), and a paragraph or bulleted list describing what you sell.**

You can use the following commands:

- **Paragraph format pull-down list.** To assign a header, use the Tags pull-down list. Type header text, highlight it, and then pull down the list to select a header level. The text changes to the appropriate header.

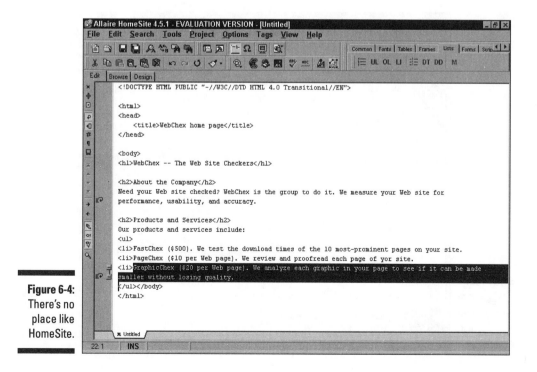

Figure 6-4:
There's no place like HomeSite.

• **Paragraph alignment buttons.** The paragraph alignment buttons are Align Center and Align Right. Highlight the text or graphic that you want to align and then click the appropriate button. The object realigns.

• **Numbered and bulleted lists.** To make a list of items into a numbered or bulleted list, choose the Lists tab and then click the button for Unordered list (bullets) or Ordered list (numbers) Select each item in the list and then click the List Item button to assign it as an item.

• **Bold, italic, and underline.** To add text styles, simply highlight the desired text and then click the Bold or Underline button. (Use these styles sparingly or your Web page will look like a hostage ransom note!)

If you want to see what the page will look like to the user, click the Browse tab. The Web page displays in its final appearance. Click the Edit tab to return to editing.

8. Add hyperlinks.

In the text that describes Web sites you use, find keywords that describe the site and select them. Then click the Anchor button. The Anchor dialog box appears, as shown in Figure 6-5.

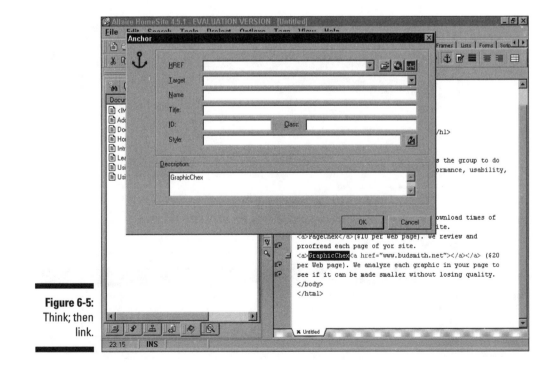

Figure 6-5:
Think; then
link.

9. **In the Anchor dialog box, type the URL of the Web site to which you want the text to link next to the HREF prompt; then click OK.**

   The text becomes a hyperlink to the Web URL.

   Avoid putting your links in unclear phrases such as "MyCo just moved to new offices" — the user won't know whether clicking the link gets them a large, slow-to-download photo of the offices, a brief text description of them, a link to your real estate agent's Web site, or something else. This lack of knowledge may frustrate your Web visitor. Instead, say something like: "Want to know more about our new offices? You can see a photo (50K JPEG image) of the new building or read the press release we sent out about the move."

10. **Insert an image into your Web page.**

    Click the Image button to bring up the Image dialog box. Click the Browse button (the one with the folder icon) to search your hard disk for the image you want to use. Then enter the size you want it to be.

11. **Continue modifying your Web page until it looks acceptable; then use the File⇨Save command to save your Web page to your hard disk.**

12. **Start your Web browser.**

    Use the File Open command (File⇨Open, or Ctrl+O in either Internet Explorer or Netscape Navigator) to open the file that you just created in your Web browser. You can see a fully usable Web page. Try clicking links to make sure that they actually take you out to the open Web.

    The only difference between your local Web page and a true World Wide Web page is that your local Web page isn't available to other Web users until you publish it on a Web server. Even if your machine is connected to the Web, it isn't a Web server unless it's running a program that responds to requests sent via HyperText Transfer Protocol — the http in Web URLs — which is the communications standard underlying the Web. (HyperText Markup Language, or HTML, is the page layout standard underlying the Web.)

Congratulations! You just created a page that can go on the World Wide Web!

Just creating this Web page is a valuable exercise for learning how Web publishing works and understanding some of its strengths and limitations. If you want to actually publish your page on the World Wide Web, check with your Internet service provider to see whether it has free disk space for Web pages. You can also use the GeoCities Web site at www.geocities.com to publish noncommercial Web pages for free. When you actually want to use your Web page or Web site for business, GeoCities offers domain name registration and Web site hosting as well. As mentioned earlier in this chapter, see *Creating Web Pages For Dummies*, 5th Edition, by Bud Smith and Arthur Bebak, (IDG Books Worldwide, Inc.) for details on how to publish a Web page.

Making Smart Graphics

If you create your own Web pages, you may find yourself creating graphics. Or when managing a Web project, you may find yourself reviewing graphics and Web pages created by others. Graphics are an area in which it's very easy to make mistakes.

You can use some simple rules when creating or reviewing Web pages to make sure that they look good and work well. Use the following checklist when reviewing your plans for a Web page:

- ✔ **Keep the file size of Web pages small.** Top Web sites keep their pages under 20 kilobytes (KB) for front pages and 50 KB for interior pages. Why? Because otherwise, many people have to wait too long for the page to appear. A typical dialup modem downloads at about 2 KB per second, so a 20 KB page takes 10 seconds to download, and a 50 KB page takes almost half a minute. Anything longer than that is just about certain to drive people away.

- ✔ **Use JPEG for most graphics.** Web graphics can be stored in either .GIF (Graphics Interchange Format) or JPEG (Joint Photographic Experts Group) format. JPEG files tend to be much smaller for photographic images and somewhat smaller for most graphics. You can test your non-photographic images in both formats, but consider trying JPEG first.

- ✔ **Link to big images.** Don't put that big "Wanted" poster image of yourself on a main page; use a small thumbnail instead. Then link off to the main image using some text such as "Want to see the big picture (50 KB)? Click here." For an example, see Figure 6-6.

- ✔ **Preload graphical menus.** One popular, but bad, idea is to use a bunch of little graphics for navigation across the top or down one column of a site. Every time a user on a slow modem wants to see another page, he or she has to wait while these little graphics haphazardly load or redisplay. Test your site on a slow modem to make sure that it doesn't do this.

- ✔ **Stick to the 216 browser-safe colors.** Only 216 colors work uniformly well on both Windows and Macintosh machines that are set to display in only 256 colors, an all-too-common choice. To find out what these colors are, check your graphics program or search for "browser-safe colors" on the Web. (CNET is a good resource.) You'll see several lists of the browser-safe colors and some details about why only these colors are safe.

- ✔ **Trust your feelings, Luke.** As Obi-Wan Kenobi said in the original *Star Wars* movies, you have to trust your feelings about how Web pages look. If you think a Web page, Web site, or a specific graphic looks cheesy or amateurish, say so — preferably before your site goes live. People's tastes vary, but very good and very bad Web graphic designs are usually plain to everyone.

✔ **Test, test, test.** Check graphics and page layouts on Macintosh and Windows machines set to use various resolutions (especially 800 x 600 and 1024 x 768) and color depths (especially 8-bit, or 256 colors, and thousands of colors). One common problem is that text that looks fine on a typical 800 x 600 laptop screen is too small to read at 1024 x 768 or higher resolution.

These instructions won't keep you out of all graphics-related problems on your Web site, but they're a good start. After you review things yourself, find someone with a graphical sense to add his or her opinion to yours. Better that you learn about problems from one tactful colleague, before publication, than from 200 flamers the day after you launch.

Although Internet Explorer and Netscape Navigator are the obvious browser-testing choices, don't forget to test your graphics — and for that matter, your entire Web site — using America Online's built-in Web browser. Certain proprietary modifications in AOL's otherwise-standard browser have been known to make some sites all but unusable. And with AOL's more than 23 million members, it's too large a pool of potential customers to turn away.

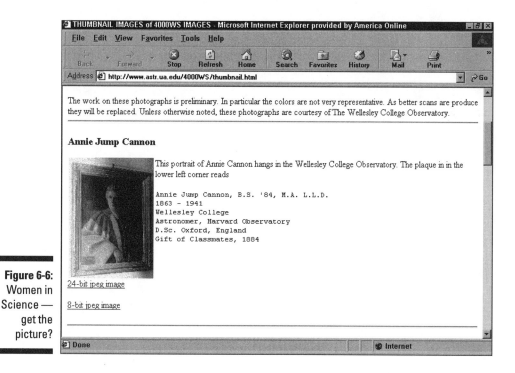

Figure 6-6: Women in Science — get the picture?

Chapter 7

Marketing on Your Web Site

● ●

In This Chapter

▶ Using your Web site to market products or services

▶ Presenting marketing information on your site

▶ Including business-related news on your site

● ●

*E*ven as the World Wide Web is about to enter its second decade, not many people understand just how powerful the Web can be as a marketing vehicle. Because the Web is still changing, using it effectively is an art that has yet to be perfected. But the same novelty factor that makes the Web difficult to use effectively also means that successful efforts are well rewarded. You can get a lot of positive attention and feedback if you do a good job of marketing on your Web site.

In this chapter, you roll up your metaphorical sleeves and plunge into the nitty-gritty of the most important ways you can do marketing work on your Web site. If you follow the suggestions in this chapter, you should be able to move quickly to the head of the class in your Web marketing efforts.

Your Web Site as a Marketing Vehicle

Different businesses depend on different ways to get the word out about themselves and their products or services. A consultant may depend on word of mouth and phone calls to business contacts to get new work. For the manager of a roadside diner, a billboard on the highway may be the linchpin of marketing. For a used-car dealer, late-night television commercials and newspaper ads may reach the key buyers. Every business has one or more established methods of advertising, and businesses that want to grow are always looking for new techniques to move themselves forward.

The Internet and the Web will continue to be the fastest-growing and most important new marketing vehicles for most businesses over the next couple of decades. If you focus now on online marketing, especially marketing over the Web, you'll be well-positioned to benefit from the growth in importance of the online world. If you wait, your competitors will probably benefit from that growth rather than you. Now is the time to decide how to use your Web site as a marketing vehicle in the future.

Coordinating your Web site with your overall marketing plan

Starting your Web marketing effort is easy if you realize that the Web should fit tightly into your more traditional marketing efforts (we refer to traditional, non-online marketing efforts as *offline* marketing in this book). Every advertisement, white paper, mailing, and press release that you create can be used as a resource for your Web site. And every marketing-related event that you attend or participate in — each trade show, product launch, or news conference — can be reflected on your Web site as well. Figure 7-1 shows a general idea of the relationship between the offline world and the Web site.

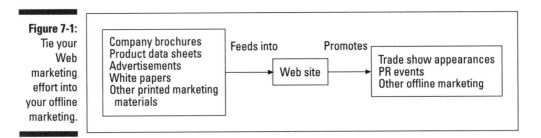

Figure 7-1:
Tie your Web marketing effort into your offline marketing.

The idea behind Figure 7-1 is that your current marketing materials feed into your Web site, and each marketing piece can be adapted for use on your site. Your Web site in turn helps promote other activities, such as trade show appearances and PR (public relations) efforts. After you've been developing and extending your site for a while, arrows pointing in the opposite direction also appear. Marketing events and seminars can be captured and put on your Web site as sound clips, movies, or even just written descriptions. And new content you develop for your Web site can be recast as printed materials to reach people who don't have access to the Web.

Another concern is fitting your Web marketing effort into your company's other online efforts. The way to predict your firm's online future is to realize that nearly every division and department of your company will eventually be reflected online. Marketing goes online first and will be foremost for a long time to come, but customer service and support, sales, hiring, and other company functions will quickly go online as well. Here are some parts of a typical company that may be represented on a Web site:

- ✔ **Marketing department.** Marketing should be responsible for the overall Web site and most of its content. Marketing-related concerns and content include the overall look and feel of the Web site, company and contact information, product photographs, descriptions and prices, information about where to buy products, and events the company is involved in.

- ✔ **Public relations.** This specialty within the marketing department deserves separate attention. PR should develop an area for press interest — if any group will depend on the Web for its first impression of you, the press will. PR should put press releases on the Web site simultaneously with release over the newswires. PR may also want to put confidential or preview information for long-lead-time press on a password-protected area of your Web site.

- ✔ **Sales department.** When your Web site captures visitor interest in your products or services, marketing and sales can work together to help deliver potential customers to the company's various sales channels. (You get a big boost in justifying your online marketing expenditures if you can show that your Web site is generating sales.)

- ✔ **Customer service and support.** Post customer service contact info and answers to common questions on the Web site. Online customer service is already very important and growing rapidly; companies reduce expenses by making the customer part of the service and support solution. Use your Web site, e-mail lists (as we describe in Chapter 11), and other online resources to involve customers in finding solutions to their problems.

- ✔ **Human resources.** Help-wanted ads can be posted on the Web site, with an e-mail address where résumés can be sent. (See Chapter 9 for more information about e-mail contact information.) A good-looking Web site helps your company attract top employees as well as customers. Marketing can help the human resources department get established on the Web site, but updating help-wanted postings is HR's job.

- ✔ **Finance.** Finance should put your company's annual report or its equivalent on the Web site, or at least make ordering a copy of your report over the Web easy for interested parties. It's very convenient for your customers, press, analysts, and others to be able to find your annual report online. However, annual reports are required to be honest, and in a bad sales year you may not want to post all the gory details on your Web site.

Out of all the departments that are involved, marketing should play the leading role in defining and developing the company World Wide Web site. It's like the old joke about the role of the chicken and the pig in a ham-and-eggs breakfast: The chicken is involved, but the pig is committed. In this story, marketing is represented by the pig. Other departments are chickens.

In addition to the preceding areas listed, other company materials may go online as well, but much of this other information appears on *intranets* — employee-only networks that often use Web browsers and servers to deliver information. An example is employee benefits information that the human resources department puts online for employees only.

Intranets aren't a direct concern of marketing, because customers don't access them. (Though one could argue that medium-sized and large companies need to market themselves to their employees, and divisions market themselves to other divisions, as well.)

A more interesting option, from a marketing point of view, is *extranets* — networks that link suppliers and customers. Though extranets may at first be used only for exchanging functional information such as order status, they can grow into marketing tools as well. If your company develops an extranet that includes customers, dealers, or others involved in the sales process, marketing should play a growing role in supplying and maintaining this content.

Web surfers frequently use bookmarks to return to Web sites and specific pages they like. Encourage your visitors to bookmark your home page and also to bookmark Web pages within your site that have information about specific products and services. Make sure that the titles of those additional pages accurately reflect what's on them so that visitors can look at the title in their bookmark list and remember why they bookmarked the page in the first place.

Designing your Web marketing effort

Before you start or expand your Web marketing effort, you should take a few initial steps. These can be formal efforts as part of a design process with storyboards and multiple levels of approvals, as described in the previous chapter, or — for smaller efforts — informal checkpoints that you keep in mind as you work on your own or with others.

The first step is to decide how you're going to separate company, product line, and product information. Each of your customers, plus suppliers, members of the press, and even your own employees, see your company through the lens of those products and services they use the most. This focus doesn't cause any problems for companies with one overwhelmingly important product or a single product line, but if you sell multiple products and services, the result may be a great deal of confusion.

From marketing online to selling online?

Because marketing is partly a sales-support activity, you need to be preparing for the day — possibly not too far in the future — when you actually sell products or services over your Web site. Analysts are adjusting their estimates and forecasts upward to accomodate surprising growth in online sales of products and services. The percentage will only continue to grow. If you don't get your share of the online-sales pie, someone else will. So start thinking now about how your marketing efforts can be extended into sales efforts in the next few years.

The following are possible ways to handle Web site organization for a company with multiple products and services:

- ✔ **Don't worry about organization.** Simply throw marketing and other information for your products and services on your Web site in a disorganized fashion, with thorough coverage of some and little of others. (This Really Bad Idea actually seems to be the plan followed on too many sites.)

- ✔ **Separate the company and its products.** The home page of your Web site needs to speak for your company and allow for easy access to company-level information. Your company home page should also point to a separate area for products. Web surfers can check out company information and then *drill down* (link to pages with successively more specific information) to the product they're interested in. You can also have bookmarkable "front pages," with a distinct URL, for your most popular products. This plan is serviceable for a new or newly expanded Web site.

- ✔ **Separate the company's markets.** A more sophisticated approach is to structure your Web site around the different markets your company and its products serve. Because customers think of themselves in terms of their interests, not your products, organizing your Web presence in this way is often the most intuitive for your customers. The Microsoft Web site is a good example of this method in use — it enables access by market, as shown in Figure 7-2. Creating a usable market-segmented Web site is hard to pull off, though, because you must include multiple paths to the same or similar information. Get experienced, professional design help before trying this approach.

- ✔ **Use separate Web sites.** If you have products that have strong constituencies, consider creating separate Web sites for those products. You can still put basic information on the company Web site, but the product site will be the home base for the real diehard users of the product. Creating separate Web sites adds difficulty in design, coordination, and planning but may considerably increase the effectiveness of your overall Web presence.

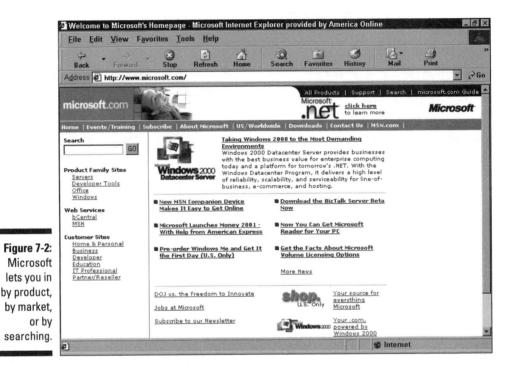

Figure 7-2:
Microsoft
lets you in
by product,
by market,
or by
searching.

One useful way to think of your Web site is as an online trade show or, if you don't do trade shows, a sales call or other customer interaction. Several of the lessons you learn in your person-to-person marketing interactions apply online as well. For instance, when you meet people in a professional context, you're usually trying to get them to do something: buy a large quantity of your product, write a positive article about your company, or feel good about their relationship with your company to put them in an upbeat frame of mind for a future pitch. Think about how to create these same effects in the minds of people who visit you online. Then identify the marketing materials that you use in various person-to-person situations and place this kind of high-priority information front and center in your Web site.

After you develop some idea of the overall structure of the marketing parts of your Web site, you're ready to identify some of the resources you can use on it. Follow these general steps:

1. **Make a list of all your marketing resources.**

   List all press releases, data sheets, brochures, ads, annual reports, white papers, and so on that you have available — even old ones. (Old resources may have information and themes that you can re-use.)

2. **For each marketing resource on your list, briefly describe what you may need to do to it before putting it on the Web.**

   "Reformat and convert to HTML" is the minimum that you need to do to each document. "Update" is another common notation, because marketing documents need frequent updating — and putting obviously outdated material on your Web site is worse than not putting up any information at all.

3. **Separate your resources into "basic marketing" and "news."**

   Pieces that have a long lifespan, such as product brochures, can be thought of as basic marketing; pieces that have a short lifespan, such as press releases and events, are news. (We describe the difference more clearly in the following section, but take a stab at making the distinction now.)

4. **Give some thought as to what to do first; if your resources are limited, consider putting your company information and in-depth information for one major product online first and then using the lessons learned to rapidly expand coverage.**

   You're likely to do a better job, and possibly even a faster job overall, by staging your effort than by trying to hit every target simultaneously.

You may want to take this opportunity to review your marketing pieces with one question in mind: What does each piece urge the reader to do? You do have to be subtle and informational with your Web marketing effort; people quickly click away from obvious hype. But even on the Web, each marketing piece needs to impel the reader to take some action he or she wouldn't have taken otherwise. With luck, that action is a step in the direction of buying your product. Double-check your marketing pieces as you ready them for the Web.

Marketing Information on Your Site

In Chapter 5, we describe what to put on a basic business Web site, including descriptive and contact information for your company. Organizing and creating a simple marketing-oriented site is easy. As your Web site gets larger and more complicated, information becomes harder to organize and update. As your Web site gets more complete, you may spend an increasing amount of your Web-related time thinking about structure and usability, and less about specific pieces of content.

As you expand your Web-based marketing effort, you may also run into some specific concerns about each of the different kinds of information you put online. Based on our experience in both hands-on and consulting roles in this very new medium, we can point out a few of the opportunities and pitfalls to help you be effective right from the start.

Understanding the vital role of press releases

Press releases are the most visible evidence of public relations on the Internet. Although they play an undeniable role in any Internet PR campaign you devise (as we discuss in detail in Chapter 14), should they play a role on your company Web site? Emphatically, yes.

Some people, including some in the press itself, look down on press releases. What could be worse — or more likely to be misleading and self-serving — than company-written news?

Yet press releases are more notable by their absence on your Web site than by their presence. Site visitors expect Web site content to be updated frequently; press releases help accomplish that. Reporters working late into the night to finish a story will visit your company site for the latest news rather than call a PR contact.

Though the press releases are bound to reflect a positive point of view about your products, services, and company, you also have a strong motivation when writing the press release to explain the basic facts that people need to know in as clear, cogent, and understandable a manner as possible. Yes, a bias exists in press release writing, but at least it's a bias the reader expects.

Many organizations prepare too few press releases — and don't post what they do prepare on their own Web site. Consider doing, and posting, a press release for every event of importance, including the following:

- ✔ Field-testing a new product
- ✔ Making a product available for sale
- ✔ Improving a product
- ✔ Launching a service
- ✔ Hosting or participating in an event
- ✔ Entering into a partnership with others
- ✔ Welcoming a new executive

Unit sales, revenue, and other financial milestones are also good press-release topics.

Must Web writing be boring?

Try to avoid being boring, but remember that most writing for the Web does need to be fairly tame. Because of its origins in academia and the military, and because people actively seek Web information themselves instead of passively receiving it, the World Wide Web has a tradition of honesty and directness that makes typical marketing hype seem misplaced. Think of Web writing as describing your company and product to a business colleague, not as creating an extremely slow-moving television commercial. Adhere closely to the established tone of existing Web writing, at least until you gain enough experience to know when you can bend or break the rules.

Press releases are an underused yet vital tool in marketing in general and especially in marketing on Web sites. The concentrated effort that goes into creating and making sure that all the information is correct in a press release makes it something you can use and re-use online and in the offline world, as well. Follow these rules for using press releases on your Web site and you'll do a better job of getting all your marketing information online:

- ✔ **When in doubt, do a press release.** An important event has happened, and you want to announce it on your Web site. What's the best way? The best and easiest method is to write a press release about the event and, if it's of general enough interest, distribute it through PR wires (as covered in Chapter 14) as well as post it on your Web site.

- ✔ **Hit the Web instantly.** Press releases should be on your Web site at the same moment that they hit the PR wires. People who hear news about your company will immediately check your Web site for information; you look bad if the information isn't there.

- ✔ **Make press releases easy to find.** Put a prominent pointer to each new release on your Web site's home page and then post the press release in an appropriate spot on your Web site. Make sure to send an electronic copy of the press release to people who may want to mention it on their own Web pages or otherwise make it known to others.

- ✔ **Link your press releases.** Your press release should include references to key business partners, customers, and others who have a role in the new event, and you can include hyperlinks to their Web sites in the online, HTML version of your press release. This approach makes you look savvy and is often greatly appreciated by those you link to.

✔ **Do a careful job with the HTML.** Carefully converting a press release to HTML so that it looks good on a Web page takes only a modest amount of time and makes you look organized and professional. Set aside an hour or two to convert and review your press release before it's sent out to the world and the rush to put it on the Web hits.

✔ **Create a text-only version.** You'll want a version of your press release that you can send out by e-mail (see Chapter 9 for instructions); make that version available on your Web site along with the HTML version. Then visitors can e-mail the release to their contacts as well — doing your marketing for you for free.

✔ **Create a .PDF file.** Many people like the look of fully formatted documents. The most popular way to reproduce this look on the Web is with an Adobe Acrobat Portable Document Format (.PDF) document. Figure 7-3 shows a site offering .PDF files, and Figure 7-4 shows an example of a .PDF file in action. Note how it allows more precise layout and better graphics than a Web page alone could support. Consider creating a .PDF file of your press release and making it available on your Web site alongside the HTML and text versions.

✔ **Go beyond the release.** You can include additional information that links from the press release, providing more details. For example, one easy-to-create and valuable tool is a Frequently Asked Questions document (FAQ), a longstanding tradition for delivering technical information online that has been successfully adapted for online marketing. (FAQs are sometimes called Q&As, for Question and Answer documents, in traditional marketing jargon.) Link to product data sheets, white papers, or any other information you can put online. Or be adventurous and include a sound or video clip from an analyst call or press conference.

✔ **Ask that others' press releases link to you.** After you earn people's gratitude by appropriately including them in your press releases and linking to their Web sites, ask for the same favor in return. When key partners, suppliers, or customers prepare press releases, ask them to acknowledge any role that your company played and to link from their HTML press release version on their Web site to your Web site.

Many of the lessons you learn in creating and posting press releases apply to other online efforts as well. Putting information up on your Web site fast; making it easy to find; linking to the Web sites of partners, suppliers, and customers; adding text-only and .PDF versions of files; and asking for mentions and links from others are all vital survival skills for online marketing. If you practice these skills as part of creating and posting press releases and then use your newfound skills 24/7 (that's "all the time," for those of you without a teenager in the house), you can go far in the online world.

Figure 7-3:
Clicking a
.PDF link
brings up
the right
article.

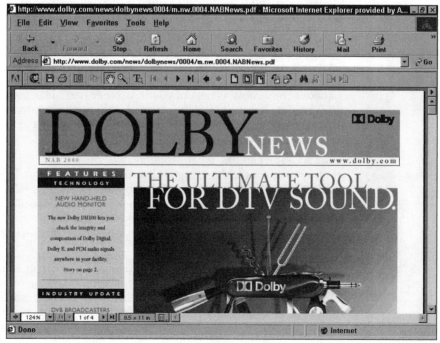

Figure 7-4:
.PDF files
show up
right in your
browser.

Putting product information online

Many companies do a fairly good job of marketing their companies online but don't give much detail about the specific products and services that their companies sell. Having a robust company presence is great, but the company really only exists to deliver products and services to people — most of the time at a profit, it hopes. Your Web site isn't finished — well, it's never really *finished,* but it's not even very good — until you provide detailed information about whatever it is that you sell.

Here and elsewhere in the book we use the word *products* to refer to both products and services — partly for our convenience and yours, and partly because you probably need to package your services in product-like fashion to market them effectively over the Web.

Here is some of the information you need to consider providing on your Web site about each product your company sells:

- ✔ **Product name and functional description.** Don't forget to include a Web page devoted to the product, by name, and a brief functional description of what the product does. If all your previous marketing has been *narrowcast* (sent to a small audience that already understands the topic) via trade-specific publications, industry trade shows, and so on, you may be new to presenting yourself to an audience as diverse as that on the Web. Explain to people, in simple terms, what your product does — even if all the explanation accomplishes is to help them realize that they're not interested.

- ✔ **Who uses the product.** Describe who uses your product and how. Go into some depth; allow your Web surfers — that is, your well-off, media-savvy, potential customers or influencers — to see themselves or someone they know as part of your customer base. Like the product's functional description, a description of who uses your product also helps your Web surfers know whether they should stick around for more information — or surf on.

- ✔ **System requirements.** Most products operate in a specific environment of other products and user activities. You can't run *Doom II* on an original IBM PC XT, and you don't need a copper pot if you don't cook. Communicate, either subtly within other text or in a specific list, what kind of environment your product is used in, what other products need to be present for it to work effectively, and what skills the user needs to have to make it work.

- ✔ **Market position.** Everyone loves a winner, and if you can identify any customer group in which your product is number one, announce it loudly. "Best-selling veeblefetzer worldwide" is the best market position to have, but "the leading veeblefetzer for the North American forest services industry" is fine, too. The markets in which you're number one are likely to be the most profitable for you anyway, so exploit your leadership position(s) on your Web site.

✔ **Customer information.** List big-name customers (with their permission, of course) or, if the numbers justify the claim, give a blanket customer description such as "used by half of the Fortune 500." Let the positive image and success of your customers reflect on you as well. For complicated or expensive products, create success stories that show how a specific customer used your product to solve a problem.

Make sure to get customers' permission before including their names on your site, but don't worry much about being turned down; most customers love the attention. Ask for permission to use their logos on your site as a link: If you exchange links with them to their Web sites, everyone gets a boost.

✔ **Awards, accolades, and (positive) reviews.** Provide external validators (see Chapter 7) showing that your product is the best from some independent point of view. Any awards, positive feedback, or positive reviews that you can mention — or, better yet, link to on another Web site — go a long way toward helping people choose your product.

Your product doesn't have to finish first in a review in order for that review to be worth mentioning on your Web site. In a so-so review, pull out any positive statement on a substantive aspect of your product and quote it. ("The easiest of the reviewed products to use" is probably worth quoting; "the easiest to remove from its packaging material" probably isn't.) If you do finish first in a review, link to it if it's online, even if it says some bad things about your product in between all the good ones. If you finish second or third, consider linking to the review, but surround the link with an explanation of the specific areas in which you're best or information about how you've improved the areas in which the reviewer found fault.

The underlying message in your product description and related information should be, "No need to look any further; this veeblefetzer is the one for you."

If visitors to your Web site are looking to buy, be sure that your site tells them how. (See the next section for details.) Even if the people reading the information are not looking to buy your type of product today, they may either make a purchase or be called on for a recommendation in the future. A distant recollection that comes out as a recommendation, even a low-key one like "I heard Acme veeblefetzers are pretty good," can help you clinch a sale. Product information on your Web site can create just this kind of long-lasting positive impression.

Telling Web surfers where to buy

One of the most important but trickiest issues for marketing on your Web site is telling visitors how to buy your products and services. Because the Web is global, everyone receives the same information simultaneously. However, because of legal restrictions in different places, language barriers, service and support concerns, or for many other reasons, you may not be able to sell the same way — or at all — to everyone who wants to buy.

The first step you can take to prevent problems is to make clear — on your Web site — any restrictions as to who can buy your product and how they can buy. Some limitations will be obvious: If you do interior-decoration consulting in Miami, you won't be expected to fly to Moscow to give a quote. But if you sell a product for one price in Green Bay and a higher price in Germany, you have to think twice before providing pricing and ordering information on your Web site.

Just as an example, consider the issue of price information a bit further. Consider a mythical company that manufactures a high-end stereo system in the Northeastern United States and sells it only in the United States and England. This company charges a higher price in England because of shipping costs, lower volumes, and higher margins expected by the English distribution channel. Now if this company puts the U.S. price of its product on the Web, English customers may start trying to get the product for the U.S. price — perhaps by ordering over the phone, or perhaps by asking a U.S.-based friend to buy for them and ship it over. English distributors will then become upset by the pointed questions some of their customers will ask them and by the lost business caused by people trying to get around the standard distribution system. This is just one example of the potential problems that can occur when you give pricing information on your Web site. Yet giving customers at least a ballpark idea of your product's price is a necessary part of encouraging them to consider buying it, so what do you do?

To begin solving this problem for your own unique situation, review the kind of pricing information you give in existing marketing and sales materials, and study the ways you've previously handled the problems of pricing differences and availability restrictions. Think about how you can continue to support your current pricing and distribution arrangements — or consider how to change them if needed.

Don't be afraid to link

Linking strategies are an important part of Web site design. You should, of course, link extensively within your Web site, but what about links to other sites — don't they just send Web surfers elsewhere, never to return? Quite possibly, yes, so link to other sites only for a good reason. Web sites you should link to include: press coverage or other sites that say good things about your company or product; sites of companies that are partners of yours; sites with industry information; or sites with information about products that are used with your own. These kinds of links not only help Web surfers find out more about your product in a broad sense but also keep them thinking of your product, as well — increasing the chances that they will return to your site.

Here are the major options available for giving pricing and distribution information online:

- ✔ **"I know nothing."** One approach is to give no how-to-buy or pricing information on your Web site. This is a sad choice, given the power of the Web to inspire sales, but a good way to defer problems until you've figured out how to avoid threatening existing sales or distribution channels by using one or more of the other approaches described here. Expect, though, to irritate — and lose — potential customers.

- ✔ **Give distributor information online.** A classy alternative to omitting how-to-buy information is to simply make your current distributor information available online so as to help your Web visitors reach their local sales outlet for your product. Figure 7-5 shows how one company handles this approach. Giving distributor information online can be tricky; for instance, people based in one country may call another country, shopping for a cheaper price. You may need to consider clever alternatives such as having only information specific to a visitor's country show up in that visitor's browser.

Figure 7-5:
Help Web surfers find your distributors online.

✔ **Give a phone number for distributor information.** You can give a phone number for potential customers to call to find their nearest distributor. (Make sure to hire and train the people in the position before posting the phone number!) This is a nice, low-key way to support your existing sales channels and get the right pricing information to the right customers.

✔ **Give an e-mail address for distributor information.** You can give an e-mail address either in addition to, or instead of, a phone number. With e-mail, you have time to think before answering tough questions and you can re-use the contact information you get from the inquiries.

✔ **Give a phone number or fax number for ordering.** "Danger, Will Robinson!" (As the robot used to say in "Lost in Space.") You can allow people to order directly from you, but don't upset your existing apple cart of sales arrangements without a lot of preparation first.

✔ **Support direct online sales.** Online selling is the logical end point of online marketing but is also a double-edged sword that has the potential to hurt more than it helps by upsetting your existing distribution arrangements. Plan carefully, and see *Selling Online For Dummies,* by Leslie Lundquist (IDG Books Worldwide, Inc.), if you plan to take this step anytime soon.

Don't tick off your distributors

We mention elsewhere in this book that one of the most important rules for marketing online is the first sentence of the Hippocratic Oath: First, do no harm — a crucial principle when you give sales information online. Don't undermine your distributors, direct salespeople, and other sales channels by undercutting them with information about direct phone sales, access to other, cheaper distributors, or secure Web-based sales directly from your site.

But wait, you say: What if the online market is bigger and more profitable than the distribution channels I'm going to undercut? Then stop, take a deep breath, and study the problem carefully. Size the Internet market opportunity coldly and realistically, taking into account the experience of others and actual and potential competition. Remember that only about 1 percent of world commerce is online as of the turn of the century. Although the near-term market opportunity for your specific products may be somewhat larger or smaller than that 1 percent, the online market for your products is still likely to be only a small percentage of your total market when you start out. Are you sure that, in going after this small slice, you won't undermine the rest of your sales pie? Review your legal obligations and, just as important, the impression you have left with your distributors, salespeople, and so on as to where they stand with you.

If you plan your move to online-supported or online-based sales carefully and make it with as little damage as possible to existing sales relationships, you'll be in the best position to come out ahead.

You leave a very bad impression with potential customers if you don't handle phone calls and e-mail messages in a prompt and friendly manner. See Chapter 10 for information on handling volumes of e-mail, and consult other resources for information on how to staff your phone lines.

Before you do anything that changes existing sales and distribution relationships, talk to people. Your existing sales channels no doubt know about Web commerce and have some thoughts or even fears about it; ask them what they think and what they would like to see you do. Never surprise your offline sales channels with new developments online; talk to them first, and give them advance, written notice and time to respond before you implement any plans. Even if the only effect of your Web site is to increase overall sales volume without hurting anybody's interests, people need time to plan and staff for that. If you do take steps that take business away from anyone, or increase sales for one channel but not others, more time and previous consultation is needed. Moving forward to help your Web visitors buy is very important; moving carefully is even more important.

News on Your Site

In Wonderland, the Red Queen tells Alice that reality is whatever she says it is. In just the same way, on your Web site, news is whatever you say it is. To be more specific, your Web visitors don't expect "news" in the *New York Times* sense on your Web site; they expect "what's new" information about recent events that relate to your company and its products. But the tradition on Web sites is to call this part of the site "news," so you should have a "news" area on your site.

We've heard it said that the most intriguing words in marketing any product are "new" and "free." The Web is already free to use (after the Internet service provider gets paid), so you have that base covered. But the word we're concerned with here is "new." We believe that people visiting your home page should see some piece of new information right up front, on the first screen of information they access, and that some brand-new information should appear there at least once a week. (The Microsoft home page, shown in Figure 7-2 earlier in this chapter, is one of the many that follow this rule.) Seeing something new makes people stop and click their way into your site rather than just surf by, and it keeps them coming back regularly.

Figure 7-6 shows an example of news on a Web site. New information appears right on the first screen of the home page and a news section is readily available. Use this approach or suffer from lack of public interest in your Web presence.

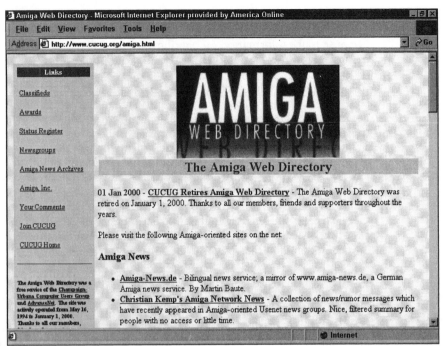

Figure 7-6:
The news is,
they quit!

So what kind of news should you put on your Web site? Earlier in this chapter, we emphasize the vital role of press releases in online marketing, but even we have to admit that not everything that happens relating to your company and products is worth a press release. Here are some of the things that you should put in the news section of your Web site:

✔ **Product developments.** Have you made any changes in your product — any at all? Anything "new" or "free" about your product? This is the place to put minor stuff such as slight revisions in software, new printings or editions of books, changes to the emission control system of a riding lawnmower, and so on. Your most devoted customers are often more interested in this kind of stuff than even your company's employees.

✔ **Trade shows.** Always let the world know your trade-show schedule well in advance. A month before the show, give details about what you'll be doing at the show; two weeks before, remind people that it's coming right up. During and after the show, post any news generated on your Web site.

✔ **Other events.** Any event you participate in — a press conference, a trade group meeting, a university hiring day — is worth mentioning on your Web site. (People who see you at these events will check your Web site to learn more about your company and will be pleased to see the event mentioned.)

✔ **Sales wins.** Any significant new customers or increases in sales? Give ammunition to your fans out there — tell them how your business is growing.

✔ **Distribution changes.** Any new sales channels or new increases in your geographic reach? Other changes in how your products are sold and delivered? Again, even arcane stuff is interesting to somebody. Let people know how your distribution is expanding.

✔ **Executive changes.** Any new hires in the executive suite? Note them in the news section.

This list is hardly exhaustive; many other kinds of events appear in online news listings. Anything that seems significant to you in your work is grist for the mill. Key customers and suppliers may have as big a stake in your company as you do; include them in all the happenings. (But trumpet only the major ones on the first page of your Web site; put the minor ones where your more dedicated Web surfers can find them.)

In each news item, try to include an action item for the reader and encourage the reader's involvement. Are there changes to a product? Tell people how to get the new one. Is a trade show coming up? Link to the trade show Web site or otherwise tell people how to attend. Did you get a big sales win? Remind people how to obtain your product themselves. You don't have to beat people over the head with your call to action, but do make sure that it's there.

Chapter 8

Getting the Most Out
of Your Web Site

● ●

In This Chapter

▶ Gathering information about visitors

▶ Improving your site

▶ Getting your Web site listed with the search engines

▶ Publicizing your site

● ●

*I*n Chapters 5 through 7, we show you how to quickly build an affordable and effective Web presence. To reach your goals in online marketing, however, you ultimately have to take your Web site further. As the old navigational charts used to say when showing *Terra Incognita,* or the unknown lands, "Danger! Monsters lurk here!" Wasting time and money is easy to do on wrong-headed Web efforts.

Luckily, you can build up to a winning Web presence that makes your existing customers happy and your prospective customers eager to become existing ones, at reasonable expense and within a relatively short time frame. In this chapter, we highlight how to find out about who visits your site, point out some of the best ways to improve your site for future visitors, and show you how to help people find your Web site.

Gathering Information about Site Visitors

As soon as any new kind of marketing effort gets past the early "gee whiz" stage — imagine the thrill of seeing your company in one of its very first TV ads, for instance — you may start to wonder how to measure the effectiveness of the new medium. The broadcasting industry has the Nielson and Arbitron ratings to help advertisers discover who their ads reach. The Web is developing powerful tools that allow you to know where your visitors go on your Web site, though the numbers gained in this way aren't yet as accepted across sites the way that broadcasting industry ratings are.

The Web is so important these days that you don't need to go to much effort to justify having at least a low-cost, low-hassle Web presence site for strictly defensive purposes — just a non-embarrassing Web billboard to prevent people from seeing you as road kill on the information superhighway. But as you start to invest more time, energy, and money into your Web site, you need to know something about the kinds of visitors you get.

At the lowest level, the information that's easy to get from your Web server software or Internet service provider (ISP) is *hits* — the number of connections made to the Web server to receive HTML files, graphics files, or any other files on your Web site. However, hits are not a good indicator of the number of visitors, because some users surf the Web with graphics turned off for speed; such users generate fewer hits even if they visit the same number of your Web pages. To effectively measure accesses to your Web site, use *page views,* the number of HTML files that have been downloaded. Ask your ISP to provide this information to you, or select Web server software that can provide it.

Techniques for gathering visitor information

You can use several different techniques for gathering information about your Web site visitors above and beyond hits, each of which may be worth its own chapter in a book on the topic. But just to get you started, here are some methods for learning about your site's visitors:

- **Reading site e-mail.** Just scanning the e-mail that comes into your site gives you some information about who's visiting and what their concerns are. (Of course, you should *answer* the e-mail, too — see Chapter 9 for more information.) Consider printing a hundred or so e-mails, arranging them by category, writing a brief cover note and summary, and passing the whole stack around to marketing, sales, customer service, and other people in your company who may be interested in what your Web site visitors have to say about the site.

- **Visitor counters.** You can easily install software to count the number of visitors you get to each of your Web pages; your ISP may even offer this service for free or for a small fee. For access to counter software, go to `www.yahoo.com/Computers_and_Internet/Internet/ World_Wide_Web/Programming/Access_Counters`. You can use a visible counter if you want others to see how many visitors you've had, or an invisible one if you want to keep the number to yourself. The information that counter software gives you is valuable feedback as to the amount of traffic you're getting on your Web site and what parts of your Web site draw the most attention. You can compare the number of hits and the cost of your site to the cost per thousand impressions that you pay for magazine ads to get a rough idea of whether your Web site pulls its weight.

Any time you see a long URL from the Yahoo! site, you can access the Web page without typing in the URL. Just go to the Yahoo! home page at `www.yahoo.com` and choose the category links that match each folder name in the URL. For instance, to follow your way to the URL in the previous bullet item, choose the `Computers and Internet` link, then `Internet`, then `World Wide Web`, and so on through the parts of the URL until you reach the Access Counters page.

✔ **Log analysis.** To get a better idea of who's coming to your site, whether they arrived there from an external link, a search engine, or a bookmark, how long they stay on your site, and the path they take through your site, you need a sophisticated logging capability in your Web server software and both software and human expertise to analyze the data. The results can help you understand what users value most on your Web site and see whether navigational problems make navigating your site difficult.

✔ **On-site registration.** One good way to gather information about your Web site visitors is to ask them to register on your site. If you ask them for their registration information, though, you need to give them something in return — an industry survey of some sort, entry in a drawing for prizes, or regular e-mail updates on changes in your Web site. (Different rewards get different kinds of people to register; try to get people who are current or likely customers.) Registration info is useful, but you have to remember that it's biased toward whatever kind of person takes the time to register.

People are rightly becoming concerned about what happens to registration information that they enter on a Web site — they don't want it to be used to make them the target of e-mail spam (as we describe in Chapter 9), junk mail in their mailboxes, or phone solicitations. Many users give false information when registering, perhaps to avoid being the target of solicitors. Reassure your visitors by telling them that you will never rent or sell their information to anyone else (assuming that such an assurance is true; if it isn't, disclose what you will do with it so that you don't lose visitors' trust). Figure 8-1 shows an example of this kind of reassurance on the Thunder Lizard Productions Web site.

✔ **Surveys.** You can do on-site or e-mail surveys of visitors to your Web site. This is much like registration, but with no ongoing relationship implied, so cash or its equivalent is a good reward. You can map survey data against log analysis data to get a pretty good idea of who's coming to visit your site. If you want only some people to respond to the survey — say, people within a certain geographic area — limit the reward or prize opportunity to people who fit your target. Everyone likes cash, so there may be less bias in the results of surveys with cash rewards than with other forms of information gathering.

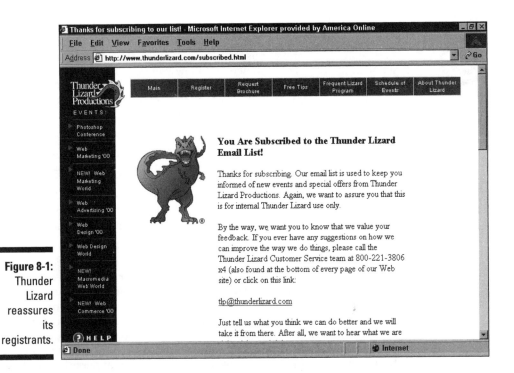

Figure 8-1:
Thunder
Lizard
reassures
its
registrants.

Unless you have a large online marketing group at your company already, you may want to consider choosing an Internet service provider or consultant who can provide some or all of these information-gathering services for you. Implementing and analyzing these measurement techniques can be technically challenging, and you may need to find someone with lots of online experience, a degree in statistics, or both, who can help you determine who's coming to see you.

Uses for visitor data

At some point in the process of planning and implementing your data-gathering effort, you need to ask yourself what you're going to do with the information you acquire. For example, if your Web site is giving you more impressions per dollar than magazine advertising, and the impressions on the Web are reaching the same kind of people as the magazine, you may want to put more of your advertising and marketing budget into the Web site.

A special kind of opportunity for Web marketing is the ability to actually use the Web to maintain and improve your relationship with a specific customer — referred to as *one-to-one* marketing. One way to do this involves using a *cookie,* a data file stored on the site visitor's machine that records the visitor's activities on each visit to your Web site.

With a cookie file, you can access information about customer visits and track their online habits on your Web site. (Users can turn off cookie capability, but the majority don't do so. You may want to ask users before creating the cookie file the first time.) Going further, you can actually modify the information you present to each of your Web visitors to fit that particular visitor's interests and habits. For example, imagine a home page of a pet store that shows three pictures, each a hyperlink: one of a dog, one of a cat, and one of a rat. Depending on which link the visitor clicks, you can offer information that interests the particular pet owner — clicking the dog, for example, may bring up an article on dog dental health. In addition, the site can include an ad for dog food alongside the dental health article and an Internet coupon for a dollar off the next visit to the pet store. In this way, the site can offer useful information that keeps visitors coming to the site, offer visitor-specific marketing information, and create visitor profiles that can be analyzed by marketing to better assess who visits. If you're interested in fine-tuning your Web marketing effort in this way, ask your ISP, Web-hosting provider, or a consultant to help.

Cookies, and other information gathered by Web sites, are a very sensitive area. The best rule if you're not certain how your visitors will react to cookies, registration, and other information-gathering techniques is to disclose, disclose, disclose. Does your site use cookies? Say so, and for what purpose. Do you ask for an e-mail address or other "personally identifiable information?" Say exactly what you will, and won't, use it for, and what other companies you work with (if any) may see it and do with it. For more suggestions on what sites can and should disclose to ease any privacy concerns by visitors, check out the Web site of the independent Internet privacy organization TRUSTe (www.truste.com).

Improving Your Site

Early in the existence of the Web, many people pulled out all the stops, creating large, attractive, highly interactive sites that cost huge amounts of money but did little to advance a company's interests in any measurable way.

This led, naturally enough, to a backlash. Many companies stopped investing in their Web sites altogether, and the Internet is littered with thousands of these "dead" or barely breathing sites — they're rarely updated, uninteresting, and looking more and more stale with the passage of time.

Now, however, many companies are starting to see real results from their Web investments. Companies that sell online report increased business; Web-based marketing and PR efforts are gathering steam and having impact in the offline world as well as simply making companies famous in cyberspace.

As your own Web efforts start to have an impact, you want to consider ways to improve your Web site — partly to meet or beat your competitors' improvements in their online presence, and partly to move toward more Web marketing or an initial effort at Web commerce.

Developing and improving your site into something really interesting and attractive brings in more visitors and results in a more effective online marketing push. Here are some of the techniques you can use to get there:

- ✔ **Improve navigation.** One of the most neglected, and most important, concerns for your site is improving visitors' ability to navigate it. A clickable graphic with major site areas listed at the top or bottom of each Web page is one starting point. More advanced navigation approaches include a site map, HTML frames with table of contents information, and a search capability for users to find specific things within your site.

- ✔ **Streamline graphics.** The single biggest irritant for many users of the Web is the slow speed with which pages load, mainly because of large graphics files. Reducing the size of the graphics files while maintaining or improving the attractiveness of the Web site is an ongoing challenge. Consider using advanced tools such as Adobe Photoshop to help you reduce the size of graphics files, or find a graphic designer with Web experience to help.

- ✔ **Create valuable content.** Creating evolving content that users want to keep coming back for is a long-term win for your Web site. One approach is to maintain and update information for your industry area, which can be as simple as a good page of links to industry-related Web sites or as complex as an ongoing survey of customer attitudes. (Give away the top-line summaries, but keep the details for yourself!) Providing information for your industry segment sends the message that you're the leader.

- ✔ **Use other Internet services.** Too much online marketing starts and stops with the Web. Use other online services described in this book to create a comprehensive online marketing effort that makes your customers and potential customers feel part of your team. Use the information on e-mail (Chapters 9 and 10), e-mail lists (Chapter 11), and discussion groups and chat (Chapter 12) to enhance and extend the customer relationship you start with your Web site.

- ✔ **Add multimedia.** When you add multimedia to your Web site, you also open yourself up to tech support questions from users who have trouble running it, and to complaints from users if a multimedia file takes a long time to load. So set modest goals initially and make multimedia additions interesting and appropriate: a brief video clip of your CEO speaking; a 3D model or virtual reality object photograph of a product to show what it really looks like or how it works. Figure 8-2 shows an example of effective multimedia use on a Web site.

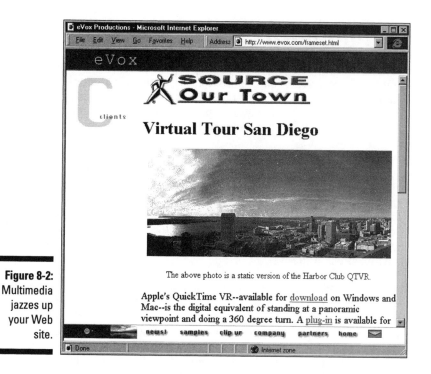

Figure 8-2:
Multimedia
jazzes up
your Web
site.

✔ **Make it interactive.** Many Web sites are adding interactivity. One popular technique is to add a guest book that allows people to comment on
your site. This can be done with text and *CGI scripts*, programs that run
on the Web server and don't risk causing problems on the user's
machine (check with your ISP for details and whether it offers this type
of service). Many other sites create more ambitious interactive effects
such as taking over the whole screen to display information, often
through Java programs. You can make using your Web site much more
engaging this way, but you also make it more expensive to design, maintain, and support, and many users object to having Web-based programs
seemingly "take over" their computer. Define your goals carefully and
identify your resources before going too far in this direction.

✔ **Create a channel for wireless access.** Wireless devices such as Palm OS
handhelds and WAP phones (that's Wireless Application Protocol) have
little tiny screens and are natural targets for focused marketing efforts.
Wireless channels work best if you have at least a couple of news items
appearing on your site a day, and if those items are short (again, the
little tiny screens).

✔ **Add online sales.** The ultimate goal for many Web sites is to make
money through direct online sales. If this is an option for you, start
planning now for when and how to get there.

Getting Found with Search Engines

Your Web site doesn't do you any good if people can't find it. The single most important tool you have to make sure that people can find your site is to get a domain name that matches your company name as closely as possible, as described in Chapter 4. That way, anyone who knows your company name can easily guess your Web URL and visit your site.

However, you also want people to find your site when they know only a product name, or maybe just the kind of product or company they're looking for. Bringing these potential customers to your site is actually cheap, easy to accomplish, and easy to check up on. Web users who look for certain kinds of sites almost invariably use search engines — more than 80 percent of Web users do so, according to several popular surveys, and search engine sites (now grown into "Web portals" such as Yahoo! and AltaVista) are among the most visited sites on the Web.

To understand how to make the search engines work to your advantage, you need to know that there are basically two kinds of Web search engines. Each kind may borrow tricks from the other, but all search engines rely on one of two basic strategies: *passive* and *active*. Passive search engines require you to register your site with them; active search engines are constantly combing the Web for new sites, and find and list your site without your knowing about it or asking for it! The strategies for successfully registering for each type of search engine are very different, as the following two sections explain.

You may come across a variety of free and fee-driven tools and services that offer to register your Web site with many different search engines simultaneously. We suggest that you *not* use these services and instead take the time to register your site — and improve it for easier finding — yourself. You're much more likely to end up in the right categories on the major search engines if you take the time to prepare for each one individually.

Registering for Yahoo!

The category of passive search engines — search engines for which you have to register your site to get it listed — is now completely dominated by the granddaddy of all the big search sites, the early leader in Web searching, and now the most popular single site on the Internet: Yahoo!, at www.yahoo.com.

Yahoo! first asks you to register your site with it and suggest an appropriate category for your site within the Yahoo! hierarchy. A Yahoo! employee, called a *Yahoo! Surfer,* then reviews your registration form and your site and assigns your site to a main category. He or she — the only thing you can be certain of is that this person probably has more fun at work than you do — also cross-references the site to other, related categories.

Marketing with chat on your site

Because chat takes place in real time, text-based chat is used by a number of companies to enhance their Web sites.

Chat's marketing role can be as part of a special event — a kind of virtual news conference to introduce a product or company development. Or it can be used for ongoing customer service and support — for example, interactive question-and-answer sessions with support technicians. Think of it as a conference call with fingers rather than voices.

Chat is well-suited to fast interactions such as technical support calls, but it does have its limitations when used for marketing. If you get more than 20 or so people involved without a firm moderator acting as talk-show host, it becomes difficult to follow who's saying what, and the incoherence level approaches infinity. If you have fewer than five people taking part, you may see long gaps while people think of something to type. As a result, e-mail lists (see

Chapter 11) are a better option if what's being discussed doesn't demand immediate back-and-forth.

If you want to control your own online chat sessions, you need to set up chat software. Setting up chat on a Web site requires that your customers have a chat "helper application" or plug-in for their Web browsers, and/or for you to run a chat server program on your Web server. Chat server software ranges in price from a few hundred dollars to thousands of dollars, depending on the number of simultaneous participants it handles and how advanced the controls are for keeping everyone in line. Some chat servers include EmeraldNet ChatBox and its sample version, ChatBox Lite (www.chatbox.net), WebMaster ConferenceRoom (www.webmaster.com), and IChat Rooms (www.ichat.com). Another approach is Java-based chat, such as that from Parachat (www.parachat.com). These sites also have examples of working chat features.

Register for Yahoo! early. Yahoo! gets *thousands* of site listing suggestions a day, and getting to yours may take some time. Remember, however, to have at least your basic content up and running before submitting, or the Yahoo! Surfer who checks your site won't find it and therefore won't list it.

The better job you do of deciding on the correct initial category for your site, the easier time the Yahoo! Surfer has categorizing it. Your effort puts the Yahoo! Surfer in a good mood and gives you a better chance that this happy person cross-indexes your site thoughtfully and carefully to the appropriate (and, with luck, large) number of additional categories. Follow these steps to register with Yahoo!:

1. **Search for your Web site on Yahoo! at** www.yahoo.com **to see whether you've already been Yahoo!'d.**

   Your site may already have been added. If so, check the listing to see whether it's categorized properly and whether the listing is up-to-date and complete. If you need to make changes to your listing, fill out a Yahoo! change form at add.yahoo.com/fast/change.

   To see Yahoo!'s description of how to register your site, start at docs.yahoo.com/info/suggest.

2. Decide on the right Yahoo! category and subcategory for your site.

Surf around Yahoo! to find the right category for your Web site. Use the Search capability for terms associated with your business and see what kinds of hits come up. Look for companies and products that compete with yours and see where they're listed to get a good idea of what would be appropriate for your own company.

The most commonly used high-level category for a company site is likely to be in the Business and Economy category. Your site may be cross-referenced in other areas of Yahoo!, but the main listing will probably go under Business and Economy. If you operate only in a specific region (in a U.S. state or a non-U.S. country), your listing should go in the Regional category. Write down the full name of any categories and subcategories that seem appropriate for a cross-reference listing.

3. Surf to the category you want to be in.

Go deep into the category listings. For instance, if you sell several kinds of jewelry, but 80 percent of your business is wedding rings, surf down into the Wedding Rings subcategory.

4. From within the correct category, click the Suggest a Site button, as shown in Figure 8-3.

The first Web page for the Suggest a Site process appears. Read it carefully for more details.

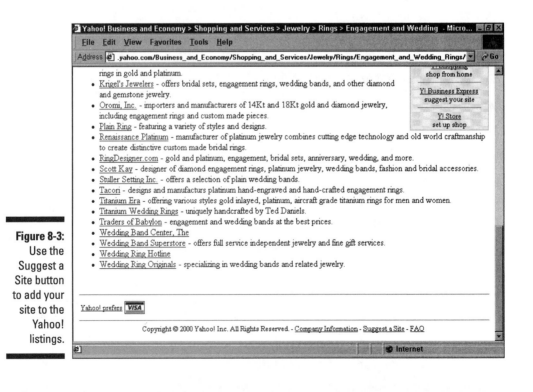

Figure 8-3: Use the Suggest a Site button to add your site to the Yahoo! listings.

5. **Click the Proceed to Step One button.**

   The Suggest a Site: Step 1 of 4 Web page appears. Part of the Web page is shown in Figure 8-4.

6. **Choose the Standard site suggestion process or the Business Express program, which is faster (one- to two-week turnaround) and costs $199.**

   The steps are the same for either choice, except that you have to add payment information for the Business Express approach. The remaining steps are for the standard, free process.

7. **Enter the title, URL, and description of your Web site in the appropriate fields.**

   - Enter your business name as the Title field.

   - Carefully enter the URL (Web address) of your home page and a description of up to 25 words.

   Yahoo! may take several weeks to process requests to add a site or change information about a site. Do a careful job of entering your information so that it will be right the first time and you won't have to enter a change request and wait for it to go through.

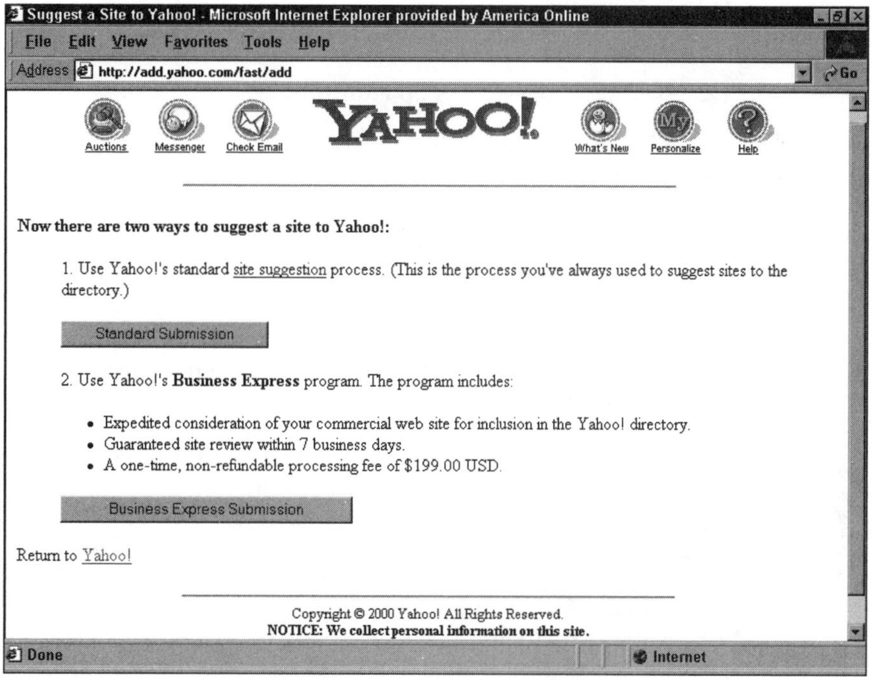

![Screenshot of "Suggest a Site to Yahoo!" in Microsoft Internet Explorer provided by America Online. Address: http://add.yahoo.com/fast/add. YAHOO! with toolbar icons: Auctions, Messenger, Check Email, What's New, Personalize, Help.

Now there are two ways to suggest a site to Yahoo!:

1. Use Yahoo!'s standard site suggestion process. (This is the process you've always used to suggest sites to the directory.)

   [Standard Submission]

2. Use Yahoo!'s **Business Express** program. The program includes:

   - Expedited consideration of your commercial web site for inclusion in the Yahoo! directory.
   - Guaranteed site review within 7 business days.
   - A one-time, non-refundable processing fee of $199.00 USD.

   [Business Express Submission]

Return to Yahoo!

Copyright © 2000 Yahoo! All Rights Reserved.
NOTICE: We collect personal information on this site.]

Figure 8-4:
Start by choosing Standard or Express submission.

Take some time to create a useful description, and keep it under the 25-word limit. If your entry exceeds 25 words, Yahoo! may edit it with results that you may not like. Include key descriptors and phrases in the Description field. For example, in a description of this book, we would use the phrase "online marketing and real-world marketing," rather than tying it together as "online and real-world marketing." Why? Because in case someone searches for the exact phrase "online marketing" in quotation marks, you want to make sure that your site shows up high on the list of hits.

8. **Click the Proceed to Step Two button.**

   The Suggest a Site: Step 2 of 4 Web page appears.

9. **Enter additional categories in which you think your site should be cross-referenced; here's where you use those full category names you wrote down in Step 2 of this list.**

   You may also want to enter any new categories that you think are needed for your site.

10. **Click the Proceed to Step Three button.**

    The Suggest a Site: Step 3 of 4 Web page appears.

11. **Enter a contact person's name, e-mail address, and company information in the appropriate text boxes, plus your Yahoo! Yellow Pages ID if you have one.**

12. **Click the Proceed to Step Four button.**

    The Suggest a Site: Step 4 of 4 Web page appears.

13. **Provide any applicable information about starting and ending dates for your site and any final comments in the appropriate text boxes; then click the Submit button.**

    A Yahoo! Surfer checks out your site, compares it to what you suggested in your submission, and then categorizes it appropriately.

Congratulations! Your site will soon be listed on the most important search directory on the Web.

Wait for your site listing to appear on Yahoo! and then check that your site listing is accurate and positioned where you want it. Try searching for it using different terms related to your business. Make sure that your site comes up at least as often as the sites of competing businesses. If it doesn't, or if at any time in the future you need to update your Yahoo! listing, use the Yahoo! change form at add.yahoo.com/fast/change. The Yahoo! change form enables you to make changes to the Description field and a variety of other aspects of your listing, as well as suggest a new category for your site.

Getting found by active search engines

Most search engines on the Web, and for other Internet services as well, are *active* search engines. Active search engines use programs called *Web spiders* or *infobots*. These programs open a Web page, read the contents, index them according to various criteria, store the results in a database, and then go on to the next Web page. The result is an indexed database of millions of Web pages.

When you query an active search engine to do a search, the engine doesn't go out and start searching the Web — that would be way too slow. Instead, the engine accesses its database and provides you with the indexed sites that match your query.

If the information in the search engine database has become outdated since the last time the Web spider checked a site, you may get a different-than-expected Web page or an error message when you go to that Web site. Given the sheer size of the Web and other online resources, the database can easily get behind — one popular Web search engine says it needs two to four weeks to index a new site. However, the information that the search engine provides is accurate most of the time, and the search engines are very useful.

Most active search engines enable you to register your site with them by simply entering your URL and e-mail address. The staff of the search site then points its spider your way so that it indexes your site sooner than if you were to wait for it to find you at random. The good news is that you don't *have* to register — the spider finds your site eventually.

Either way, with most active search engines, the Web spider finds the key-words for your site and creates that entry in the search engine database. This is in contrast to how, with Yahoo!, you decide the appropriate description for your site. And Web spiders, like real spiders, don't have much in the way of brains — they simply go out on the Web and index all the words in every Web page they find without knowing which words on a given Web page are the important ones. Some engines simply treat the first words they encounter as the most important; others use different weighting criteria. Your job: to make those first words count so that your site appears high on the "hits list" when a search engine user enters keywords appropriate to your Web page.

The following steps suggest that you make some small changes to the HTML tags in your Web page. You can do this work yourself, if you know HTML or are willing to get your hands dirty (the changes are really pretty simple, and you can use a simple text editor such as Windows Notepad or Macintosh SimpleText to make them). Or you can find a colleague or consultant who knows how to use HTML to make the changes for you. For an introduction to common HTML commands, see *Creating Web Pages For Dummies,* 5th Edition, by Bud Smith and Arthur Bebak, *HTML 4 For Dummies,* by Ed Tittel and Stephen James, or *HTML 4 For Dummies Quick Reference,* 2nd Edition, by Deborah and Eric Ray, all from IDG Books Worldwide, Inc.

Here's how to make it easier for Web search engines to bring the right kinds of users to your Web page.

1. **Modify your home page's title for "findability."**

   Every Web page can have a title that appears at the top of the Web browser window and that is also used by search engines and other Web tools to find appropriate Web pages. The title can include your company name, area of business, product names, or any keywords by which you would like to be found.

2. **Add <META> tags to your home page for "findability."**

   The <META> tag is an HTML command that allows search engines to more easily find your site. Add the following <META> tags between the <HEAD> and </HEAD> tags of your Web pages, with your own information inside the quotation marks in the content= areas:

   ```
   <META name="description" content="Dummies Consulting does
         marketing consulting for high-technology
         companies.">
   <META name="keywords" content="online marketing, online,
         marketing, high technology, Web, Internet,
         dummies, geniuses, veeblefetzer">
   ```

Most of the HTML editing software available includes features for adding <META> tags. See the documentation for your Web page editing tool to learn how to add HTML tags directly.

A Web page, shown in Source mode with a summary and <META> tags useful for searchability, is shown in Figure 8-5. You can view the source HTML document in Netscape Navigator by choosing View➪Page Source. You can do the same in Internet Explorer by choosing View➪Source.

Some companies have gone to extremes in their <META> tag content and have used rival company and product names as keywords. The idea is that someone searching for a specific product will be directed by a search engine to the Web site for the competing product instead. This is not only bad business but also may incur legal liability; several lawsuits have been filed over this issue.

Always include one odd, new word in the <META> tag for keywords so that you can test whether each search engine has added your newly updated Web page yet. In the example in these steps, we use the word *veeblefetzer*.

3. **Upload your modified page to your Web server so that it is available on the Web.**

4. **Go to the major search engines and tell them whatever they need to know to list or reexamine your Web site.**

   Here are the URLs for submitting your site with some of the most important search engines:

- **AltaVista:** www.altavista.com/av/content/addurl.htm

- **Excite:** www.excite.com/Info/add_url.html

- **HotBot:** www.hotbot.lycos.com/addurl.asp

- **GO Infoseek:** www.go.com/AddUrl

- **Lycos:** home.lycos.com/addasite.html

- **Many, many additional search engines:** www.the-vault. com/easy-submit

As you add your URL, check the search site for information on how long the search engine takes to index new sites. Expect not to see your site listed for at least one week and as long as four weeks.

5. Use your test keyword to test each search engine weekly and see whether your site has been added yet.

As soon as your page shows up, test that search engine with several different kinds of search terms that customers are likely to use to find Web pages like yours. See whether your Web page shows up in the listings. If it's among the top ten hits for crucial keywords that relate to your business, good job! If not, modify your <META> tags, adding the needed keywords, and try again.

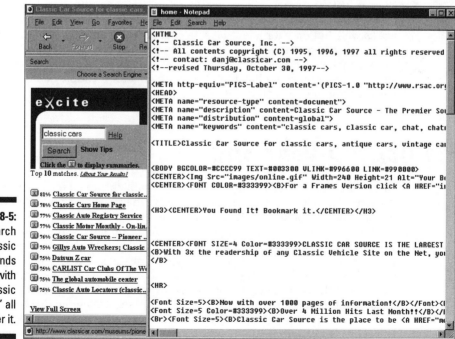

Figure 8-5: A search for "classic cars" finds a site with "classic cars" all over it.

If your Web page doesn't show up near the top, use the View Source command in your Web browser to inspect the Web pages that do show up first. Take a look at the `<META>` tags in those pages and see what key-words to use to make your own site rise to the top.

6. **When you're happy with the performance of the search engines on your Web pages, ask some colleagues and customers to try searching for businesses and products like yours — and tell you the results.**

This whole process is a lot of work but it's some of the most important work you need to do for your online marketing presence. Your Web site is most likely the cornerstone of your entire online presence, and it's vital that people who are interested in companies and products like yours be able to find your site.

If you really want to make yourself accessible, consider listing the specific Web pages for each of your key products and services with Yahoo! and the various active search engines. That way, people go straight to the exact Web page they need to get the product or service they want — from you, not from someone else.

Many people test a new Web site by uploading it to their Web server, making it available on the Web, and simply not telling more than a few people where it is. This kind of testing allows you to see how features such as CGI scripts (if your Webmaster uses them) work under "live" conditions and allows you to test how long your Web pages take to download across the Internet. This works well, but only for a few days, because if there are any links to the page, active search engines find it. (Yes, people have stumbled across valuable secrets by following links from active search engines.) To protect your test site or secret site, don't link to it, take it down after a couple of days, password-protect it, or move it frequently to different Web page addresses.

Publicizing Your Site

One of the most talked-about topics in Web publishing is publicizing your Web site. There's a difference, though, between publicizing your Web site to people who are looking for it and putting the word out to vast masses of Web surfers through banner ads, aggressive linking campaigns, and spam. You *do* want to get the word out to your customers and potential customers, which means that you want to include your URL on business cards and press releases and also make your site easy to find via the various search engines, as we describe earlier in this chapter. However, you *don't* necessarily want to spend a lot of time and money — having your Web banner ad displayed on a popular site can cost thousands of dollars — trying to get random Web surfers to stop by your site. Here are some of the common myths of why you should widely publicize your Web site:

✔ **To get more visitors.** Getting more visitors to your Web site sounds okay, but it doesn't do you much good if the people who visit aren't potential customers for your products. Getting randomly selected people to — in most cases, briefly — browse your Web site probably doesn't do them or you much good.

✔ **To show people you're online.** This was a good reason five years ago when being online meant you were technically savvy. However, these days it's news if a company is *not* online, and the online public is not likely to be impressed by the simple fact that you have a Web site.

✔ **To let people know your URL.** How much work does it take to remember the CNET, Netscape, or Yahoo! URL? None at all. If you know the company name, you know the URL. If your company has an easy-to-guess URL, you don't need to help people remember it; if not, turn back to Chapter 4 and go get one.

Developing an effective publicity strategy

Okay, so you should never publicize your Web site, right? No, that would be going too far. Here are the steps to take in deciding how to appropriately publicize your Web site:

1. **Determine what you want from your Web visitors.**

   Web sites are hard to perfect because they must meet the needs of several different groups, including customers, potential customers, press, financial analysts, and even employees. What do you want people in each group to take away from their visit to your Web site? Put the answer in the form, "With my Web site, I want to increase their likelihood to . . ." and include one primary goal for each group. Then analyze your Web site to make sure that it accomplishes your stated goal for people from each group.

2. **Develop a Web site you're proud of.**

   Sure, you can start out with a bare-bones, cover-your-assets Web presence for people to find when needed, but that's different than trying to actively bring people to it. Until you've made your Web site really worthwhile, don't make extra efforts to bring it to people's attention.

3. **Figure out where the ducks are.**

   If you're a duck hunter, you don't go to Paris for the start of the duck hunting season — you go to a cold, dark, predawn duck blind on some half-frozen lake somewhere. Same with Web publicity: Don't put a banner ad on CNET for tens of thousands of dollars and attract random Web surfers. Instead, figure out where your potential customers are and publicize your site there. For instance, if you are selling baked hams online, try to exchange links with food-oriented sites. And consider paying one or more search engine companies a fee to put up a banner ad for you each time someone searches for the word *ham*. (For more on Internet advertising, see Chapter 13.)

4. **Do initial publicity to some ducks.**

    Decide on some initial efforts to draw people from among your targeted groups — your potential customers, trade press from within your industry, and any other group you really want to visit your site. These efforts can include a print mailing, an e-mailing, a targeted press release, or other means.

5. **Measure the results.**

    Carefully compare who visits your site before you make a publicity effort and then again after the blitz using the techniques we describe in the "Gathering Information about Site Visitors" section, earlier in this chapter. You can get a quick read on who's seeing your publicity by asking Web surfers in your company whether they've seen it. But also do a more detailed analysis of the number of visits you get and whether your desired results — visits by people from certain kinds of companies, viewings of specific Web pages, registrations for information, downloads of specific files — are being achieved.

If you follow this process, you'll do the right kind of publicity and get good results that you can not only be proud of but also cost-justify thoroughly.

In the radio industry, the conventional wisdom is to not advertise a new format for a radio station — for example, a change from news to talk or from rock to rap — until a few weeks after the change. The reason is that radio listeners may sample a changed station once and then not come back unless they really like what they hear — and just after a change, there may still be glitches in the on-air experience for on-air talent and production staff, and therefore for the listeners. In keeping with this guideline, many radio stations make sure that they're firing on all cylinders before publicizing their new format. Consider following a similar strategy in publicizing your Web site.

Expanding your publicity efforts

When you've developed a Web site that you're proud of — that is, one that has at least basic company, product, and service information, tells visitors how to buy whatever it is you sell, is easily found by anyone using a major search engine, and is one of the better sites, or even the best site, among your direct competitors — then it's time to milk your Web site for all it's worth. That means doing some real publicity work, both in the offline world and online.

Two factors influence the amount of benefit you get from visits to your Web site. These factors can be expressed as two questions: How impressive is your Web site? And what sales impact do you get out of visits to it?

The more impressive your Web site and the more sales impact you get out of Web site visits, the more publicity you want to do. Figure 8-6 expresses this idea roughly in a conceptual graphic form.

The idea here is that the more impact your Web site has on sales and the more impressive your site is, the "hotter" it is and the more deserving of publicity. A really hot site — one that is a first-class, award-winning site and that drives a significant portion of sales for one or more of your products or services — should get a substantial part of your total company publicity effort. For sites that do somewhat less, publicize somewhat less. Here's how we see the publicity effort:

- ✔ **Cold.** Your site neither stands out on the Web nor has much impact on sales. (The vast majority of company Web sites live here, and in many cases, that's okay.) Make your site findable, as described earlier in this chapter. Add your Web site URL to business cards and company stationery to give an impression of being technologically up-to-date and to remind your regular customers to visit you online. Make sure that your Web URL is in all e-mail signature files, as we describe in Chapter 9.

- ✔ **Warm.** Your site beats competitors and noticeably increases sales. Push to get the URL on printed company materials and include it in any broadcast ads that you do. Do cute things like matchbooks, *tchotchkes* (freebie giveaway trinkets), and so on with your Web URL and a catchy slogan. Start doing press releases when you make major changes to the site or reach visitor or sales milestones related to it.

- ✔ **Hot.** Your site is first class or wins awards and drives many sales. Pay for carefully targeted Internet ads to pull in traffic; issue regular press releases about awards, sales, and additions; advertise the site directly in the offline world; start developing online sales capability.

You can fine-tune your efforts based on the strengths and weaknesses of your site's impact. For instance, if your site isn't all that impressive but still drives many sales, put all your effort into targeted publicity among likely buyers, but don't waste money trumpeting your site outside those groups. Or if your site is award winning but has little direct impact on sales, advertise it in a low-key way to broad audiences; it's a real plus to your company's image but not a real plus to revenues. In either case, consider ways to increase the site's impact.

The important thing for most people to understand is that the vast majority of Web sites live in the "cold" zone and don't merit an active, costly publicity effort by themselves. Promotional costs related to this kind of competitive but low-key Web effort should be incidental. Only when you invest more in your Web site and see results from that investment do you need to step up the publicity effort.

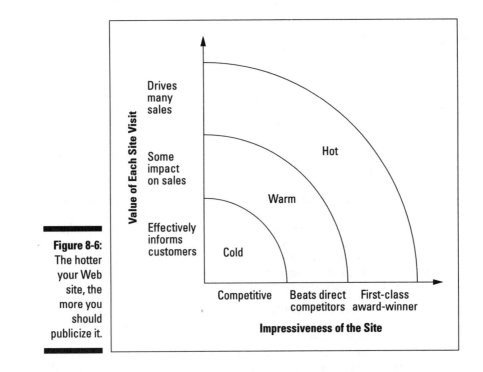

Part III
Marketing with E-Mail

The 5th Wave   By Rich Tennant

"I like getting complaint letters by e-mail.
It's easier to delete than to shred."

In this part . . .

*T*he Internet is more than just the Web. And some of the most effective Internet marketing comes from one of the Internet's oldest components: e-mail. E-mail markets your company or product in every individual message, targets groups effectively in bulk, and builds a sense of community online.

Chapter 9

E-Mail Marketing 101

• •

• •

*A*lthough the most important single element in your online marketing strategy is your World Wide Web site, effective marketing requires going well beyond pretty HTML pages. The Internet offers a wide variety of other marketing vehicles that rely on the decades-old guts of the Internet — plain, unadulterated text.

This Wonderful World of Text includes electronic mail (e-mail), automated e-mail lists (commonly called *listservs,* after the most well-known product, LISTSERV, used to manage them), and public discussion groups known as newsgroups and their real-time equivalent, chats. A convenient way to think of these text-based Internet services is as a continuum, as shown in Figure 9-1, that starts with one-to-one communication (e-mail), moves to one-to-many information (bulk e-mail, described in Chapter 10, and e-mail lists, or listservs, described in Chapter 11), and ends with many-to-many discussions (newsgroups/chats), described in Chapter 12. Online services, also described in Chapter 12, support e-mail and their own newsgroup-like online forums.

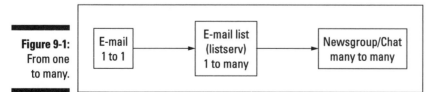

Figure 9-1:
From one
to many.

| E-mail 1 to 1 | → | E-mail list (listserv) 1 to many | → | Newsgroup/Chat many to many |

E-Mail: The Common Denominator

If Helen of Troy had the face that launched a thousand ships, e-mail had the body — body text, that is — that launched a thousand Internet domains. (Not to mention tens of thousands of both good and excruciatingly bad marketing campaigns.)

E-mail is exceedingly valuable to marketers for three reasons:

- ✔ **E-mail is ubiquitous.** Every Internet account subscription includes electronic mail capabilities, whether the subscriber has signed up with an Internet service provider (ISP), has Web access through work, or uses a commercial online service, such as America Online (AOL). Hundreds of millions of people have e-mail — many more people than the subscriber base of any single ISP, online service, or the user base of the World Wide Web. If someone is online, he or she has e-mail; even many mobile phones can now receive e-mail. E-mail is the lowest common denominator — it ties everyone on the Internet together with its common, reliable method of transmitting simple text information.

- ✔ **E-mail is cheap.** As pay-by-the-hour online subscriptions were replaced by flat-rate, all-you-can-eat digital buffets, composing and delivering an e-mail message came to cost nothing more than time. There are no printing or postage costs. On the receiving end, no special equipment is required to read an e-mail message other than e-mail client software — and that software is included as a part of productivity software suites, in America Online's subscriber software, and in the leading Web browser packages, Netscape Communicator and Microsoft Internet Explorer (as Microsoft Outlook Express), the latter of which is shown in Figure 9-2.

- ✔ **E-mail is easy.** Jotting an e-mail message requires no more skill than that required to type a brief note and click a Send button. Reading an e-mail message is likewise simple, requiring only an installed base of computer users with literacy skills.

As a result, e-mail — whether as an individual message, as a bulk message, or as part of an automated e-mail list — is the universal "killer app" to reach anyone online.

Ever wonder why the marketing newsletter you send to your customers doesn't arrive in all their mailboxes at exactly the same time? Or why the e-mail that someone promised would get to you in seconds may take minutes or hours to reach you? The delay is not necessarily because the sender is slacking off. More likely, the delay resides in Internet mail servers and the route the message has to take. If a mail server at either end is overloaded or shut down for some reason, or if a major Internet backbone is backed up, messages don't move as fast as they theoretically could. So if that promised order or response to a marketing pitch doesn't show up when you expect it, don't blame the sender — it could be that the message is "in the mail."

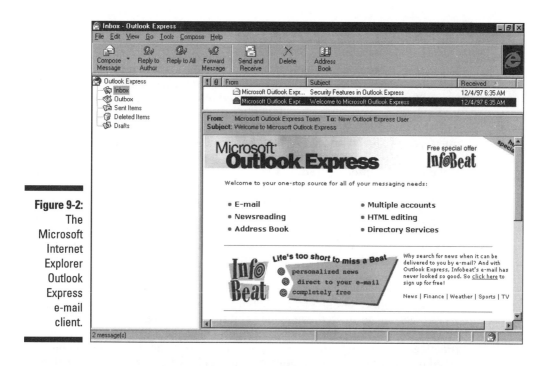

Figure 9-2:
The
Microsoft
Internet
Explorer
Outlook
Express
e-mail
client.

A brief history of e-mail

To say that e-mail is *why* the Internet came into being in the first place is not a stretch: ARPANET, the precursor of the Internet as we know it today, was envisioned as a system that would ensure that critical research and military installations could stay in touch with each other, even if parts of the network were destroyed. And the predominant way to stay in touch was with boring, text-based e-mail.

Although e-mail has been around for a long time (both of the authors have been using it since the mid-1980s), it wasn't very effective for marketing until the early 1990s. Up until that point, many online services with e-mail — such as BIX, Delphi, MCI Mail, Prodigy, and CompuServe — did not directly connect to the Internet or allow

a seamless exchange of messages among themselves. People were divided into separate, virtually walled online communities by their choice of online services.

In the early 1990s, *Internet gateways* (methods to translate proprietary online service e-mail address and message formats into Internet-friendly form) finally enabled users of different online services to send text-only e-mail to each other — joining the many who already had Internet e-mail access through an Internet service provider, university, government agency, or other source. With the barrier to text exchange among online services finally eliminated, e-mail became a critical marketing tool.

Basic E-Mail Netiquette

E-mail is a one-to-one medium, meaning that e-mail is inherently personal. In fact, because it arrives directly at a person's computer in his or her office or home, it seems more personal than printed direct mail. Just as offline marketing vehicles such as direct mail include certain dos and don'ts (do include a call to action; don't deliver it postage due), certain basic rules of Internet etiquette, or *netiquette,* apply to e-mail. (As the term suggests, *netiquette* is a set of unwritten rules for polite and courteous behavior that have become embedded into Internet tradition.)

Just because you use the Internet for marketing doesn't mean that you can ignore or sidestep appropriate netiquette — if you do, you run the risk of running headlong into another quaint Internet tradition, the *flame.* Flames are very direct e-mail responses to offensive messages, responses bearing all the subtlety of someone attempting to dispatch a troublesome spider with a nuclear device.

Netiquette applies not just to e-mail but also to other text-based Internet services (such as automated e-mail lists and newsgroups) and even to the text on your Web site. Although using netiquette may seem like a commonsense practice, it's amazing how uncommon that practice can be when someone is faced with a new communications medium. Follow these rules as a starting point to becoming netiquette-savvy — you'll find that they're critical to doing effective online marketing:

- ✔ **Keep it short.** Reading a short message with short paragraphs is still much easier than reading a doctoral dissertation in e-mail. And with brief, short paragraphs, your marketing message is less likely to get lost in an overabundance of gray text.

- ✔ **Don't type in all capital letters.** Typing in all capital letters is a sure way to communicate that you're new to the Internet. It doesn't matter whether all you're trying to do is draw attention to a special offer. IT'S INTERPRETED AS SHOUTING, and no one likes to be yelled at (even if it's well-deserved).

- ✔ **Avoid emoticons.** Marketers should eschew the use of *emoticons,* also called *smileys* : -). Using punctuation to simulate inflection can easily be overdone and come across in business dealings as inappropriately cutesy, unprofessional, or patronizing. If in doubt, don't :-(. Just clearly say what you mean in words.

- ✔ **Be aware of Net-savvy abbreviations.** Understand the dense e-mail abbreviations that are a type of keyboard shorthand, including such common acronyms as IMHO (In My Humble Opinion), BTW (By The Way), LOL (Laughing Out Loud), and ROTFL (Rolling On The Floor, Laughing). As with emoticons, know them well (so that you can respond to their use when customers e-mail you) but use them sparingly yourself, and only then if you know that the audience will react positively to them.

Flame on!

Flames are, in their own way, an art form. Many denizens of the Internet have spent years perfecting the craft of using text to slam someone up against the wall. And if you're a marketer and make a misstep with e-mail, odds are you'll feel the heat.

As mentioned elsewhere in this chapter, *flames* are overtly hostile and in-your-face messages that are commonly sent to those who obviously and repeatedly break rules of netiquette (after what is usually a polite first reminder). Such broken rules include TYPING IN ALL CAPS, posting a message that has nothing to do with the topic of an automated e-mail list or newsgroup, or sending the ultimate flame-bait: *spam,* messages that are blatant, and unsolicited, advertisements.) Flames also grow out of initially low-key online exchanges.

One of our favorite flames is the carefully crafted and lengthy religious tract that a client of one of the authors received after said client made the mistake of sending a spam to every attendee at a trade show. The e-mailed response made an indirect yet valid point — the client was as interested in reading about someone else's religious beliefs as the initial recipient was interested in reading the client's unsolicited ad.

If you're ever on the receiving end of a flame, the best response is usually none at all. Unless, of course, you enjoy the Internet equivalent of a firefight, the *flame war.* We don't, under any circumstances, recommend that you cultivate a taste for getting into such a battle. Although they may entertain bystanders, flames almost always reflect badly on you and your company's reputation — no matter how right you may be. If you respond to a flame, be level-headed and offer to deal with any complaint the instigator may have. Or just pick up the phone and call the person instead of continuing to bludgeon each other online.

Ironically, flame wars frequently begin over a simple misunderstanding as opposed to any great disagreement, thanks to text's inability to display nuances that are present in vocal inflection or facial expressions. Many online discussions turn partly or totally into flame wars until the participants either walk away — or their cinders are swept away.

The preceding tips are just a few netiquette basics required for good online marketing. For a more exhaustive list of smileys, abbreviations, and other tips, check out *E-Mail For Dummies,* 2nd Edition, by John R. Levine, Carol Baroudi, Margaret Levine Young, and Arnold Reinhold (gasp) from IDG Books Worldwide, Inc.

The Elements of E-Mail Marketing Style

Netiquette's implied rules of online courtesy are, by and large, defensive; the main goal of using netiquette is to avoid being seen as an idiot. But beyond simple netiquette, you (and the others you work with) have to write e-mail that works for you, not against you. You can take a couple of proactive steps to make sure that all your company's e-mail is a consistent, positive force for marketing. This advice applies to whether you're responding to an individual e-mail query or sending e-mail to a large group of people (as covered in Chapter 10).

Although we're not great fans of company policy manuals (many of which seem to exist for the sole purpose of providing jobs for company policy manual writers), distributing a list of e-mail guidelines for those handling e-mail from the outside world is a good idea. In this section, we suggest three approaches that can be the basis for your own, more company-specific list.

Write "dressy casual"

Because e-mail is so quick and easy to compose, writers often have a tendency to slip into too much informality and let spelling, grammar, and proper capital-ization slide. Don't let your e-mail undermine your personal image and your company's image. Although the style that is used to write an e-mail shouldn't be formal, it shouldn't be sloppy, either — especially now that many e-mail pro-grams, including the Messenger component of Netscape Communicator 4.73 (as shown in Figure 9-3), include integrated spell checkers.

If you need to aim for a style, consider the handwritten business thank-you note. Such a note is personal — without being too informal — brief, and to the point.

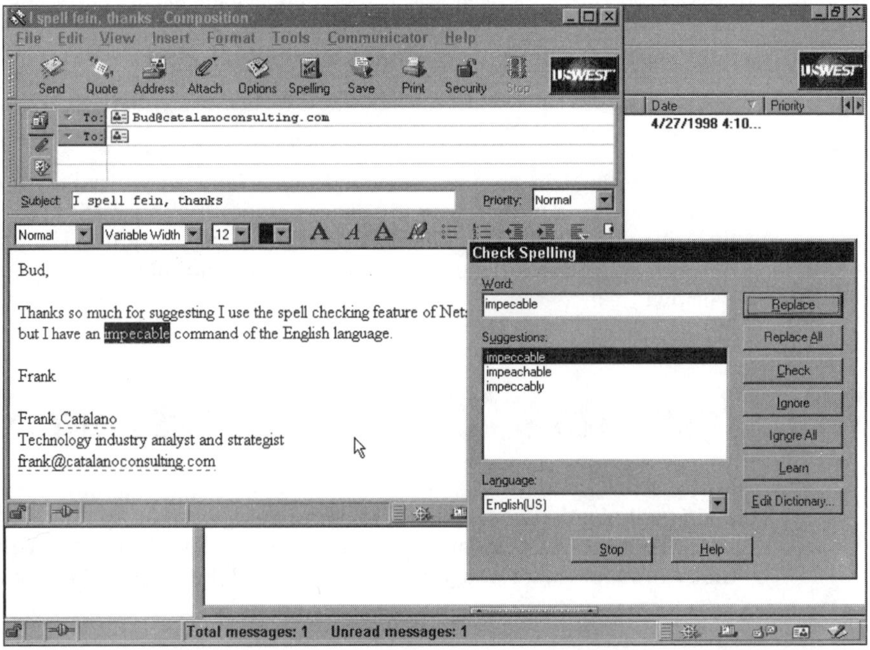

Figure 9-3:
Checking spelling in Netscape Communi-cator, just to be safe.

Be polite

E-mail coming from your company is stamped with a return address — your company's domain name. (If you don't have an easily recognizable domain name and e-mail address that reflects your company name, see the instructions in Chapter 4 on how to change them.) If your e-mail message is going to someone who doesn't know much about your company, that person's first impression about your professionalism and demeanor comes from your e-mail message. If you're having a bad day, letting your mood and feelings affect your e-mail to vendors, prospects, customers, or business partners is a bad idea.

So grin while you're writing business e-mail — even if it hurts.

Don't be afraid to be forwarded

E-mail, unlike paper mail, is easily forwarded.

The upside of easy forwarding is that a useful message can go to anyone and everyone who may benefit from seeing it.

The downside of easy forwarding is that a blistering message — such as your candid opinion of your boss's toupee — can be forwarded to anyone and everyone (including your boss) just as effortlessly — and not just immediately after you send it, but again and again for a long time to come. Some wag may even create a Web site devoted to the e-mail message and immortalize the blunder for posterity.

One of us was graphically reminded of the permanence of e-mail after having published a column observing that America Online was the largest and most successful commercial online service. A reader responded with a copy of an e-mail message — also written by the columnist — complaining about AOL's customer service and wondering how it could possibly stay in business very long. The e-mail was dated October 1989. The column appeared in 1996. As the sender wryly commented, "Guess you didn't buy the stock either, eh?"

Either write your message in such a way that it can be forwarded widely without offending anyone, or include the words "private" or "please don't forward" in the message. Then cross your fingers and hope that such requests are honored. But like a public figure who tells a reporter that a controversial comment is "off the record," don't expect your request to be honored unless you know the recipient very, very well.

Making Every E-Mail Do Its Share

At the end of every e-mail, as with a paper letter, you'd normally sign your name. E-mail has the advantage that it can automate the process — and provide a potent marketing tool — with something called a *sig file* (short for *signature file*).

A sig file is several lines of text that automatically appear at the end of every e-mail, automated e-mail list message, or newsgroup posting that you create. Sig files are optional but can be powerful reminders of who you are and what your company does. Sig files can range from the whimsical, including favorite quotations and fanciful job titles, to unabashed plugs. Some samples of sig files are shown in Figure 9-4. But the best approach for marketing with a sig file is informational: conveying who you are, what you do, and how people can reach you.

Figure 9-4:
Signature files range from the sublime to the ridiculous.

```
+------------------------------------+-----------------------------------+
| Sherlock Holmes                    | Mail:   sherlock@holmes.co.uk     |
| Consulting Detective               | Web:    http://www.holmes.com     |
| 222B Baker Street                  | Fax:    (01) 555-5555             |
| London, England U.K.               | Voice:  (01) 555-0000             |
+------------------------------------+-----------------------------------+

===================================================================
Dr. Doolittle                     * FUN ARMADILLO FACTS #5
drdoolittle@aol.com               *
animaldoctor@mouse-potatoes.com   * These nocturnal animals eat ants,
http://www.drdoolittle.com        * termites, snakes and even carrion.
===================================================================
```

Don't dismiss a sig file's effectiveness because it's simple text at the end of an e-mail message. It's simple text at the end of *every* e-mail message that you, or anyone in your company, sends. It provides contact information, reinforces your brand and corporate identity, and provides a measure of consistency across all your outgoing communications. It is likely the cheapest, easiest way to repeatedly push your key marketing message without appearing, well, pushy.

Keep sig files short. A general rule is to make a sig file no more than four to six lines of text. If your sig file is longer than that, your signature may threaten to exceed the length of a message; worse yet, some newsgroups and e-mail lists automatically *clip* (reduce the size of) your sig file to keep it within what they consider acceptable limits.

For example, if you run a science fiction bookstore, a good marketing sig file for you might read as follows:

```
Jules Verne
Where No Reader Has Gone Before Books (Seattle, WA)
The biggest science fiction bookstore in the universe.
www.wherenoreaderhasgone.com 206-555-5555
```

You often don't need to include dashes or other separators between your e-mail message and the sig file; many e-mail programs automatically insert them. Try sending a message to yourself to test your sig file and see whether a separator is necessary.

The key elements of a good sig file include:

```
Your name, your title
Your company name
Your company tag line, slogan, or description
Your phone number(s)
Your Web URL
```

Keep in mind that sig files don't have to include your e-mail address; the recipient already has that simply by getting your e-mail. However, if you use an automated response program (called a mailbot) or use your sig file on messages that you have others send for you, it makes sense to include your e-mail address in your sig file as well.

Signature files can serve one other purpose if you or any of your employees send personal mail, newsgroup postings, or e-mail list contributions from a business domain: They can contain a disclaimer if the message is for personal, not work, reasons. ("Any opinions expressed are my own and not that of my employer" is boring, but it does the job. Many such disclaimers are far more creative.)

Creating a sig file is relatively straightforward and can be done for both the Microsoft Outlook Express portion of Microsoft Internet Explorer and Netscape Communicator, as well as for standalone e-mail clients (such as Qualcomm's Eudora), newsreaders (such as Microsoft Outlook's newsreader), and even America Online software (version 5.0 was the first with support for sig files, which AOL calls Signatures).

The following sections tell you how to create sig files for the three most popular Web browsers: Microsoft Outlook Express, part of Microsoft Internet Explorer 5.0; the e-mail client in Netscape Communicator 4.73; and America Online 5.0. The steps in these sections are very similar to the steps that apply to creating sig files for other programs not listed here.

Creating a signature file in Microsoft Outlook Express 5

In Microsoft Outlook Express 5, follow these steps to create a sig file for all your e-mail messages:

1. **Launch Outlook Express.**

2. **Choose Tools⇨Options.**

   An Options dialog box appears. The General tab is selected.

3. **Click the Signatures tab.**

   The Signatures dialog box appears.

4. **Click the New button.**

   In the Signatures field, Signature #1 appears and is highlighted.

5. **In the Edit Signature field, you have two choices: You can either type your signature in the empty Text field at the top, or you can choose the File option and specify a text-only signature file that you've already created.**

   For this example, we use the Text option.

6. **Type your signature in the Text field; then click the radio button to the left of the word Text.**

   The radio button may already be selected, which is fine.

7. **Above the Signature field, click the check box to the left of the words. Add signatures to all outgoing messages.**

8. **Click the OK button in the Signatures dialog box.**

   The Signature dialog box closes.

Now, whenever you create an e-mail message in Outlook Express, the signature that you created is automatically appended to it. The preceding steps are similar to those that you can use to create a signature file for newsgroup postings.

Creating a signature file in Netscape Communicator 4.73

The steps for creating a signature file in Netscape Communicator 4.73 require you to create the file separately and then tell Communicator where to find it. Follow these steps to create a signature file:

1. **Go into any word processing or text processing program (including Windows Notepad or Macintosh SimpleText).**

2. **Create a new document.**

3. **Type in your signature text as you want to see it, including carriage returns.**

4. **Save the file by giving it the filename "sigfile" (or any other name — we use "sigfile" in this example) in text format.**

   Remember the directory in which you saved the file.

5. **Launch Netscape Navigator.**

6. **Choose Edit⇨Preferences.**

   A Preferences dialog box with a list of options on its left side appears.

7. **Click the plus sign (Windows) or arrow (Macintosh) adjacent to Mail & Groups on the left side of the dialog box.**

   Additional options appear below Mail & Groups.

8. **Click "Identity" when it appears under Mail & Groups.**

   The right side of the dialog box changes to Identity preferences.

9. **Click the Choose button to the right of the Signature File field.**

10. **Navigate through your hard disk until you find the file that you created and named "sigfile" in Step 4 (which should appear as "sigfile.txt").**

11. **Click "sigfile.txt" to select it.**

    The Identity portion of the Preferences dialog box appears again, indicating the file that you've chosen as your signature file, as shown in Figure 9-5.

12. **Click the OK button.**

    The Preferences dialog box disappears.

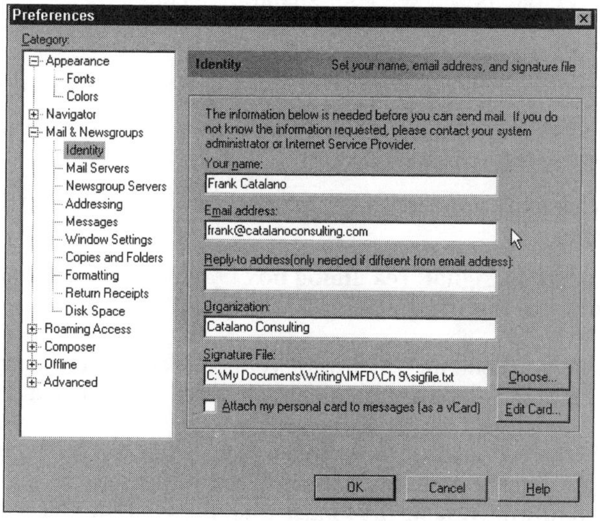

Figure 9-5:
Selecting a signature file in Netscape Communicator.

Now, whenever you create a new mail message or a newsgroup posting with Netscape Communicator 4.73, your signature automatically appears at the bottom of the message, separated from the message by a series of dashes.

Creating a signature file in America Online 5.0

Even though you may not use America Online for business e-mail, an appropriate sig file for all your outbound AOL personal messages can help cross-promote your business (and some small businesses do use AOL for business e-mail accounts):

1. **Launch America Online.**

2. **Choose Mail Center⇨Set Up Mail Signatures.**

   The Set up Signatures dialog box appears.

3. **Click the Create button at the bottom left.**

   The Create Signature dialog box appears.

4. **Type a name for your signature in the Signature Name field.**

   The name can be anything, such as "Business Signature."

5. **Type your signature in the Signature field.**

   Use any combination of fonts or font sizes, but understand that those font selections will be visible only to other America Online members; non-AOL recipients will see your signature as plain text.

6. **Click the OK button.**

   The Set up Signatures dialog box reappears. The name of the signature that you just created should be highlighted.

7. **Click the Default On/Off button.**

   A red check mark appears to the left of the name of the signature that you created.

8. **Close the Set up Signatures dialog box by clicking the X in the upper-right corner of the window.**

Now, every time you send an e-mail with your AOL account, the signature that you just created will be automatically inserted (as shown in Figure 9-6).

To sig or not to sig? A business-oriented signature file can seem clumsy at the end of more personal or chummy messages. Very short messages can also seem "weighed down" by a sig file longer than the content you're sending. Be ready to delete the signature lines before you send your e-mail message if they seem out of place.

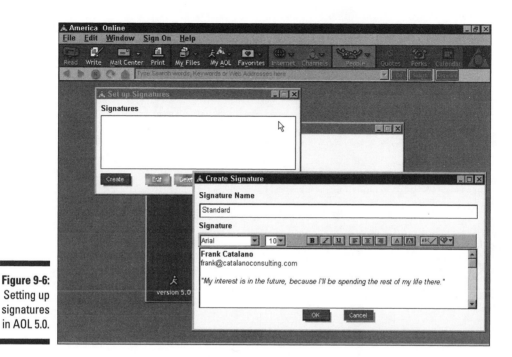

Figure 9-6:
Setting up
signatures
in AOL 5.0.

Chapter 10

E-Mail by the Pallet

In This Chapter

▶ Handling high volumes of e-mail

▶ Using mailing lists

▶ Weighing the pros and cons of spam

▶ Avoiding being labeled a spammer

*G*etting started with e-mail marketing is a lot like poking a small hole in a dam and walking away: Before you know it, you've got more dam water than you can handle. In some cases with e-mail, you may simply be responding to the flood; in others, such as with newsletters or e-mail marketing campaigns, you may be purposely creating it.

In both cases, though, you need methods and tools to manage e-mail so that your prospects become customers and your customers stay customers. And so that your business doesn't float downstream, caught up in the current.

Processing E-Mail by the Pallet

If you have a company Web site and it includes any e-mail addresses at all, there's no way around it: You're going to get e-mail. E-mail can come to any addresses you have listed on your site, and it may even come addressed to generic e-mail addresses that your customers are used to seeing on *other* sites — addresses such as sales@yourdomain.com, info@yourdomain.com, or webmaster@yourdomain.com.

The types of messages you're likely to receive can run the gamut:

✔ Inquiries for details about products or services

✔ Comments from existing customers about product experiences

✔ Requests for customer service or support

✔ Résumés from job seekers

✔ Inquiries from potential business partners about joint ventures or promotions

✔ Complaints about things people in your company did or didn't do

✔ Spam and wacko mail from people in close personal contact with Regulus IV

✔ Orders for your products

No matter how little interest you think that your Web site may generate, it almost always generates more e-mail than you expect.

Planning for the flood

Before blasting your e-mail address or addresses to the Internet world, plan how to channel the potential flood of incoming e-mail into information streams that you can handle. Here are some planning tips:

✔ **Write and post a detailed FAQ.** One of the best ways to deal with a potential e-mail flood is to prevent it. Anticipate the kind of questions you're likely to get asked repeatedly, answer them, and post the questions and answers very obviously on your Web site in a Frequently Asked Questions (FAQ) document. FAQs don't eliminate incoming e-mail but they do help reduce the volume of routine requests.

✔ **Place all contact information on one Web page.** Rather than leave your visitors guessing who to contact, make finding the right address for a person or department easy by creating an "About Us" or "How to Contact Us" Web page that includes every salient e-mail address in your company, and link to that contact page from every other page on your Web site. The presence of this page prevents visitors from having to guess addresses and send their messages to the wrong people inside your company, thereby either delaying your firm's response or preventing a customer from ever getting a response at all. Figure 10-1 shows one such contact page for the computer industry trade publication *InfoWorld*.

✔ **Embed a** `mailto:` **link behind each text e-mail address on a Web page.** A `mailto:` link enables visitors to click directly on the e-mail address. Doing so spawns a new e-mail message and sends you the mail without requiring visitors to type your e-mail address. (This assumes, of course, that the visitors have put their e-mail server information in their browser program's preferences, but that situation is something over which you have no control.) The key is to make it easy for visitors to contact you if they're set up to do so. Visitors who don't have their preferences set to take advantage of `mailto:` links can still send you e-mail; they just have to go through a bit more effort (cutting and pasting the visible e-mail address from the Web site into their e-mail client software). Embedding `mailto:` links into Web pages is supported by most popular Web page creation tools.

Figure 10-1:
A contact
page for the
computer
trade
publication
InfoWorld.

✔ Create aliases for departments or functions. E-mail server software — whether maintained by your ISP, your Web-hosting service, or your company — usually allows creation of an *alias* that is, effectively, an e-mail address that points to one or several other e-mail addresses. Thus, the alias of `sales@yourdomain.com` could point to the sales receptionist who would read each incoming e-mail and either respond to it or forward it to the right person in your organization for a response.

Similarly, `custsvc@yourdomain.com` could automatically forward mail to the people in your organization who handle customer-service inquiries. You can make up aliases for almost any function or even for short-term promotions, such as `contest@yourdomain.com`.

Most ISPs and Web-hosting services assist you in setting up aliases. If the mail server resides within your company, your mail server software can be configured to assign aliases.

Make sure that someone in your organization is ultimately responsible for verifying that every e-mail sent to a specific alias is answered or otherwise appropriately dealt with. Because an alias may point to several addresses within an organization, assigning a lead person within that group to ensure that no message falls through the cracks is a good idea.

Should you put an e-mail address on your site?

Presumably, if you're reading a book called *Internet Marketing For Dummies,* you're planning to do some kind of online marketing (or you just have a Renaissance approach to recreational reading). But online marketing can be, when implemented fully, an intensely interactive, two-way process. If customers know that you're online, they expect to do more than just read about your products or services on your Web site. They want to get in touch. And the easiest way for them to do that, once at your Web site, is through e-mail.

The best sites — and organizations — realize that e-mail can be a powerful communication tool that can further bond current and potential customers to them. Other sites treat e-mail as more of a problem than an opportunity.

If you have doubts about your ability to handle a large volume of incoming e-mail, a good initial step to gauge the response you may get is to put a single e-mail address on your site. If the response is overwhelming, temporarily remove the address and use the information in this chapter to help you plan how to handle all the mail you receive from your Web site promptly and in a way that your customers, vendors, and business partners — and even the occasional channeler of alien intelligences — can appreciate.

If the e-mail flood threatens to drown you — but you don't want to turn off the spigot — it may be time to examine some electronic Customer Relationship Management (eCRM) software packages or services. eCRM software and services run the gamut of handling how companies interact with their customers, but some packages focus primarily on e-mail management: making sure that every incoming e-mail is routed, tracked, and dealt with properly. Packages include Talisma Enterprise Edition from Talisma and eGain Mail from eGain Communications; many more are available. However, be prepared to pay for the added convenience, with prices typically starting in the thousands of dollars for the software, although some (such as those from Talisma and eGain) can be outsourced as services hosted on the vendor's systems for slightly less cash.

The 24-hour rule

Pretend that you've just written an old-fashioned paper letter to a company to request information. You've spent time typing the letter, printing it, preparing an envelope, putting a stamp on the envelope, and sticking the envelope into a mailbox. If you get a response in one week, perhaps two, you're satisfied.

Now, pretend that you've called a company's customer service number and left a voice-mail message. You've spent the time dialing the number and asking your question. You expect a response the next business day (or perhaps in two business days, at most). Your expectation is based, in part, on how much effort you put into your end of the communication and, in part, on the speed of the communications mechanism.

Finally, pretend that you've sent your request in an e-mail message. Unlike a paper letter, e-mail is very easy to compose, can be sent with a mouse click, and is usually delivered almost instantaneously. So with e-mail, unlike with either paper letters or voice-mail messages, customer expectations for a prompt response are higher.

The best rule to follow is to send out at least a brief answer to all e-mail inquiries within one 24-hour business day.

Unanswered e-mail comes with a potentially high cost: You are likely to find yourself with a dissatisfied customer or, at the very least, a customer who questions your commitment to customer service. On the Internet, a dissatisfied customer can quickly spread the word about your perceived shoddy service through online discussion groups (such as newsgroups, message boards, or chat rooms), automated e-mail lists, and individual e-mail messages to friends — the very same vehicles that we're talking about using as marketing tools. And, like other e-mail messages, such negative messages can hang around for years in easily accessible online archives. Unless used with care, the Internet marketing sword can easily become double-edged.

Introducing automatic mail

If you're getting a large amount of e-mail, automating the reply process may be a tempting option. The most common method of automating responses is by using a program known variously as a *mailbot, infobot,* or — our preferred term — *autoresponder.*

These programs respond to incoming e-mail by checking the subject line for specific words (for example, *brochure request*) or by looking for a specific incoming address or alias (for example, info@yourdomain.com) and then shooting off a reply with canned materials, untouched by human hands.

Autoresponder programs and automated e-mail lists, or listservs (covered in Chapter 11), can do many of the same things. The major distinction is that autoresponders are designed to evaluate each incoming message according to some criterion, such as the subject line or incoming address, and then send a predetermined (and, we hope, appropriate) response to the sender. Listserv e-mail lists receive messages from the members of that list and then duplicate and send the messages to all members of the list in order to facilitate discussions.

Autoresponder programs reside on the mail server maintained by you, your Internet service provider (ISP), or your Web- and mail-hosting service; ISPs and Web-hosting services can usually set up such programs for a small or no monthly fee in addition to your normal monthly ISP or Web-hosting charge.

If you are running your own mail server, you can get an autoresponder program from a variety of sources. Some of the better-known shareware programs are PromaSoft Autoresponder and Rubberband, available from various shareware

Web sites. Some mail server and automated e-mail list programs, such as Lyris from Lyris Technologies (www.lyris.com), also include autoresponder features.

Throughout this book, we recommend various shareware and freeware programs to jump-start your Internet marketing efforts with minimal out-of-pocket cost. But just because you can't find a software program online to meet your specific needs one week doesn't mean that the perfect application won't be there the next. Shareware offerings change often, and more and more shareware is being released, not only for the various flavors of Windows 9x and the Macintosh OS but also for workstation operating systems such as Windows NT/2000 and Linux. Check shareware sites — such as ZDNet (hotfiles.zdnet.com), Dave Central (www.davecentral.com), PCWorld.com's Fileworld (www.pcworld.com/fileworld) and CNET's Shareware.com (www.shareware.com) — frequently for updates to old favorites and new releases. And remember, if you like the shareware, register and pay for it: That's how new shareware gets written.

The Internet has a strong UNIX heritage. Despite the progress that Internet tools have made in moving to Windows and Macintosh, quite a few of the powerful server programs are designed to work only, or best, on UNIX servers. Unless you like getting your hands dirty, have a UNIX-based Web server, and are familiar with such arcana as *vi* (short for visual editor, an obtuse UNIX text editor), you're better off outsourcing such services as autoresponders to your Internet service provider or Web-hosting service. Who knows? Someone at your ISP may actually like working with UNIX.

Using autoresponders autoresponsibly

The bright side of autoresponder programs is that they can make responding to every e-mail within 24 hours brain-dead simple. When an incoming e-mail arrives to an alias, the autoresponder automatically sends a reply.

The dark side of autoresponder programs is that they can become a crutch if overused. They automatically send out canned materials — and nothing else — to someone who may actually have a specific, legitimate question that requires personal attention.

Our advice: Use autoresponders carefully. Make sure that your visitors clearly understand that, when you promote e-mail addresses that are handled by infobots, the response will be automated. (You can, for example, use a Send an e-mail to brochure@yourdomain.com to receive our product literature automatically **message on your Web site.**) In the body text of the automatic response, include a follow-up e-mail address that leads to a mailbox read by a real, live human. That way, customers can send an e-mail to the second address if the canned information doesn't answer their questions.

Home of the e-weird

Not every e-mail message you get will be easily classifiable, and some may be, well, downright strange.

Because sending you an e-mail message is so easy, you may get off-the-top-of-the-head questions (or questions designed simply to irritate) that have nothing to do with your products, your business, or even your life. These e-mail messages may take the form of either flat statements or questions, such as "When your company was founded, the moon and stars were in perfect alignment" or "What's your company strategy for the unification of Europe?"

Because it's difficult to tell whether the sender is a 12-year-old with too much time on his or her hands or a potential multimillion-dollar client

testing your responsiveness, the safest tack is to take a deep breath, let the query sit for a few minutes, and then do your best with a straight-forward, but very brief, response.

Another option is to practice writing the neutral response that puts the offbeat question back in the sender's lap — "We've never actually considered it that way. Why do you ask?" — and hope that the response is clearer (or doesn't come at all).

A final approach is the classic one that was used to great effect by Lucy in Charles Schulz's *Peanuts* comic strip. When confronted with deep, philosophical questions by Charlie Brown, Lucy paused and then carefully noted, "We had spaghetti at our house three times last week."

If you use an infobot to answer each and every e-mail promptly, think of your automatic response more as an acknowledgment than as a real response. Tell the sender, "Thank you for your e-mail. We're sending you this automatic confirmation to let you know that we received your message and will respond within 24 hours (or the next business day)." Then live up to that promise.

Delivering E-Mail by the Pallet

At times, you may want to send out *bulk e-mail* — the same e-mail message sent to dozens, hundreds, or thousands of people simultaneously. Following are some possible reasons for sending bulk e-mail:

- ✔ You're having a sale and want to let preferred customers know about it early.
- ✔ You're shipping a new product and need to contact prospects who asked to be notified when it's available.
- ✔ You've created an enhancement to a product (or have found a defect) and need to advise current owners immediately.
- ✔ You're changing your phone number, location, or even your e-mail address, and your customers, vendors, and business partners need to know.

E-mailing this information one message at a time is not very efficient (or smart). The solution for the bulk e-mail situation is to make and maintain lists of e-mail addresses. Essentially, you're creating different groups of individual e-mail addresses, and you're creating each group of addresses for a specific purpose.

Creating an e-mail mailing list

The most basic way to create simple e-mail lists for a specific, small group of recipients is with your e-mail client software. (Much larger, and more flexible, automated e-mail lists are covered in Chapter 11.) Netscape Communicator, Microsoft Internet Explorer, America Online, the Microsoft Outlook family (Outlook Express, Outlook 98, Outlook 2000, and so on), and Qualcomm's Eudora are just a few of the many programs that can handle groups of addresses in their address books, as shown in Figure 10-2.

There is also a plethora of commercially available bulk e-mail programs, some with nifty features — for example, the ability to customize the body of every e-mail message with the recipient's name. You can find trial or demo versions of a number of these on shareware sites (listed in the *Internet Marketing For Dummies* Internet Directory, in this book). But be careful — many of these are similar to programs used by spammers to send unwanted, unsolicited bulk e-mail. And messages sent by "spam-friendly" bulk e-mail software is routinely identified and deleted by ISP spam filters. Don't make mistakes that could put you in that not-so-elite spammer club (see "Spam: Cons and a Few Pros," later in this chapter).

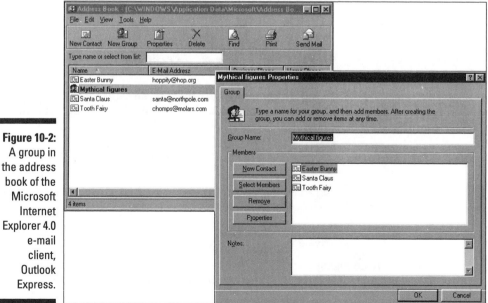

Figure 10-2: A group in the address book of the Microsoft Internet Explorer 4.0 e-mail client, Outlook Express.

The sources of the e-mail addresses that you group can be as varied as the types of information that you plan to send via e-mail:

- ✔ **Existing customer lists.** You may already have these if, at some point, you have asked your customers for an e-mail address in response to mailings, product registration, and the like. (If you don't already collect e-mail data, start now — just make sure that you disclose to your customers how you will use it.)

- ✔ **Requests for information generated by visits to your Web site.** Ask for an e-mail address from every visitor who requests more information, orders a product, or otherwise interacts with your company online.

- ✔ **Customer lists from business partners.** For example, a bookstore may get a list of e-mail addresses from a publisher so that the store can announce the publication of a new book. However, this can be tricky, and you should check with your business partner to make sure that the potential recipients have given their okay to receive e-mail from a third party.

Privacy on the Internet is a hot topic and isn't likely to cool off as long as the Web is considered a key part of doing business. This applies especially to the marketing use of private information. The short advice we can offer: Disclose, disclose, disclose. Reveal explicitly and often exactly — both when you gather the information and in a specific "privacy policy" area of your Web site — how you plan to use e-mail addresses and other personal information gathered through your online marketing efforts. Don't mislead people or go beyond the publicly stated boundaries you set. The long advice: Check out Chapter 8, "Getting the Most Out of Your Web Site."

A fourth source of e-mail addresses is permission-based e-mail services. These services provide lists of e-mail addresses from people who have specifically asked to receive information on certain topics, such as by checking a check box on a Web form they've filled out. These opt-in services are very different from e-mail address "harvesters" that gather up every public e-mail address on the Web and sell them to you, making it possible for you to do indiscriminate unsolicited bulk commercial e-mail (a.k.a. "spam").

Permission-based e-mail services are still relatively new; many are unproven. And there's the trust factor — you need to trust that the services truly are fully "opt-in" (that is, people on the list have actually given their permission to be on the list) and aren't simply tattered bulk-address harvesters in new, fashionable togs.

If you're thinking about using an opt-in, or permission-based, e-mail list, check its reputation first. General feedback sites such as Deja.com (www.deja.com) and Epinions.com (www.epinions.com) may be able to provide general guidance, whereas marketing-specific sites such as ClickZ (www.clickz.com) and I-Advertising (www.i-advertising.com) routinely have discussions about e-mail list issues. Both of the latter also have fully searchable archives.

If you're feeling especially daring, go to an opt-in e-mail list's Web page and sign up for an opt-in list yourself. Take note of how well the list discloses what it will do with your e-mail information. Is it clear that you should expect to receive offers via e-mail? And how easy is it to opt out should you change your mind after you've opted in? If you're not comfortable with how the list gathers names, odds are that your prospects from that list won't be the most receptive to your e-mailings.

Don't confuse "opt-in" with "opt-out" lists. Opt-out lists include names indiscriminately without regard to whether the recipient really asked to receive any messages. The only way someone gets removed from an opt-out list is to specifically ask to be removed. Based on several e-marketers' personal experience, opt-out lists are far less responsive than opt-in lists and can lead to a "spammer" label being slapped across your business. When in doubt as to the type of list, you yourself should opt out — of using any questionable list.

Creating the right message

The obvious first step in sending e-mail messages to a list of people is to write the message; the second step is to address it; and the third is to hit the Send button. Resist such immediate temptation. The ease with which e-mail can be composed and delivered to dozens (or perhaps hundreds) of recipients doesn't always allow time for the kind of reflection and revision that other marketing materials (such as brochures, direct mail pieces, and print ads) force upon their creators. Make yourself take the time. Before e-mailing anything to a group, step back and do this quick reality check:

- ✔ **Are the tone and style of your message consistent with your image?** The elements of e-mail marketing style noted in Chapter 9 — write "dressy casual"; be polite; and keep it short — apply as much to mass e-mailings as they do to individual responses, if not more so. Many of your group e-mail messages may be sent to prospects who are only casually interested in what you have to offer but will quickly note anything off-putting about the message's tone or content.

- ✔ **Do you tell enough?** If the message is likely to be seen by people who aren't intimately familiar with your company or product, you need to provide enough background information to satisfy them. Don't forget basics, such as your company name, product or service name, and contact information. (Even those who should know better make this mistake: We've seen at least one e-mail news release that was sent out by a public relations agency to promote a new software product to the press — but neglected to reveal who the software's publisher was.)

✔ **Do you sell enough?** No matter what the purpose of your mass e-mail, it should contain a call to action. If your message is designed to announce a new product, say where it can be ordered. If the message is designed to advise that your phone number has changed, remind the recipients to update their address books. Do it without undue hype — e-mail, remember, is a personal medium — but definitely do it.

✔ **Do you make it easy to get off of the list?** Even though people may have at one time asked to be notified about new products or other company information, they may at some point change their mind. The first or last sentence in any bulk e-mailing should provide clear, straightforward instructions on how a recipient can keep from getting any further messages from your business. These "remove" instructions should require no more effort than sending an e-mail back to you — and should be honored immediately.

✔ **Does your message really need to be communicated by e-mail?** Although this advice may sound heretical in a book about Internet marketing, not every communication needs to be sent as an e-mail message. If your message is complex, detailed, or controversial, consider another delivery vehicle, such as direct mail or a personal phone call. The same e-mail message that you can send in an instant can be returned just as quickly, with new red-hot commentary, if what you're trying to say is not clear or if your message is seen as insulting.

Finally, reread the message and make sure that you've briefly answered all the questions the recipient may reasonably have — either in the text of the message or on a Web page to which the message points. Doing so can cut down the amount of time you spend dealing with confused responses and lower the irritation level of a recipient looking for the information.

The (not yet) golden age of wireless (e-mail)

As digital mobile phones, handheld and Pocket PC devices, and two-way pagers proliferate, so does the incentive to send marketing e-mail to this new class of e-mail device. But currently there are severe limitations on the display of wireless e-mail.

The bottom line: Unless your marketing message is very short and is communicated very well by straight text, don't target wireless e-mail devices. If your message does work within these restrictions, you'll need to decide what kinds of wireless device you want to reach: Spelling out your key points in fewer than 150 characters meets the e-mail limit on many digital mobile phones, whereas keeping the length within 500 characters works with one "grab" of a Palm VII, for example.

This might mean that your subject line effectively is the message, with a brief call to action following in the body of the e-mail. Think of it as an opportunity to hone your editing — or your haiku — skills.

Getting the mechanics right

After you have the message worded the way you want, the next step is making sure that the message will read the way you want — not the wording, but the formatting. If the message is unattractive to read, odds are that it won't be read, or your company won't be presented in its best light. E-mail messages can get very creatively munged through various e-mail formatting options and in how the recipient's e-mail client software decides to display it. Some key considerations:

✔ **Is the message strict ASCII text?** Some e-mail client software (including the America Online mail client, Qualcomm's Eudora, and browsers that support HTML mail, including Microsoft Internet Explorer's Outlook Express and Netscape Communicator) enable users to send electronic mail with colored text, varied fonts, and underlining. Unfortunately, those features aren't readable by Web-based and many other e-mail clients, which display only plain text and carriage returns. Refrain from using bells and whistles that may look cool to you but could cause your message to frustrate and confuse your recipients.

✔ **Are you using short line lengths with fixed carriage returns?** Keep text on each line to no more than 60 characters and embed a hard carriage return after each line. That forces the lines to neatly "line" up as you intend and can help avoid the stair-step effect that occurs when e-mail client software assigns its own carriage returns, repeatedly, both on the sender's and the recipient's end.

✔ **Are you sending blind carbon copies?** Unless your message is going to only a handful of people, you probably don't want everyone who gets the message to see the names and e-mail addresses of everyone else who gets the message. To avoid this, use the blind carbon copy (or bcc:)

HTML Mail: Temptation and trap

Both Netscape Communicator 4.0 and higher and Microsoft Internet Explorer 4.0 and higher have integrated a feature known as *HTML Mail* into their e-mail capabilities. (Netscape created HTML Mail first, if you're keeping score.) Just as HyperText Markup Language (HTML) enables Web browsers to display graphics, HTML Mail enables you to embed graphics, Web page links, and stylized text (among other things) in e-mail messages.

You may be tempted to jazz up a dull text e-mail message with HTML Mail features. Our advice:

Don't, unless you're absolutely sure that everyone who is receiving the message (or is likely to be forwarded it) can read HTML-formatted mail.

If not, you fall into the trap of sending a perfectly good message that is virtually unreadable by a strictly text e-mail program, as shown in Figure 10-3. What your recipient sees: plain text, infested by ugly HTML tags.

option in your e-mail software. Here's how: Rather than choose To: or Cc: when addressing the message to the list, choose Bcc: in order to suppress the visibility of the complete address list. The recipients who don't have to scroll through a long list of names before getting to the body of the message will likely appreciate your thoughtfulness. This also protects the privacy of recipients.

- **Do you include a reply address?** If someone does a "reply all" to your bulk e-mail, make sure that every response doesn't go to everyone else who got the initial bulk message. (In this case, misery does not love company.) Most e-mail clients allow you to insert a specific "reply to" address for responses. To play it safe, also include reply instructions at the end of each message — if appropriate, with a warning to not "reply all."
- **Have you been the guinea pig?** Before opening the floodgates, trickle one copy of the message to yourself (preferably sent from one e-mail address at one domain to a second, different e-mail address at a different domain; for example, send a test message from your hosted Web service to an America Online account). This type of dress rehearsal identifies any weird formatting problems that could irritate those who receive your message; it also gives you one last look at the message's content. For large e-mailings, repeat this test on several colleagues.

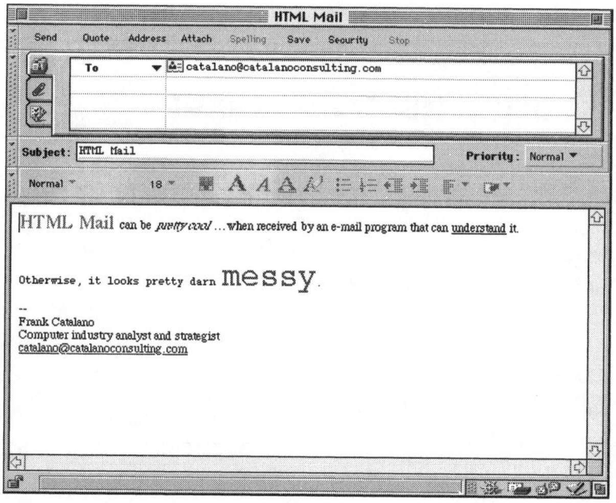


```
Subject:     HTML Mail
Date:        12/05  9:14 AM
Received:    12/05  9:15 AM
From:        Frank Catalano, catalano@catalanoconsulting.com
To:          Frank Catalano, catalano@catalanoconsulting.com

<HTML>
<FONT COLOR="#3EA9C0"><FONT SIZE=+2>HTML Mail </FONT></FONT>can be <I>pretty
cool</I>...when received by an e-mail program that can <U>understand</U>
it.
<BR> 
<PRE>Otherwise, it looks pretty darn <FONT COLOR="#E81631"><FONT SIZE=+4>
messy</FONT></FONT>.</PRE>
--
<BR>Frank Catalano
<BR>Computer industry analyst and strategist
<BR><A HREF="http:www.catalanoconsulting.com/catalano/">
catalano@catalanoconsulting.com</A>
<BR>     </HTML>
```

Figure 10-3: HTML-formatted mail, before and after.

Spam: Cons and a Few Pros

As certain as summer turns to fall, wine turns to vinegar, and a solitary clothes hanger turns into dozens when not watched, new online marketers turn to thoughts of sending e-mail en masse to prospects who have never even contacted their company. The word for such a Net byproduct is *spam*. (Other words come to mind, too, but we can't print them here.)

The appeal of this automated e-mail equivalent to the cold call is seductive. After all, if a company is already sending out e-mail to large lists of its own contacts, why not just buy an e-mail list from a third party and see how many e-mail recipients on the list bite? Sending a few hundred — or a few thousand — more e-mail messages has little incremental cost.

Unfortunately, cost isn't always measured in dollars. Cost is also measured in good will and legal uncertainty. Most Internet service providers, Web-hosting services, and commercial online services such as America Online, EarthLink, AT&T, and many, many others have strict policies forbidding their subscribers from sending spam. The penalty is usually a warning and/or suspension of service on the first offense — and termination of service on the second offense.

A brief history of spam

On the Internet, the word *spam* is not shorthand for "shoulder pork and ham." The apocryphal story about the word's origin in the online world is that *spam* is an acronym for "self-propelled advertising material." Other Internet lore credits the classic *Monty Python* sketch set in a restaurant in which every menu item (emphasized by a group of Vikings chanting "spam spam spam spam" in the background) is some variation of the luncheon meat. And to most users of the Internet, the electronic version is not nearly as tasty as the Hormel version.

The more modern version of spam gained widespread notoriety in early 1994, when the law firm of Canter & Siegel, run by a husband-and-wife team, posted a message to Internet discussion groups known as *newsgroups* — the subject of Chapter 12 — advertising Green Card services for immigrants. The team didn't pick one, or two,

or a dozen appropriate newsgroups. The same message was posted to thousands of newsgroups, whether the newsgroup topic was cooking or cave art. This novel action was a real shock to many Internet users because online commerce over the Internet, let alone this kind of in-your-face assault, was just getting started.

The backlash was immediate and loud. Tens of thousands of hostile responses (or *flames*) inundated the originators, overloading their ISP, costing the duo its Internet access, and reportedly leading to the ISP and Canter & Siegel threatening to sue each other over the matter.

Since then, *spam* has commonly come to mean any unsolicited commercial message indiscriminately sent via e-mail, distributed through an e-mail list, or posted to a newsgroup. An example is shown in Figure 10-4.

```
Subject:    $7,000 LOAN--NO PAYBACK EVER!!!!!!!
Date:       11/24/97 10:49 PM
To:         spammaillist@nowhere.com

Look First: Trash Later

I look forward to getting home in the evenings and checking my mailbox so that I can count the
amount of money I have received for the day. You can be in my position too,by counting as much as
$200-$400 each day. This is real and I am a real person on a mission to achieve financial freedom.
Do not give up on this and do not throw this aside because I tell you without reservations, that
this does work!! I am glad that I did not throw this away when I received it because I am now
going to the bank to make deposits instead of withdrawals! Join me and the others by gaining your
own financial freedom and continuing this process by sharing it with whomever you come in contact
with because the more you share, the  more money you make.

You may have an interest in receiving an INTEREST FREE LOAN, even if you have had CREDIT PROBLEMS
IN THE PAST. Well, read on because this one can really bring the CASH FAST! And it only costs a
minimum.

$7,000 LOAN--NO PAYBACK EVER!!!!!!!

Time: 12-30 days

Interested? Read on.

WOULD YOU LIKE A $7,000 LOAN THAT NEVER HAS TO BE REPAID?

You can definitely get up to $7000 within a few weeks and you willnot have to pay it back. This
program is designed to raise money fast.It is VERY inexpensive to participate in because it's been
designed to be run totally online, there are no postage or name list expenses! Read this over and
carefully follow the instructions. It has worked very well for me each time that I have used it.
```

Figure 10-4:
A typical
spam
message,
modified to
protect the
guilty.

In addition, several large ISPs and online services have been aggressive in filing lawsuits against spammers who they believe have fraudulently sent e-mail to their subscribers or misappropriated their e-mail services. (A couple of years back, one Northwest regional ISP estimated that it bounced at least 10,000 fraudulent spam messages each day.) And several states, starting in 1998, passed anti-spamming laws that provide for severe penalties for spammers.

So take any inclination to spam with a grain of salt. Perhaps even an entire lick.

Spam is also commonly known as *unsolicited commercial e-mail, bulk e-mail,* and *junk e-mail.* But as Shakespeare once noted about a rose by any other name, spam still smells — and tastes — the same.

If you're uncertain whether your mass e-mail message will be viewed as spam, think of your message as a fax. Would you spend the personal time and effort to send this person a fax with the same information? If so, your e-mail message probably won't be regarded by the recipient as spam.

Why spam offends

Most businesses new to online marketing don't intuitively understand why spam generates such a vehement response among those who receive it. With flat-fee Internet access having overwhelmingly supplanted pay-by-the-hour service, it's easy to conclude that no one should object. But rightly or wrongly, spam generates as much controversy as discussions of religion, politics, or the clubbing of baby seals. Many recipients see it as an intrusion that steals time, an intrusion much more odious than paper junk mail. Why? Here are some possible reasons:

✔ **Too easy.** For regular mail, the costs of creating effective copy, printing it, and spending money for postage erect an effective "barrier to entry" to amateurish offers that appear more often at home on hand-lettered yard signs than in mailboxes. (When was the last time you were sent direct mail for illegal cable television descrambler boxes, miracle vitamin cures, or instant weight-loss products?) Spam is much easier to create and send, and this ease leads to e-mail that's not relevant to a recipient's interests.

✔ **Too confusing.** It's hard to tell from the subject line of an e-mail message — much more so than the design, text, and graphics on a printed return envelope — whether a message contains an unwanted commercial offer.

✔ **Too personal.** The rejection of mass e-mail messages may simply result from the fact that e-mail is considered highly personal by recipients because e-mail is a far more informal method of communicating than paper mail, arrives inside their homes or directly to their work computer, and thus seems to be a violation of that personal space.

No matter what the reason, increasing numbers of spam messages seem to be crowding out other messages in many e-mail boxes as more Internet-unsavvy businesses discover the Internet and users gain experience in freely handing out their e-mail addresses. Flat-fee account or not, an all-you-can-eat buffet isn't very tasty when most of the serving plates contain the same unwanted dish.

Spam I am?

Not all e-mail trying to sell something is spam. Before sending mass e-mail, consider these three questions:

✔ **Did the recipient request the information?** If someone wants information from you, it's not unsolicited — the recipient is likely to be more upset if you *don't* provide the information. Do note in your message that it is in response to the recipient's query (and don't lie about the request; that's a common spammer tactic).

✔ **Do you have an existing business relationship with the recipient?** If the recipient is a past or current customer, vendor, or business partner of yours, your mass e-mail message is probably not spam.

✔ **Are you acting on behalf of a business partner who has the customer relationship?**

This situation is a bit more tricky. For example, if you own a bookstore and are using a book publisher's mailing list to let someone know that you're carrying that publisher's book, you're a step removed from the process by which the mailing list was created. You're trusting that the publisher's list is clean and not *harvested* by a third party from e-mail addresses in newsgroup messages or America Online profiles. You also need to explain clearly to the recipient why you're sending an e-mail message to your business partner's customer.

Generally, if you can answer *yes* to any one of these questions, then congratulations — your e-mail passes the anti-spam sniff test and isn't likely to offend many recipients.

Avoiding the spammer label

Sending spam is never, ever a good idea. But all it takes is one naïve misstep and you can open yourself up to hate e-mail and even have your Internet domain *blacklisted* — that is, blocked from sending e-mail to customers of many ISPs — because you inadvertently released a torrent of unwanted messages to recipients who promptly complained to their ISPs.

Here are common errors to avoid:

- ✔ **Misidentifying commercial e-mail.** In the subject line, make clear that the message is commercial in nature. Include your company name if possible. Do not, under any circumstance, use red herrings frequently used by spammers such as "Information Request," "Extra Income," or the dreaded "Free Stuff!!!" (Exclamation points are almost always an indication that the correct next step for the recipient is to hit Delete.) In the "from" line, make it clear which company sent the message.

- ✔ **Going on and on.** Keep the message short. If the recipient erroneously got put on your e-mail list, scanning and deleting a brief message seems (to our gut-level check) less offensive than doing the same to a long one.

- ✔ **Having a nonworking return address.** Some companies that sell software for bulk e-mailing crow about their capability to forge, or fake, a return e-mail address so that hostile responses don't go to the sender but rather to some other unsuspecting Internet user's address or domain. Make sure that your `replyto:` address works. Test it before sending. Put yourself in the customer's shoes: Would you patronize a store that couldn't be found when you decided to respond to an offer?

- ✔ **Using offensive, unbelievable, or unethical pitches.** Much spam goes out to advertise things that people don't want to talk about in polite society, such as the hugely controversial but fast-growing online porn industry or ways to hijack cable service. Don't tarnish your good name by including anything dubious in your messages — even if you mean it as a joke (remember, dry humor translates poorly in text). Sending offensive pitches puts you in the same league as those who spam.

- ✔ **Acting slowly on remove requests.** Include, both at the beginning and the end of your e-mail message, clear, simple instructions on how a recipient can avoid getting any more unsolicited e-mail from you. And honor all these requests immediately, before your next e-mailing.

Just in case we didn't make it clear: Don't spam. Ever. Those who think there's a responsible way to spam may also think there's a responsible way to con the elderly, destroy the rain forest, or wash red sweatshirts with white underwear. Spam is the most offensive, and least effective, Internet marketing tactic. It is, simply put, a Bad Idea.

Chapter 11

Building Community with E-Mail Lists

· ·

· ·

Keeping in touch with customers and prospects can be done one at a time, individual e-mail by individual e-mail. Or, you can do it through manually created and maintained lists of e-mail addresses in your e-mail program or contact-management software. But soon you may want to communicate with your customers and prospects, regularly, as a group — or have them communicate with each other in an ongoing, public e-mail community. If that's the case, you can automate the entire process thanks to e-mail lists.

E-mail lists are one of the most powerful forces available for creating a user community. This community will very quickly let you know about defects in your products and services as well as what you do right. If you fix the problems and publicize the positive comments (with permission, of course), you can do an awful lot to build your business through an e-mail list. In this chapter, we show you how to use e-mail lists to market your business, from finding the right e-mail lists covering your interest or industry to discovering how to create and promote your own mailing list.

Oh yeah — don't forget about the Directory portion of this book (the yellow pages) in which you can find the addresses and instructions for a number of online marketing-related e-mail lists.

What's an E-Mail List?

Although the meaning of *e-mail list* is crystal-clear to longtime Internet users, the term can confuse many marketers because of how people use the term *mail list* in the nonvirtual world.

An Internet e-mail list, unlike a direct mail list, is *not* a collection of e-mail addresses you buy or rent for the purposes of blasting them with advertising. Though collections of e-mail addresses are sometimes offered for sale on CD-ROM (usually through offers that make you wonder whether they ship in a brown-paper wrapper), these are generally e-mail addresses harvested from Web sites and public discussion groups without the knowledge or consent of the address holders. Blast a true Internet e-mail list with advertising and you may likely earn a place of honor on someone's publicly posted blacklist. An Internet e-mail list is a self-selecting community of online users who choose to either receive information (such as newsletters) or discuss specific topics completely by e-mail. These two types of Internet e-mail lists are referred to as *announcement lists* (the one-way kind) and *discussion lists* (for two-way interaction).

Internet e-mail lists differ from mailing lists you create in your e-mail software (see Chapter 10) because they're largely automated — participants can add or remove themselves from the announcement or discussion list. And in the case of discussion lists, e-mails sent to a single e-mail address are automatically distributed to everyone else on the list, as shown in Figure 11-1.

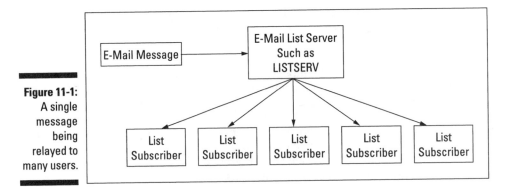

Figure 11-1:
A single message being relayed to many users.

Subscribing to an e-mail list

At the heart of every Internet e-mail list is a *list server,* the software program that keeps the list running smoothly. Several list server products exist, of which LISTSERV from L-Soft International is the best known. All list servers respond to subscription-related commands sent by e-mail.

A brief history of e-mail lists

E-mail lists are a good marketing tactic because of their long history as a trusted resource, their ability to target audiences, and their potential to nurture brand loyalty. E-mail lists predate just about everything that's well known about the online world, including the World Wide Web, America Online, and spam. The first Internet mailing lists were distributed in the mid-1980s over Bitnet, a worldwide network that connected academic and research institutions (the first general interest e-mail list is widely thought to be SF-Lovers, appropriate for a forward-looking technology). E-mail lists now provide newsletters and discussions for almost every conceivable interest — everything from computer product debates to how to breed Golden Retrievers to Internet marketing. And because they're so specific to an interest or industry, they are excellent marketing resources and tools.

So the only thing you need to participate in an e-mail list is the ability to send and receive e-mail. That's the beauty of e-mail lists: Unlike newsgroups (see Chapter 12), you don't have to seek out the discussions; when you sign up for an e-mail list, e-mail messages arrive in your e-mail box for you to peruse at your leisure.

One e-mail list works pretty much the same way as another when it comes to subscribing, no matter which e-mail list program runs them. To get on an e-mail list, for example, you generally do the following:

1. **Find the name, topic, and e-mail address of an interesting e-mail list and send an e-mail message to the list administrative address, which is typically** `listserver@host.domain`.

   (See "Finding the right list," later in this chapter, which covers how to identify an interesting list as a marketing resource.)

2. **In the body of the e-mail, type the word** subscribe, **followed by the name of the list you want to subscribe to, such as:**

   subscribe listname

   The various e-mail list servers may require a different subscription routine, such as typing **subscribe listname** in the subject field, or some other similar wording. Be sure to pay careful attention to the instructions for the specific list you want to join.

   Some list servers then send back a confirming e-mail message asking whether the person at the submitted address really wants to subscribe. (This confirmation prevents the electronic equivalent of the fun-filled prank, which many people perfected in high school, of sending in magazine subscription cards with the names and addresses of unsuspecting victims.)

LISTSERV versus listservs

Few things beat being first in marketing. Just ask Kleenex, Fiberglas, or Xerox. Their names, much to their trademark attorneys' dismay and their marketing managers' delight, have become nearly synonymous with their product category.

The first automated mailing list program widely used for electronic discussions was developed in 1986. LISTSERV was originally available only for IBM mainframe computers — what mainframe junkies like to call "big iron" and personal computer users like to call "dinosaurs." LISTSERV has spawned more than 150,000 public mailing lists, versions for UNIX, VM, OpenVMS, Windows NT and Windows 95/98, and several competitors. Prominent UNIX competitors are Majordomo and ListProc, and many sophisticated Windows 95/98 and Windows NT/2000 list servers have also been developed over the past few years.

Yet because LISTSERV was the first e-mail list software product, its name has forever been linked to automated e-mail lists. You may frequently hear e-mail lists referred to simply as "listservs." It may give lawyers heartburn, but that kind of generic fame is priceless in marketing.

As soon as the list server receives the confirming e-mail back from you, you become a subscriber to the list. Your first message from the list is likely to be a welcome message that includes salient details such as the list description, list dos and don'ts, how to send an e-mail to all list members, and a command reference — including how to unsubscribe from the list.

From then on, you get every message sent to the list, until you send an **unsubscribe listname** command to the list administrative address. Of course, "every message sent to the list" can fill up your Inbox pretty fast. That's why most e-mail lists support a Digest option, as explained shortly.

If you're tempted to delete an e-mail list's welcome message, resist. The most important item in that e-mail is the command reference — and the administrative address to send list commands to.

Almost all e-mail lists maintain two separate e-mail addresses: the *list address*, the one to which you send messages that you want every other list subscriber to see, typically listname@host.domain, and the *administrative address*, the one to which you send commands or requests such as **subscribe**, **unsubscribe**, **help**, and so on, typically listserver@host.domain.

If you nuke the welcome message and don't have a photographic memory, you won't know where to send the **unsubscribe** command when the time comes to leave the list. And other list subscribers find few things more irritating than having to wade through lots of messages demanding "Help! I've fallen on this list and I can't get off! Unsubscribe me!" We know. We've done it.

Some e-mail lists also have a Web page so that you can sign up for the list directly from your Web browser, including the Dummies Daily mailing list, shown in Figure 11-2. This type of Web page makes remembering commands and the administrative address less critical, but you still have to remember the site URL if you ever want to make changes. So don't toss the welcome message.

Variations on an e-mail list

As you may expect with something automated, e-mail lists have variations on their one-message-to-many theme. E-mail lists are commonly thought of primarily as discussion lists. But one variation is the announcement, or *broadcast*, list for missives such as electronic newsletters. Examples of these newsletters are the Dummies Daily lists from IDG Books Worldwide, Inc., the AnchorDesk news service from ZDNet, and Dispatch lists from CNET. Announcement lists can be huge: L-Soft, the maker of the LISTSERV e-mail list software, knows of one list server with nearly 5 million subscribers (the server listserv.women.com). That's a lot of e-mail addresses for a single alias to point to, and far more work than you likely want to manage yourself.

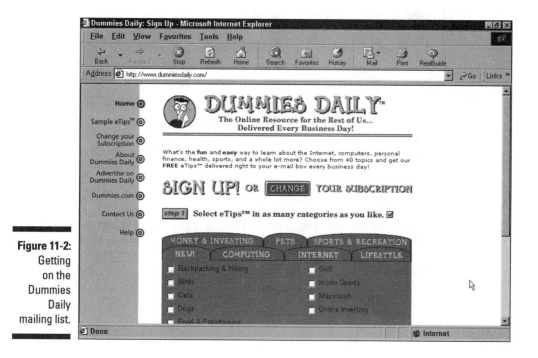

Figure 11-2:
Getting on the Dummies Daily mailing list.

But what discussion and announcement lists have in common is that they completely rely on e-mail for delivery, and list participants, or subscribers, can easily add or remove themselves from the lists. Discussion lists can even be more varied.

Moderated versus free-for-all

On your garden-variety discussion list, you find very little filtering. An e-mail sent to the list address automatically goes to everyone else on the list. A major drawback, however, is that unless list participants police themselves vigorously, these unmoderated lists tend to become overgrown with personal notes, single-line "Thanks!" messages, and the occasional inedible spam.

Enter the moderator. On a moderated discussion list, e-mail messages first go to the moderator to be reviewed for appropriateness and then are sent on to everyone else on the list. A moderated discussion list is very much like a Letters to the Editor section, in which an editor makes sure that the messages are relevant to the topic, don't ramble, and don't endlessly repeat previous comments. Moderators also can throw a wet blanket over *flame wars* and hostile message exchanges (see Chapter 9), and that alone is worth the selection of a moderated list over an unmoderated one.

Individual messages versus digest

When a discussion e-mail list gets popular, or its participants get really enthused or cranky, the number of messages that arrive in your e-mail box can quickly become overwhelming. Many lists have a Digest mode to help manage this kind of list traffic.

Digests are simply compilations of messages that arrive either once a day or after a certain number of messages are processed, as shown in Figure 11-3. The upside of choosing a Digest mode is that you get far fewer e-mail messages from a list, and following how separate discussions develop can be much easier. The downside is that the messages won't be as timely. Unless you need to make snap business decisions based on a list discussion, the downside probably won't pose a problem.

If you're not sure how busy a list is, choose Digest mode when you first subscribe. You can always switch to reading messages as they're sent later. The instructions on setting your list subscription to Digest mode or to individual messages mode are in the initial welcome message — another reason not to delete it.

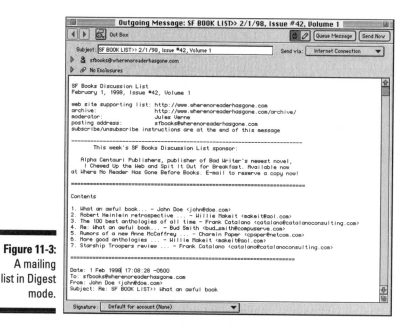

Finding and Using the Right E-Mail Lists

As with e-mail, e-mail lists require a light touch if you want to use them to market your products. The guiding principle is that e-mail lists are informational, meaning that typical marketing messages (which often emphasize style at the expense of substance) don't fit in well. But if you can avoid marketing hype and provide solid information, e-mail lists can be a valuable part of your overall Internet marketing mix.

Benefits of participating in an e-mail list

Discussion e-mail lists make good marketing vehicles for you as a participant for several reasons:

- ✔ **Discussion e-mail lists are highly targeted.** Discussion e-mail lists spring up around specific interests and, if they have a moderator, stay true to those interests.

- ✔ **Discussion e-mail lists are free.** Almost all e-mail lists charge nothing to subscribe. Some discussion lists and many broadcast newsletter lists are supported financially by small ads in the messages themselves rather than by subscription fees.

✔ **Discussion e-mail lists are communities.** Discussion e-mail lists consist of people helping people, whether that help is in the form of providing solid information on where to find a dog breeder, what the hot new science-fiction books are, or how to troubleshoot software problems. For better or worse, regular list participants become like neighbors. If you can add value to the community, you and your business both become good neighbors.

Participating in discussion lists

The easiest way to gain experience in using e-mail lists for marketing is to take part in an existing list (see the section "Marketing to a discussion list," later in this chapter, for more on marketing techniques). But first you need to find the right list for your industry or interest and then use the right approach in posting to the list.

Finding the right list

Although tens of thousands of e-mail lists are available, the right one may not be easy to find. Unless a list administrator chooses to publicize the list, it can be virtually invisible to nonsubscribers because all traffic between the administrator and subscribers travels directly between subscribers and the list administrator by e-mail.

But several excellent resources routinely scour the Internet for e-mail lists and collect what they find in one place. A few examples, most of which overlap in their list listings, are the following:

✔ **Liszt** (www.liszt.com): A huge list of e-mail lists, shown in Figure 11-4, including a search engine to cull through more than 90,000 public and private lists as well as details on how to get more information about each list. Liszt is owned by the list-management site Topica, which itself hosts a number of private and public lists.

✔ **Publicly Accessible Mailing Lists** (paml.net): Stephanie da Silva's painstaking — and long-running — compilation of public e-mail lists with a search engine and descriptions.

✔ **CataList** (www.lsoft.com/lists/listref.html): L-Soft International's searchable database of e-mail lists that use the LISTSERV list server.

✔ **Topica** (www.topica.com): A large directory of e-mail lists, easily searchable, from a site that also hosts mailing lists. This directory includes both Topica-hosted lists and others.

Don't subscribe to an e-mail list based on the list name alone; you may be unpleasantly surprised. For example, searching for *golden* in the Liszt database brought up more than 20 lists identified by minor variations on the word *golden* in their list names, including e-mail lists for the Golden Key National Honor Society, Golden Age Comics, Golden Oldies, and people whose surnames are Golden. But the search brought up only one for Golden Retrievers — the goal of the search. Before subscribing to a list, use an e-mail list search engine and pay attention to any tips the search engine provides to make sure that the list name describes what you think it does, or you could be barking up the wrong tree.

Marketing to a discussion list

After you've found and subscribed to the perfect discussion lists, you're almost ready to dive in with your marketing message. But stay on the side of the pool for a bit longer.

A discussion e-mail list is nothing more than a one-to-many exchange of e-mail messages. So all the rules for e-mail described in Chapter 9 — keep it short, don't type in ALL CAPS, create an effective signature, don't spam, and so on — apply just as much to e-mail lists, if not more so.

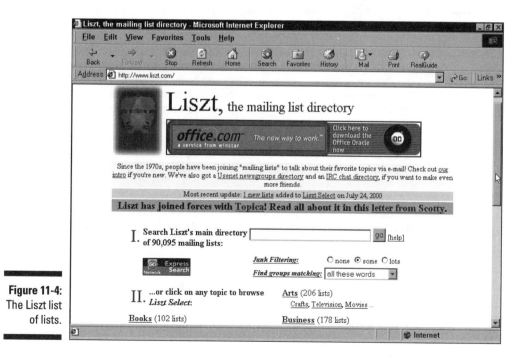

Figure 11-4:
The Liszt list of lists.

E-mail lists about marketing

E-mail lists can be an online marketing resource as much as a marketing tool. Three lively marketing lists are the I-Advertising Discussion List (www.i-advertising.com), with more than 12,000 subscribers, the Online Advertising Discussion List, also known as Online Ads (www.o-a.com), with some 10,000 subscribers, and the ClickZ Forum (www.clickzforum.com) from the Internet marketing Web site ClickZ.

These moderated lists are good examples of Internet resources for online publicity, promotion, advertising, and general marketing, with the occasional spam debate tossed in.

There's also no shortage of marketing-focused announcement e-mail lists in newsletter clothing.

Michael Tchong's irreverant Iconocast (www.iconocast.com) and a variety of dispatches from ClickZ (www.clickz.com) are just two picks from a high-quality litter.

And even though it ceased operations in 1996, the Internet Marketing Discussion List is a classic example of how nothing on the Internet ever dies; it just gets archived. Inet-Marketing has left its searchable — and quite valuable — list archives at www.i-m.com.

Finally, don't forget to consult the Directory portion (yellow pages) of this book for a few more online marketing e-mail lists worth checking out.

Before contributing anything, *lurk*. A poorly-thought-out e-mail message is read by only one person, but a similarly ill-considered discussion list submission can be read, remembered, and replied to by thousands. So read the e-mail list messages for one to two weeks before participating. That way, you get a good feel for the tone of the list, what the current hot topics are, and who the key players happen to be. You also find out whether the e-mail list provides Frequently Asked Question (FAQ) documents. FAQs often have details on issues that have been discussed ad infinitum (and even ad nauseum) on the mailing list. So lurk before you leap.

Another consideration for marketing in discussion e-mail lists is the fact that most of them are for customer service or for open, honest discussion of an agreed-on interest. Anything that feels like marketing hype within the list will be ignored, at best, or cause people to drop the list, at worst. You know the feeling when a good friend suddenly starts trying to get you to buy things from him so that he can move up in a network-marketing scheme? That's how e-mail list users will feel if you suddenly start pitching them directly.

After you dive into a discussion list, keep the following dos and don'ts in mind to avoid sinking to the bottom:

  ✔ **Do informational marketing.** Discussion lists are exactly that: discussions. They shouldn't be monologues or chest-beating exercises. Be helpful. If someone is having problems in your company's area of expertise, answer the question directly. If you have a product or service that may help solve a problem, answer the question directly and provide a very brief, casual reference to your product.

One method may be to write, "Several products may be helpful. One is produced by us, (insert product name here). Other similar products are made by (insert competitors' names here)." Your corporate ego may not like having to mention competitors, but the goal is for users to see you as a long-term, useful resource. And if your name and company appear in the signature at the end of the message, readers who need a product like yours may contact you first.

✔ **Don't cut and paste marketing materials into messages.** Many times the information you want to send to answer a question or elaborate on a thought exists in your current marketing materials — but those are written in an upbeat, cheerful, even inspirational tone that is usually inappropriate for e-mail lists. Take the time to write the facts in a tone appropriate to the e-mail list.

Participating in your company's e-mail lists

One common scenario that you may find yourself in is as a subscriber and contributor to an e-mail list run by someone else in your own company. For example, your company may run a customer support e-mail list for a product for which you do the marketing. Such lists commonly wander into broader topics, and if so, the list becomes a good vehicle for the occasional marketing message. Follow these suggestions:

✔ **Read the list.** You should read any e-mail list that directly concerns your product, but especially a list from your own company. You can glean quite a bit of useful information from the comments, and you need to be there to respond to flames or cries for help that are marketing oriented rather than customer-service oriented.

✔ **Tread lightly.** Remember that someone else is doing the heavy lifting of creating the list and maintaining it. Don't take over the list by posting to it at length or with great frequency.

✔ **Start slowly.** Give brief responses to messages that directly concern you. Watch for responses to your postings that tell you whether your comments are welcome as part of the list.

✔ **Develop relationships.** Send e-mail directly to individuals on the list who bring up topics that the list as a whole doesn't need to know more about. Put people from the e-mail list into your own list of people to whom you send key marketing e-mail messages.

✔ **Consider posting press releases.** One of the authors used to post shortened, text-only versions of press releases to his company's customer-service-oriented list, after establishing himself on the list and with apologies for the long, nontechnical message. List members generally appreciated the information because it was positioned as an unusual interruption of the list's normal business and not followed up by further marketing hype.

✔ **Do stay on topic.** Do you have an annoying acquaintance who somehow manages to bring any conversation around to focus on him or her every time? If you mention your company or product every time you participate, you risk the same reputation. In moderated lists, you also risk having your messages never appear and getting extra scrutiny from the moderator for any subsequent messages you send.

Equally odious is forwarding messages containing virus hoaxes, jokes of the day, or pornography if the list doesn't discuss, respectively, computer viruses, humor, or sex. Some lists may not only revoke your subscription but also take even more drastic measures for off-topic mail. The welcome message for a dog enthusiast list ominously warns that punishment can go as far as "a lifetime flea curse on your dwelling."

✔ **Don't respond in public every time.** You don't need to publicly answer every question posed in a discussion list, especially if your response involves recommending your company or product for a particular situation. Reply directly to the person who sent the message.

✔ **Do be positive.** While wearing your marketing hat, think long and hard before saying anything negative about anyone or anything. It's amazing how far your e-mail message can get forwarded — and anything you say reflects not only on you but also your company.

✔ **Don't spam.** What you do in the privacy of your individual e-mail account is your business (see Chapter 9). But the fastest way to have your subscription to a discussion list stopped is to send unsolicited commercial e-mail for a product or service to everyone on the list. Not coincidentally, it can also destroy any progress you've made in building your reputation on that list.

✔ **Do a two-pronged approach.** Subscribe to e-mail lists that appeal to potential customers and to e-mail lists that appeal to your industry peers. If you own a bookstore, this may include some lists for science-fiction enthusiasts and others for independent booksellers. Be equally helpful on both. Whereas one cultivates customers, the other cultivates your reputation within the industry — and few mind being thought of as an industry expert.

Creating Your Own E-Mail List

Over time, you may find that you don't just want to participate in e-mail lists; you want to create one of your very own. Perhaps other lists aren't specific enough to your or your company's interests, or you have to support a product your company makes, or you have responsibility for distributing company information that you think many people would want to see, or maybe you want to establish yourself as an expert in your field.

In all cases, your own e-mail list — discussion or announcement/newsletter — could fulfill your needs.

E-mail lists are particularly demanding of one resource: time. Many e-mail list moderators put in several hours each *day* reviewing messages, to say nothing of list administration tasks such as dealing with misdirected subscription requests or the Psycho Factor (that very small, but very real, percentage of list subscribers whose only role in life, it seems, is to drive the moderator crazy). This estimate doesn't include the time required to physically set up the list server software and hardware — a good reason to outsource the technical aspects, as we describe a little later in this chapter (see "Setting up a simple list server"). Before moving ahead with creating your own list, make sure that you can carve out the time to make it successful.

Benefits of creating an e-mail list

Just as you can derive many marketing benefits from participating in e-mail lists, as described earlier in this chapter, you can reap potentially even more benefits in creating one:

- ✔ **E-mail lists are highly targeted.** By creating a list, you define the breadth and depth of the topic area and, in turn, know that people who make the effort to subscribe are actively interested in that topic. The topic can be focused on your products, industry, or related subjects.

- ✔ **E-mail lists are delivered.** What's more compelling: Having people need to seek out your marketing message by searching for a Web site, or having that message automatically show up in their e-mail? (Consider this the definitive example of a rhetorical question.)

- ✔ **E-mail lists build communities.** A lively e-mail list can create a feeling of shared purpose among subscribers and actually turn mere customers into fans of your product or service, especially if they believe that they have a say in its direction and if you, as a representative of your company and a carefully trained Internet marketer — you're reading this book, aren't you? — take an active part in the list as well.

- ✔ **E-mail lists position you as a leader.** Being seen as the source of a good, active list gives both you and your company a reputation as experts in the list's subject matter, especially if the list has a lot of informational value.

Determining which type of list to start

After you decide that an e-mail list is a good thing to have and you give some thought as to the topic of your initial list, you have two flavors of e-mail list from which to choose: discussion list or announcement list. Here's a more detailed description of the two types of lists:

- ✔ **Discussion lists** are interactive lists that can be used by customers to discuss how best to use your product, by your company and customers for product support, or by anyone in your industry to debate the importance of industry trends. For example, you can create a list moderated by someone in product support for those subscribers interested in learning more about every nuance of your product from you and from other experienced customers. Or you may want to start a list that updates developments in your industry for comment by the list subscribers.

- ✔ **Announcement lists** are one-way lists that go from the sender to a group of recipients and don't allow the recipients to reply to the members of the list as a whole. Your company can use these broadcast lists to announce new products and weekly specials or provide industry and company news. For example, you might create a list strictly of news releases for press and analysts and another list for dedicated customers to give them early notice of sales or special offers. Another approach is to create a regular newsletter for customers and prospects. A simple announcement list newsletter for a music store, for example, may include new product information and tips from manufacturers and other readers, along with the mention of any upcoming sales.

Balance *come-on* with *content* in your announcement lists. Include tips and tricks on using your product and other information, such as announcements of upcoming conferences and events, that may prove useful even for someone not actively looking to buy. That way, you increase the chances that your e-mail message will be opened — and the potential that readers may change their minds about not planning to buy when they scan the specials.

If you're uncertain about what topics to focus on in your new discussion or announcement list, see what others in your industry or related industries have done. Visit one of the several mailing list search engines on the Web (see "Finding the right list," earlier in this chapter) and browse the list descriptions to get some ideas.

Consider creating matched pairs of announcement and discussion lists as well. Whereas an announcement list provides one-way information, a related discussion list gives subscribers the opportunity to analyze and comment on the information.

Done properly, a good e-mail list or set of lists can:

- ✔ Reward core customers by providing timely information that they can't easily get anywhere else.

- ✔ Reduce the need for paper newsletters and catalogs, saving printing and postage costs for mailings to online customers.

✔ Enable your customers to support each other by answering questions, taking some of the pressure off your customer service, technical support, or sales staff.

Here's how the fictional Where No Reader Has Gone Before science-fiction bookstore uses e-mail lists:

✔ **New release announcement list,** updated as often as daily with whatever new book releases have just shown up at the store.

✔ **New release discussion list,** encouraging customers to post their own reviews and debate the merits of new releases.

✔ **Author signing announcement list,** containing news of when book authors come to the store.

✔ **Science-fiction convention discussion list,** with news of upcoming science-fiction conventions, the bookstore's participation, and subscriber tips on what to expect and who goes.

✔ **Futurist discussion list,** a bookstore-sponsored but not bookstore-oriented discussion list on "how to build the future we want."

Even if the purpose of your list is informational, you can advertise in your own marketing vehicle. Consider putting a brief, four-to-eight-line, text-only "ad" for one of your products at the bottom of your discussion list digest. Just clearly separate it from the discussion list text with dashes or some other clever punctuation mark :-).

Setting up a simple list server

You have a "buy versus rent" decision when it comes to running a list server: should you install and run the list server software yourself (buy), have someone else do it for you (rent), or simply take advantage of a free service? Here's how the three choices shape up when implementing an e-mail list:

✔ **Gratis.** Several Web list-hosting companies have sprung up over the past couple of years, providing free list hosting and straightforward Web-based e-mail list maintenance. The catch? In exchange for the free list hosting, your list subscribers usually have to put up with a text ad at the bottom of each list message. Still, it's not a bad option when you're starting out; it lets you focus on the content of the list rather than its technical operation. Free e-mail list services include Yahoo!'s eGroups (`www.egroups.com`), Topica (`www.topica.com`), and Microsoft's ListBot (`www.listbot.com`). For a flat monthly or annual fee, some services offer the option to not have ads appear in list e-mails.

✔ **Renting.** Contact your Internet service provider or a third party and ask it to host your e-mail list. Many ISPs, developers of list-server software, and Web and e-mail list-hosting companies provide this service for as little as $5 to $10 a month to start (but it can run in the hundreds of dollars a month for lists numbering in the tens of thousands of addresses). Some of the many companies providing high-volume, outsourced list services include L-Soft, Innovyx, Lyris, SparkList, and FloNetwork.

✔ **Buying.** Find the right list server product and install it on a PC that you can use as a list server. List server products are available for UNIX, Linux, Windows NT/2000, Windows 95/98, and Macintosh. Don't forget to factor in the hours you spend installing, figuring out how to use, and running the server. A good starting point for finding list-hosting software is reading the `comp.mail.list-admin.software` newsgroup.

Another way to think through the "buy versus rent" decision: If your company already maintains its own mail server, then buying makes a lot of sense. If your company already has its domain hosted on an ISP and uses a dial-up service to get access to it, then having the ISP host the list ("renting") or using a free list service makes more sense.

UNIX is no fun. There, we've said it. But some popular list-server packages are available only for UNIX, or reserve their most advanced features for their UNIX versions. Because of this — and the unexpected challenges involved in setting up any Internet server product — we strongly suggest letting someone else host your e-mail list if you're thinking of using a UNIX version. Then you can focus on providing the best content.

Probably the best-known list server product is L-Soft International LISTSERV (`www.lsoft.com`), available for VM, OpenVMS, UNIX, Windows NT, and Windows 95/98. Two major competitors, CREN ListProc (`www.cren.net`) and Great Circle Associates Majordomo (`www.greatcircle.com`), are available only for UNIX. A growing number of strictly Windows and Macintosh list-server products are available but may lack the features and automation of their UNIX brethren.

List servers like — and many require — you to install them on a computer with a dedicated connection to an Internet mail server. You can install list-server software on a PC that you regularly use to dial in to your ISP, but you can easily wind up with long mail download times as your list-server software transfers waiting messages to and from the mail server.

Whether you host your list server yourself or have someone else do it, it helps to know in advance the steps involved in configuring a list server.

L-Soft has helpfully released its LISTSERV for Windows 95/98 product as shareware. You can find it on L-Soft's Web site (`www.lsoft.com/download`). There are also many demo, trial, and shareware list servers available from various shareware Web sites that you can try. And, of course, there's the simplest approach: Using one of the free, Web-based e-mail list services described earlier.

To set up a simple mailing list with LISTSERV for Windows 95/98:

1. **Using your Web browser, download LISTSERV for Windows 95 Shareware Version link from the L-Soft Web site (**`www.lsoft.com/download`**).**

   Follow the links to the download on the L-Soft Web site to begin the download. Follow your browser's instructions to save the file (Win95.zip) to your hard disk, and unzip the compressed file.

2. **Double-click the win95 folder.**

3. **Double-click the file named setup.exe.**

   The LISTSERV setup program launches. The InstallShield Wizard eventually prompts you to install the program in a new directory that it creates, called C:\LISTSERV\.

4. **If you don't want to install the program in the default directory, click Browse and choose another directory.**

5. **When prompted to create the directory, click OK.**

   You're asked to approve creating the Program icon LISTSERV for Windows 95.

6. **Click OK.**

   LISTSERV is now installed. You're prompted to configure LISTSERV for the first time. Configuring LISTSERV includes providing the following information in a series of dialog boxes:

   - **The Internet host name, in the form** `listserv.xyz.com`. This is the Internet address of your mail server.

   - **A host name alias, if you have one.**

   - **The From: name you want to appear on outgoing list server messages.** The best choice for this field is either your organization name or the name you want to give your list, for example, `WidgetList`.

   - **A password to protect creation of new e-mail lists.** This password keeps other people familiar with using LISTSERV from tampering with your e-mail lists.

   - **The Internet e-mail address of the person in charge of the list server.**

   - **The name of the machine through which Internet mail is delivered.**

- **Whether you want to configure a Web interface to the list archives, and where required files can be found and stored.** Creating such an archive is a good idea — doing so allows you to easily post past discussions from your e-mail list to your marketing Web site.

As soon as you enter this information, configuration is complete.

7. Double-click the LISTSERV (Main Program) icon to run LISTSERV.

Starting a list in LISTSERV requires using a text editor such as Windows Notepad to make a *List Header.* The List Header has a specific format and standard keywords to which you assign values, which are settings to tell LISTSERV whether the list is open, sends confirmation messages to subscribers, is moderated or not, is *announce only,* (this is the term LISTSERV uses to mean announcement list, as we describe in the section "Determining which type of list to start"), and so on. The details of the various keywords and possible values for the List Header are described extensively in the LISTSERV Help file included with the program. The list header is then sent by e-mail to your list server, and you are the proud owner of a new LISTSERV e-mail list.

List management takes place through a text-based, command-line interface that opens in Windows, as shown in Figure 11-5.

Figure 11-5: LISTSERV: The good, the powerful, and the ugly.

```
SMTPW                                                    _ □ ✕
Auto  ▼  🔲 🔳 🔳 🔳 🔳 A
Enter your command:
help
9 Dec 1997 16:02:44 From LISTSERV@NT.XYZ.COM: help
*
* LISTSERV(R) version 1.8c - most commonly used commands
*
* Info      <topic|listname>      Order documentation
* Lists     <Detail|Short|Global> Get a description of all lists
* SUBscribe  listname <full name> Subscribe to a list
* SIGNOFF    listname             Sign off from a list
* SIGNOFF    * (NETWIDE           - from all lists on all servers
* REView     listname <options>   Review a list
* Query      listname             Query your subscription options
* SET        listname  options    Update your subscription options
* INDex      <filelist_name>      Order a list of LISTSERV files
* GET        filename filetype    Order a file from LISTSERV
* REGister   full_name|OFF        Tell LISTSERV about your name
*
* There are more commands (AFD, FUI, PW, etc). Send an INFO REFCARD for a
* comprehensive reference card, or just INFO for a list of available
* documentation files.
*
* This server is managed by:
*   catalano@catalanoconsulting.com
```

Powerful? You bet. Ugly? Better people than ourselves have been known to flee screaming from better interfaces than this.

Now that you have a taste of what's involved in installing a list server, perhaps it's worth considering the call to that e-mail list-hosting service. Or starting with a free Web-based service. Admittedly, this version of LISTSERV is a port from UNIX and has the ugly text-based underpinnings of that otherwise very powerful operating system. Other list-server programs written specifically for graphically based operating environments such as Windows and the Macintosh may be simpler to set up and use than LISTSERV, but the learning curve for any such program is still akin to picking up a second language.

Maintaining Your E-Mail List

Like gnats and sitcoms, e-mail lists have life cycles. You don't just create an e-mail list and walk away (or, in software product parlance, "launch and forget"), hoping that a list will do well without guidance. E-mail lists, to be successful in meeting your marketing goals, have to be nurtured. Some milestones in the life of an e-mail list include:

✔ **E-mail lists give birth.** Don't be afraid to split off and create a new list from a very busy one if you see a significant amount of message traffic on a particular related subject. If *Cheers* can beget *Frasier*, your creation can have offspring as well.

✔ **E-mail lists evolve.** The focus of an e-mail list can wander to a different take on a subject — from customer support to industry news — or even off to a different subject entirely. You may need to ask someone else to take over a list that wanders too far from your original purpose for it, or simply redefine the list to fit the direction that the list subscribers have taken.

✔ **E-mail lists die.** If list traffic declines to the point at which maintaining a discussion proves difficult, then kill the list (after warning the list readers, of course).

Running an e-mail list — discussion or announcement — takes time: time to manage and create the content; time to handle requests that can't be automated (such as dealing with subscribers who are having trouble with list-server commands); and time to think about where you want the list to go. If you can't commit the time, don't start the list — otherwise, you risk irritating potential and current customers.

Do take the time to do one other thing while your list is aborning: Examine all the technical features of the list-server service or software you're using. List servers are increasingly flexible and powerful, automating many tasks far beyond message posting, subscribing, and unsubscribing. The more tasks you can hand off to the list server, the less time you'll need to spend on maintenance of the list.

The one task that may take more time than you expect is managing the content in a discussion list. With an announcement list, it's obvious that you'll be responsible for the content: If you don't write anything, the newsletter (or other e-mail announcement) doesn't go out.

The twilight list

Murphy's Law applies as much to the Internet as it does to every other endeavor in life. Some common pitfalls of maintaining an e-mail list yourself:

✔ **A weak, or no, moderator.** Make sure that you have a good moderator for any discussion list you sponsor. Nothing looks quite so unprofessional as having an e-mail list infested with off-topic posts about alien landings and the occasional "Your company sucks!" message — especially if it's not met with an appropriate response. Poor moderation can lead to "topic creep," and if a list loses its focus, it reflects badly on you as the sponsor.

✔ **File attachments.** Most lists discourage attaching files to the e-mail messages that make up the list. Do the same. Not only do attachments dramatically slow list download times for subscribers, not all users have either the programs or the machine to open every file. You also risk liability should you allow a file attachment that turns out to contain a computer virus to go to subscribers.

✔ **Unsubscribe hell.** Hard to believe (well, not really), but people delete the welcome message with the unsubscribe instructions. Expect it to happen and for the occasional "unsubscribe me now, [expletive deleted]!" message to be submitted to the list. One ounce of prevention is to automatically attach unsubscribe instructions at the bottom of the digest version of your list, or send out a weekly or monthly reminder message about how to unsubscribe. (You can use the same vehicle to remind people to tell their friends about the list.)

But a discussion list needs just as much thoughtful work on the content. The moderator is as much glue as god. It's up to the moderator to keep discussions on track, politely weeding out (or never letting be posted) duplicate comments or those messages that are written only to be disruptive. A good moderator learns the flow of a discussion — when it's hot and when it needs a little prompting in the form of a moderator post to keep the topic moving and not trapped in circular arguments.

Promoting Your E-Mail List

As soon as your e-mail list is up, market it widely to help it get running. A discussion list, for example, is only as strong as its subscribers. (Too many lists die for lack of participation when a little promotion would have helped build them into a valuable resource.)

Marketing approaches to consider:

- ✔ **On your Web site.** Make signing up for your e-mail list easy. Include a link to an online sign-up area, as shown in Figure 11-6. If you don't have an online form for signing up, include a list description on your site with the list administrative e-mail address and detailed subscription instructions.

- ✔ **In mailings to customers.** Do all you can to get the e-mail address of all new customers as they order or receive your products, and to build up a database of existing customers' e-mail addresses. Then include an invitation to participate in your discussion list in customer e-mailings.

- ✔ **In newsgroups.** Post brief announcements about your e-mail list in appropriate industry or interest newsgroups (for more on newsgroups, see Chapter 12).

- ✔ **In e-mail list directories.** Submit your list to Liszt (www.liszt.com), Publicly Accessible Mailing Lists (paml.net), Topica (www.topica.com) and the List Exchange (www.listex.com), as well as other directories of mailing lists.

- ✔ **In your signature file.** Include the administrative e-mail address for your list in your signature file, with a comment such as "E-mail listserver@ host.domain to find out about our newsletter."

- ✔ **In your e-mail list.** For an announcement list, encourage subscribers to forward the messages to friends or colleagues they believe would be interested. Include subscribe and unsubscribe information at the end of every mailing.

- ✔ **On other e-mail lists.** If related industry or interest lists exist, politely send them a brief announcement of your new list. A long-running list, NEW-LIST, focuses on announcing new e-mail lists (http://listserv. classroom.com/archives/new-list.html), as do several other lists.

Tread lightly when promoting your list on someone else's e-mail list (unless the sole purpose of that list is to announce new lists). The best plan is to first send a private e-mail to the list administrator or moderator asking whether he or she would mind such a post — it is, after all, that person's list. Treat him or her as you want people who post to your list to treat you.

Several companies have also popped up with the express purpose of marketing mailing lists to potential subscribers. List Partners (www.listpartners. com), for example, establishes affiliate programs for lists along the same lines as affiliate programs for Web sites. However, keep in mind that you'll pay for these services in cash or advertising (included in your list messages): paying the list marketer, the subscriber referrer, or both. So do the free stuff first.

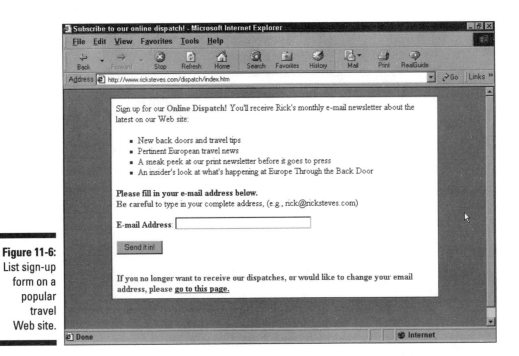

You also may want to subscribe to one of the e-mail lists specifically about lists and marketing them: List-Moderators (list-moderators.com), Mailing List Owner's Discussion Group (www.mail-list.com), and List-Tips (list-tips.com) are just a few examples.

As for your offline marketing effort, make sure that you mention your e-mail list in brochures, direct mail pieces, and the appropriate ads. When done correctly, an e-mail list not only keeps your customers in touch with you but also keeps you in touch with them — even when they don't regularly visit your Web site.

Part IV
Even More Internet Marketing

In this part . . .

Getting your marketing message around the Internet can go far beyond your Web site and e-mail. Use this part to learn how to work effectively with discussion groups, develop and measure an online advertising campaign, and prepare Internet public relations efforts.

Chapter 12

Speaking Up with Discussion Groups and Chat

. . . .

In This Chapter

▶ Understanding newsgroups and other discussion groups

▶ Finding the right discussion groups

▶ Mining discussion groups for marketing information

▶ Marketing in discussion groups

▶ Marketing in chat rooms and channels

. . . .

*I*f e-mail is like a private conversation and e-mail lists resemble kaffee-klatches, *discussion groups* are akin to open meetings in the town square. Like any open meeting, discussion groups have their own tone, regular participants, and unwritten rules of polite conduct.

Discussion groups are similar to e-mail lists in that they are formed around common interests, but are different in that, for the most part, they are accessible to anyone, without special permission. Think of them as public bulletin boards rather than private chain letters. To participate in discussion groups, you can use nothing more than your standard Web browser, or, for some types of groups, *newsreader* software (either on its own or as part of a Web browser).

The power and peril of discussion groups is in their public nature:

> ✔ **You can't afford to ignore them.** Discussion groups can spread news, good or bad, very fast. In 1994, a posting on the Usenet newsgroup `comp.sys.intel` identified a flaw in the floating-point unit of the Pentium chip. Intel publicly ignored the problem for weeks, allowing speculation — and anti-Intel sentiment — to ramp up in newsgroups. It eventually spilled over into the mass media, and Intel was forced to offer to exchange the Pentium chips — all thanks to newsgroup messages.

✔ **You can't afford to irritate them.** Discussion groups are by far the touchiest online communities when it comes to unsolicited advertising messages, and it's a touchiness earned the hard way. In 1994, the law firm of Canter & Siegel posted a message advertising Green Card services for immigrants on thousands of Usenet newsgroups that had nothing to do with immigration — and the firm's principals immediately became the poster children for *spam*. Ever since, discussion groups have been hypersensitive to inappropriate commercial messages.

Discussion groups come in several flavors. The predominant type is *Usenet newsgroups*, the granddaddy of all Internet discussion groups. Newsgroups have several close, and younger, relatives. On America Online, they're called *message boards*; on CompuServe, they're called *forums*; and on many Web sites such as Slashdot.org, AnchorDesk.com, and Apple.com, they're simply called *boards* or *discussions*. In all cases, they are discussions of specific areas of interest that engender a strong sense of community.

Usenet newsgroups are a subset of discussion groups in general. But because they set the standard — and because they're still so prevalent — Usenet newsgroups are what we emphasize for your marketing efforts in this chapter. Techniques for marketing to other kinds of discussion groups on individual Web sites and commercial online services are similar. So when we talk about discussion groups, we're talking about all kinds of discussion groups, including Usenet newsgroups. When we specifically talk about Usenet newsgroups, we're addressing only what applies to this revered elder.

Understanding Usenet Newsgroups

Even though they aren't the sexiest things online (and may be completely ignored by new Internet users), Usenet newsgroups are generally easily accessible by anyone with Internet access. And their very public, many-to-many communication can be both a useful resource and headache to the online marketer.

Each newsgroup is an ongoing and changing collection of messages, also called *articles* or *postings*, about a particular topic as defined by the founders and sometimes moderators of the newsgroup. Tens of thousands of Usenet newsgroups have been formed as part of this volunteer-run, spread-out electronic bulletin board system featuring discussions ranging from favorite actors to flawed microprocessors. Each has its own character — and, not surprisingly, characters.

News over the "back fence"

The name *newsgroup* is in some ways misleading. Although frequently very valuable and sometimes newsworthy information is posted to a newsgroup, the Usenet definition of news isn't the same as the mass media definition — which, from the point of view of one of the authors who's a former reporter, may not be a bad thing.

More typically, the news you find on a newsgroup is of the conversation-over-the-backyard-fence variety, from back in the days when neighbors actually conversed over back fences. Both have scandalous gossip, strong opinions, helpful tips, and an occasional piece of real "news." These elements of newsgroup discussions can be very useful to marketers who are trying to gauge perceptions about their product or industry.

Organized side-to-side and top-down

Unlike Web site-specific discussion boards, Usenet is an actual network, which simplifies subscribing to, and searching, all available Usenet newsgroups from a single point.

Plus, newsgroups are organized in a hierarchical structure that makes it easier to figure out where discussions about your product or industry may be taking place.

A brief history of Usenet newsgroups

Newsgroups are more properly called *Usenet newsgroups* because Usenet is where newsgroups reside. Usenet itself is short for *user network*. It started in 1979 as an electronic bulletin board for exchanging public messages between two North Carolina universities.

Newsgroups are carried on *news servers*, which are computers that are maintained by Internet service providers, educational institutions, businesses, or other parties that want to be a part of Usenet. When a message is posted to a newsgroup, it first goes to the news server that the sender is connected to. From there, the message is fed to other news servers that carry the newsgroup, which in turn distribute it to still more news servers that carry the newsgroup, as shown in Figure 12-1. The process can take days, which can be aggravating to a marketer trying to follow a discussion — especially when, occasionally, a *response* to a message shows up on a local news server before the initial message does.

The eight *mainstream hierarchies* for newsgroups are as follows:

- ✔ comp: Computer topics
- ✔ humanities: Fine arts and the humanities
- ✔ news: Issues relating to Usenet newsgroups
- ✔ rec: Recreational activities and hobbies
- ✔ sci: Science
- ✔ soc: Social issues and culture
- ✔ talk: Debate of unresolved issues
- ✔ misc: Topics that don't fall into the other seven

The alt, or alternative, hierarchy is not considered one of the Big Eight, but in alt newsgroups you find some of the, shall we say, most creative and free-flowing discussions, including alt.backrubs, alt.revenge, and alt.barney.dinosaur.die.die.die. A number of other hierarchies exist, some of which are widespread, others of which are limited to specific news servers or geographic areas. For example, a Seattleite can check out the seattle hierarchy.

Related newsgroups start with the same abbreviated set of letters, and each distinct subtopic is separated by a period.

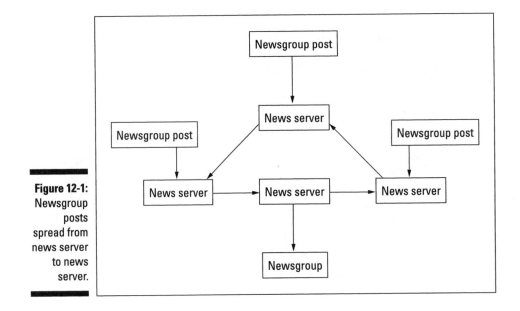

Figure 12-1:
Newsgroup
posts
spread from
news server
to news
server.

Usenet newsgroups versus AOL and CompuServe boards

They've gone by the names online forums, message boards, bulletin boards, roundtables, and Special Interest Groups. But these America Online and CompuServe discussions are variations on the broad category of discussion groups.

So how are the discussions on America Online and CompuServe different from Usenet newsgroups?

✔ **Top-down.** The services set the rules for discussions and the *moderators*, people who actually monitor the discussions, strictly enforce them. Most Usenet newsgroups are unmoderated.

✔ **Members only.** Discussions are open only to members of the service. Although numbering in the millions, this membership base is still just a subset of the hundreds of millions of people who can read Usenet newsgroups. And those same Usenet newsgroups can be reached by AOL and CompuServe members from within their services.

Therefore, you should emphasize marketing efforts on Usenet newsgroups first for the broadest possible audience, including AOL and CompuServe members who "step outside" their home online service.

✔ **Focus.** America Online is aimed more at home users; CompuServe, more at professional and business users. Discussions on both of these online services reflect this more targeted approach than discussions in Usenet newsgroups.

The best approach to America Online and CompuServe? Use the skills you gain in Usenet newsgroups and consider these online services a supplement to, not a replacement for, Usenet newsgroup marketing. If you're going to market on AOL and CompuServe at all, the most cost-effective method is through their discussion boards.

Cat lovers (or pet food marketers) who start with the rec newsgroups find that they need to look within the rec hierarchy for rec.pets, and then further into rec.pets.cats, where they see a number of cat-related newsgroups such as rec.pets.cats.anecdotes and rec.pets.cats.health+behav, but thankfully no rec.pets.cats.die.die.die. Other newsgroups are structured in the same way.

Setting Up a Newsgroup Reader

Before you can monitor or take part in Usenet newsgroups, you need to set up the newsreader software that lets you find, read, and post newsgroup messages.

Why newsreader software? It's necessary only for Usenet newsgroups, not all discussion groups. Recall that newsgroups aren't part of the Web but rather part of Usenet. Web site–specific discussions require just your Web browser (usually with Java capabilities), whereas America Online discussions require AOL software.

Although numerous standalone newsreaders are available for both Windows and Macintosh, recent versions of both Netscape Communicator and Microsoft Internet Explorer include basic, and basically good, newsreader software. You can start with the Newsgroup component of Communicator 4.73, or with the Outlook Express software included with Internet Explorer 5.0.

If you later decide that you need more advanced features — such as filtering out duplicate messages that are posted to more than one newsgroup, automatically monitoring newsgroups at predetermined intervals, or searching among a group of messages by keyword — you can easily switch to another newsreader. Many choices are available on shareware and freeware Web sites. Start with Dave Central (www.davecentral.com), CNET's Shareware.com (www.shareware.com) or ZDNet (www.zdnet.com/downloads/hotfiles.zdnet.com). Then, do roughly the following no matter which newsreader software you choose:

1. **Get the name of the news server from your ISP.**

   A Usenet news server address is usually something like news.host.domain — for instance, for CompuServe users, the news server is named news.compuserve.com.

2. **Launch the newsreader software.**

3. **Indicate the news server name in your newsreader software's preferences.**

4. **Connect to your ISP to download all the newsgroup names from the news server.**

5. **In the newsreader software itself, subscribe to the newsgroups that interest you.**

Figure 12-2 displays how the Outlook Express component of Microsoft Internet Explorer handles Usenet newsgroup subscriptions.

Newsgroups and e-mail lists share the same terminology when you sign up for one or the other — you *subscribe*. A newsgroup subscription is little more than selecting the name of the newsgroup in your newsreader software. You don't get a confirmation e-mail or a welcome message as you often do when you subscribe to an e-mail list. You just see a list of newsgroup postings that you can choose to read or ignore. You then work with individual newsgroup messages much as you would e-mail messages, including replying and forwarding.

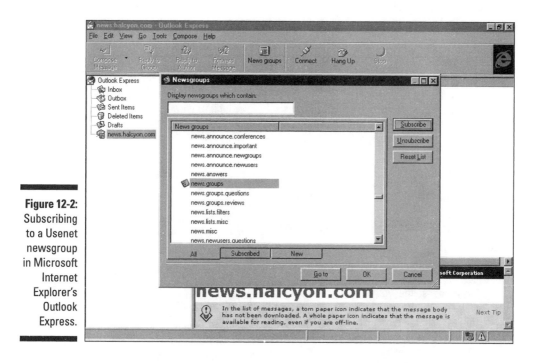

Figure 12-2:
Subscribing
to a Usenet
newsgroup
in Microsoft
Internet
Explorer's
Outlook
Express.

A good way to familiarize yourself with Usenet newsgroups is to first subscribe to the newsgroup alt.barney.dinosaur.die.die.die (assuming
that your news server carries it). It's typical of the odd humor, conspiracy
theories, and flames found in many Usenet newsgroups. If you enjoy alt.
barney.dinosaur.die.die.die — and the authors do, even though the
one with a younger child *likes* The Purple One — you'll like newsgroups.

Other newsgroups can help you familiarize yourself with newsgroups in general: news.newusers.questions, for asking questions about how to use
newsgroups, and news.answers, for FAQs on a wide variety of newsgroups.

Finding and Mining Discussion Groups

Even more so than e-mail messages or e-mail lists, discussion groups such as
Usenet newsgroups require a light — even feather-like — marketing touch. All
discussion groups are informational marketing to the *n*th degree — no hype,
no sales pitches, and definitely no spamming, unless you enjoy walking
around with a target on your virtual back.

Discussion groups versus e-mail lists

Discussion groups (such as Usenet newsgroups) and e-mail lists (see Chapter 11) have much in common. People with specific interests contribute text messages and participate in moderated and unmoderated discussions.

Yet the two have several important distinctions:

✔ **Discussion groups are sought out, not delivered.** E-mail list messages show up automatically in e-mail boxes. You need to actively seek out a discussion group to find and read it.

✔ **Discussion groups are threaded.** Discussion groups organize messages in a kind of outline format so that you read only the specific message exchanges on certain topics, or *threads,* that interest you. An e-mail list discussion is linear; that is, you get all the messages in the sequence they're sent, whether you care about all the message topics or not.

✔ **Discussion groups don't require a participant to formally sign up.** Unlike e-mail lists, which require a special "subscribe" e-mail to start participating, all you need to take part in a discussion groups is an up-to-date Web browser.

Because of the similarities between them, you can find some e-mail lists duplicated as discussion groups, many as Usenet newsgroups. You can either subscribe to the e-mail list or participate in the discussion group.

If timeliness is important to you, the identical e-mail list is the better choice — if the discussion group is a newsgroup — because of the time lag involved in newsgroup messages traveling from news server to news server. If timeliness is less critical, you may prefer the organized, threaded format of the equivalent discussion group to the strict time-received ordering of e-mail list messages.

Conversely, you can get a lot of information out of discussion groups by reading them as a resource for what others are saying about your company and your competitors.

Much of what you can do with Usenet newsgroups — search and participate from a single point — is not available with other types of discussion groups. That's because newsgroups are part of a network, Usenet, which ties them all together. Discussion boards are limited to a specific Web site, and America Online's and CompuServe's message boards and forums are available only to members of their respective online services.

Finding the right Usenet newsgroups

Before diving in as a Usenet newsgroup participant, get your feet wet to see whether your company — or your competitors — is the subject of any newsgroup chatter. If this brings to mind the horrifying possibility of having to peruse every one of the hundreds of messages in each of the thousands of newsgroups on a news server, don't worry: That's why you use Deja.com and multipurpose search engines such as AltaVista.

- ✔ **Deja.com (**www.deja.com/usenet**)** bills itself as having the largest archive of Usenet discussions on the Internet. Since its founding in 1995, it has grown to the point of having millions of visitors each month searching the contents of Usenet newsgroups.

- ✔ **AltaVista (**www.altavista.com**)** is a general-purpose search engine (as we describe in Chapter 2) but it allows the choice of either a Web or Discussion Groups (which on AltaVista includes Usenet newsgroups) search — a useful option. You can also find this option on other popular search engines.

We recommend that you start your searches with Deja.com because of its completeness. In fact, several of the other Web search engines (including America Online's Web site) rely on Deja.com to provide their newsgroup search capabilities, so you may as well go right to the source.

Even if you don't use newsreader software, Deja.com allows you to post a new Usenet newsgroup message directly from the Deja.com site — a handy and time-saving shortcut.

Here's how to start your search:

1. **Go to Deja.com by launching your Web browser and typing** www.deja. com/usenet **in the Address (Microsoft Internet Explorer) or Location (Netscape Communicator) field.**

   The Usenet Discussion Service page for Deja.com appears.

2. **In the field for Search Discussions, type the keywords or phrase for which you want to search.**

   If you are searching for a proper name or phrase — such as a product or company name — surround it with quotation marks.

3. **Click** Search.

   A list of specific newsgroup messages that match your search appears on a Web page.

4. **Scan the list of message names and the newsgroups from which they come for any messages that interest you. Click the message name to read the message.**

   The message appears; an example is shown in Figure 12-3.

5. **Click** Thread: **to read the entire newsgroup discussion that led to, or was spawned by, the specific message.**

6. **If you are reading a message and you want to find out how prolific the author of the message is — to see, for example, whether the person has expressed a strong opinion or an interesting insight about your company or a competitor — click the author's name.**

   Deja.com checks its message database to find any other messages posted from the same e-mail address and provides a summary. Click `Get all messages` to the right of the author's name to read the individual messages.

Try variations on this theme: Enter the name of the industry you're in, or search the "past" Deja.com database rather than the "recent" one for messages from more than a few months back. The "past" database often provides good historical perspective for discussions and opinions that permeate the current newsgroup database.

You'll frequently get newsgroup message search matches that have nothing to do with your company, competitors, or industry, but you have the ability to narrow your search with the Power Search option to the right of the Deja.com search box.

When you find a newsgroup that shows up repeatedly in your Deja.com searches for your company or competitors, make a note of its name. Then, the next time you launch your Usenet newsreader, subscribe to that group and use it as an ongoing source of information.

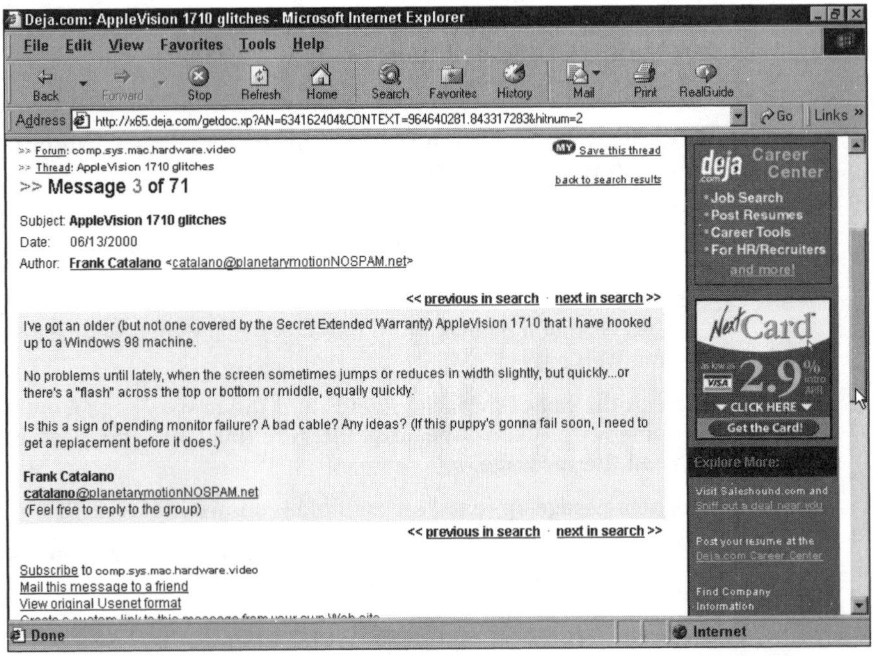

Deja.com: AppleVision 1710 glitches - Microsoft Internet Explorer

File　Edit　View　Favorites　Tools　Help

Back　Forward　Stop　Refresh　Home　Search　Favorites　History　Mail　Print　RealGuide

Address 　http://x65.deja.com/getdoc.xp?AN=634162404&CONTEXT=964640281.843317283&hitnum=2 　Go　Links »

>> Forum: comp.sys.mac.hardware.video　　　　　　　　　　　　MY Save this thread

>> Thread: AppleVision 1710 glitches　　　　　　　　　　　　　back to search results

>> **Message 3 of 71**

deja Career Center

• Job Search
• Post Resumes
• Career Tools
• For HR/Recruiters
  and more!

Subject: **AppleVision 1710 glitches**

Date:　06/13/2000

Author:　**Frank Catalano** <catalano@planetarymotionNOSPAM.net>

　　　　　　　　　　　　　　　　<< **previous in search**　**next in search** >>

I've got an older (but not one covered by the Secret Extended Warranty) AppleVision 1710 that I have hooked up to a Windows 98 machine.

No problems until lately, when the screen sometimes jumps or reduces in width slightly, but quickly...or there's a "flash" across the top or bottom or middle, equally quickly.

Is this a sign of pending monitor failure? A bad cable? Any ideas? (If this puppy's gonna fail soon, I need to get a replacement before it does.)

Frank Catalano
catalano@planetarymotionNOSPAM.net
(Feel free to reply to the group)

NextCard
as low as 2.9% intro APR
VISA
▼ CLICK HERE ▼
Get the Card!

Explore More:

Visit Saleshound.com and Sniff out a deal near you

Post your resume at the Deja.com Career Center

Find Company Information

　　　　　　　　　　　　　　　　<< **previous in search** · **next in search** >>

Subscribe to comp.sys.mac.hardware.video
Mail this message to a friend
View original Usenet format

Done　　　　　　　　　　　　　　　　　　　　　Internet

Figure 12-3:
Reading a newsgroup posting on Deja.com.

Finding the right non-Usenet discussion groups

The right Usenet newsgroups for your marketing efforts are significantly easier to identify than the right Web site-specific discussion board, America Online message board, or CompuServe forum. Newsgroups are part of the searchable Usenet network; other types of discussion groups, such as those on Slashdot.org (as shown in Figure 12-4), may or may not have any central clearinghouse.

We've covered Usenet newsgroups in the preceding section. Where to start for other kinds of discussion groups?

- ✔ **Ask a coworker or colleague.** Business associates may already participate in specific discussion groups on America Online, CompuServe, or Web sites that would be of interest.

- ✔ **Ask customers.** In routine contacts with customers you know well, inquire whether they participate in any discussion groups that your company should know about.

- ✔ **Browse competitor or industry trade group Web sites.** Threaded discussion groups are increasingly commonplace on Web sites. Check the sites of your competitors, allies, or industry trade groups for any discussion boards they may have.

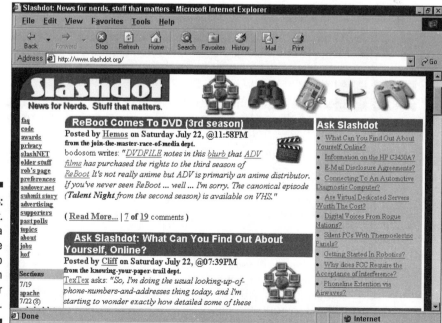

Figure 12-4: Slashdot.org, a Web site devoted to discussion groups for nerds.

Marketing in financial discussion groups

If you search for information about any public company on the Internet, you're likely to find that many of your search results are from financial Web sites that are discussing its stock. These are great sources of information and a good way to get investors' perspectives on a company. But if you're employed by such a company, or by a competitor, be very careful about posting to financial discussion boards.

In a financial discussion group, comments that might normally be okay around an espresso stand could be seen as an attempt to drive your stock up — or a competitor's stock down. If in doubt, leave commenting on such boards to designated people within your company: If you work for a public firm, that's likely to be investor relations or the CFO. You really can't market in financial discussion groups, but you can check for competitive and erroneous information and alert the right people internally.

You can add any appropriate discussion groups to your list of bookmarks (or, in Microsoft Internet Explorer and America Online parlance, Favorites or Favorite Places) in whatever Web browser you use.

Monitoring discussion groups

What, exactly, should you look for when monitoring discussion groups through Deja.com or your Web browser?

- ✔ **Frequency.** How often are you, or your direct competitors, mentioned in the discussion groups? If competitors are far more prevalent, your company or product may not be as visible online as you think. If none of you is mentioned, you have an opportunity to be first.

- ✔ **Recency.** How recently have you or your direct competitors been mentioned? A dramatic change over time may signal trouble or a company on the rise — or fall.

- ✔ **Tone.** Are posts about your company pleasant or hostile? If you encounter a lot of discussion group hostility — especially from customers who are unhappy with your customer service — you may be getting a wake-up call for immediate action. Take special note if someone comes to your defense — or if others join in to help make your firm an online piñata.

- ✔ **Content.** Do specific topics dominate conversation about your company? The topics of conversation may reflect an area in which your company excels or lags. You get extra points if discussion groups reflect your offline (print, radio, or other marketing channel) marketing messages without your prompting.

✔ **Influencers.** Do any discussion group message authors routinely write about your company or products? If the posts are positive, the author may be an influencer to carefully cultivate. If posts are negative, you may want to have an honest, private e-mail discussion with the author about the gripes. (Or, if you don't want to leave a paper trail because you don't know how the person will respond, arrange to talk by phone.)

Make checking Deja.com, other newsgroup search engines, or other discussion boards for mentions of your company and products a regular routine. Even if you're already regularly reading some discussion groups, your company may suddenly become a hot — even flaming — topic in a newsgroup that you don't monitor. Monitoring what's being said about your company online is a prerequisite to effective marketing online.

Participating in discussion groups

Given that discussion groups (including Usenet newsgroups) can be very touchy, as evidenced by the Green Card spam we mention at the beginning of this chapter, it may be easy to convince yourself that your company's best strategy is just to sit on the sidelines and watch what's being said, perhaps stepping in only when things get a little out of hand. (This attitude is something like Bill Cosby's classic approach to child rearing: Parents don't want justice, they just want quiet.)

Such a defensive strategy may be comforting or, in some cases, appropriate. But you should seriously consider taking an active role in discussion groups by posting messages and responding to discussion threads. If you don't, you miss out on the benefits of being proactive in discussion groups:

✔ **Being seen as an expert.** Being helpful on a discussion group that appeals to your peers, business partners, or customers positions you as an expert in your business area. In addition, being an expert on a discussion group is a lot less expensive and time consuming than being an expert in person — traveling to speaking engagements or writing articles for industry magazines — and it makes a very public impact among those you wish to influence who are on the Internet. (Not that you shouldn't still give speeches and write articles. A good track record online might even help you get these opportunities.)

✔ **Getting the word out.** Remember the kids' game "Telephone" in which you sit in a circle with other kids, quickly whispering the same phrase to each other around the circle until you get to the person who started the phrase and find that the original message is completely garbled? The same holds true for your marketing messages: The farther removed the recipient is from the information source (you), the more likely your corporate actions are subject to being misinterpreted or misunderstood. You can avoid having this happen in discussion groups by making sure that your company's messages come from someone at your company in customer service, marketing, technical support, or another appropriate department. And should you find erroneous statements about your company posted on a discussion group, quickly identify yourself as an employee of your company and post the truth of the situation so that the false impressions can be stopped in their tracks.

✔ **Becoming known for responsiveness.** An active company voice in discussion groups implies that your company is approachable and actually wants to get feedback. Quick response provides a human touch to your online presence, even if it comes through a remote, text-only medium.

On top of all this, discussion groups share the e-mail list benefits of being highly targeted, free, and a home to online communities, as we discuss in Chapter 11.

The Pentium lesson

Hostility in discussion groups is ignored at your own peril — especially if the hostility has any factual merit. Intel found this out the hard way by not actively monitoring, and promptly responding to, newsgroup discussions.

In 1994, a mathematician discovered that some of his calculations were off and finally narrowed down the cause of the errors to what he believed was a flaw in the first Pentium chip that affected advanced math functions. His findings were posted in messages on a CompuServe forum and in the Usenet newsgroup comp.sys.intel.

Intel did nothing publicly while other newsgroup participants weighed in on comp.sys.intel with their own confirmations of the Pentium flaw. Within days, the controversy spilled into other newsgroups and then into the press — possibly the first time, but certainly not the last, that a major news story "broke" online.

Yet it took several weeks for Intel president Andy Grove to post a message on comp.sys.intel acknowledging that a problem existed. His message did little to encourage participants to expect a fix. Continued outrage on comp.sys.intel, amplified by other newsgroups and the mass media, forced Intel to offer an exchange program for anyone with the early, flawed version of the Pentium processor.

Intel has learned from this very expensive lesson, both in terms of goodwill and hard costs. When a bug in later Pentium processors was reported on comp.sys.intel in 1997, Intel representatives were quick to respond to concerns posted in the newsgroup. What could have been a major public relations disaster — again — was quickly and skillfully averted. It's a good example of a company learning from an early "miscalculation."

Avoiding getting F*****Company.com

When dot-coms started dropping like flies in early 2000, a Web site rose to the challenge of tracking rumors and confirmations of layoffs and bankruptcies. Though it had a challenging name for journalists who wanted to report on it (and no alternate URL), it was a useful hotbed of fact and innuendo.

F*****Company.com also had a discussion group — the FC Message Board — where the various rumors were dissected and new ones added. Perhaps more so than most discussion groups on Usenet and elsewhere, this discussion group was one worth monitoring — for fear that your company would be featured.

Conversely, discussion groups can cause great damage to your company or product reputation if you don't see or respond to negative messages:

- ✔ **The appearance of flames.** Some of the questions, complaints, and statements directed toward your company and products in discussion groups can be sarcastic, mean-spirited, and cruel. Others — perhaps the worst ones — can be calm, dispassionate, painstakingly researched, and overwhelmingly negative. If not responded to rapidly and respectfully, these well-researched critiques can turn into flames spread by other participants — and grow into a fire.

- ✔ **The persistence of venom.** Some discussion groups maintain their own archives, and many are routinely archived in databases such as Deja. com. Anything that has been written about your company — or that you've written in response — lives on in archives long after the controversy dies down.

- ✔ **The "urban legend" effect.** Rumor and misinformation can spread as easily as factual information and take on a life of its own on the Internet as the topic leaps, like a wildfire, from discussion group to discussion group. Examples include the long-lived "Good Times Virus" hoax, which has persisted in e-mail exchanges for more than six years, or the many variations on the "dying boy needs cash/greeting cards/and so on" message.

The fact that your presence can help avoid these problems is an excellent reason to participate in discussion groups — and to be careful about how you participate.

The tools you need for participating in discussion groups are right in the Usenet newsgroup newsreader software that you set up earlier in this chapter, or in your Web browser. Just follow your specific software's instructions on how to post a discussion group article or message — you'll find that it's similar to sending e-mail.

Marketing to Discussion Groups

The right way to market to discussion groups recalls the old instructions on porcupine mating habits.

Q: How do you market to discussion groups?

A: Very carefully.

Each discussion group (including that subset, Usenet newsgroups) is a community with its own unique culture, tone, history, and citizens. Violating that culture can make your company as popular among group participants as a bartender at a temperance rally.

Handle discussion group marketing with an even softer pair of kid gloves than you use with e-mail or e-mail lists. Discussion group marketing is informational marketing with a vengeance. If a golden rule for discussion group marketing exists, it's "Help, don't sell." For tips on helping, see Chapter 11.

Creating your own Usenet newsgroup

You've got a newsreader. You've got a topic. Why not start your own Usenet newsgroup? As tempting as it sounds, it's not a trivial task.

Complete details on what it takes to create a Usenet newsgroup are in FAQs posted in the newsgroups `news.announce.newgroups`, for the mainstream hierarchies, and `alt.config`, for the alt groups. But suffice it to say that creating a new newsgroup requires you to first come up with a newsgroup idea that doesn't duplicate an existing group, and then submit a proposal, and then wait several weeks for the results of a public vote. The `alt`, or alternative, newsgroups require no vote, but a proposal is highly recommended to encourage news server administrators to look favorably upon your group so that they'll carry it; then again, the reality is that `alt` newsgroups aren't as widely carried as the mainstream hierarchies.

You also need to sweet-talk a current Usenet site into getting the group going. Or, you need to have a computer to use as a news server with enough storage space to hold a whole bunch of other newsgroups. Oh, and don't forget to track down an existing Usenet site to feed your news server news postings.

If your discussion doesn't have to be distributed throughout Usenet, one alternative is to create a private discussion group on your server or Web site, as many companies have done. But that requires a fair amount of technical knowledge and discussion group software (or outsourcing the whole thing and simply managing the content, an option we prefer).

A better idea: If you want the control and focus that running a finely crafted newsgroup implies, but don't want to go through the difficulties of creating one, read Chapter 11 and consider starting an e-mail list instead.

Everything that applies to e-mail and e-mail lists applies to discussion groups: Keep it short; don't type in ALL CAPS; create an effective signature file; don't spam; lurk first; stay on topic; don't respond in public every time; be helpful; and be positive. Because of the very public nature of discussion groups, this kind of Scouting Code for Internet participation may apply even more strongly in discussion groups than in private e-mail messages, described in Chapter 9, and e-mail lists, described in Chapter 11.

Consider these variations on, and additions to, the aforementioned themes unique to discussion groups:

✔ **Read the FAQ.** Unlike e-mail lists, discussion groups don't have welcome messages to outline tone, topic, and rules. However, Usenet newsgroups (and, potentially, other discussion groups) do have Frequently Asked Questions (FAQ) documents that are usually posted regularly. Look for one the first time you scan a newsgroup's messages. A searchable repository of newsgroup-specific FAQs is on the World Wide Web at www.faqs.org/faqs/, as shown in Figure 12-5. Newsgroup FAQs are also found in the newsgroup news.answers.

✔ **Read, then post.** Posting to a discussion group without first getting a feel for appropriate message tone can be like wearing shorts to a church in North Dakota in the middle of winter. Discussion group tone varies widely with topic — the tone and what's embarrassing to mention differ among, for example, the newsgroups alt.sex, misc.forsale, and sci.physics. And remember that, when it comes to discussion groups, not all are in English. Spend some time reading message threads before contributing your own messages.

✔ **Craft a clear subject line.** Unlike e-mail and e-mail lists, message threading means that the only part of your message a discussion group reader may ever see is the subject line — a reader has to be motivated to click the message title to view the entire message. Make the subject line count without crossing the line into spam-like hype. In an automotive newsgroup, rather than "About cars" when posting a tip, try "Clearly diagnosing carburetor problems." In a book newsgroup, rather than "New release," write "New release by William Gibson." Some discussion groups also use a specific format for the subject line; for example, game groups may include the name of the specific game in all subject lines. Follow the tradition. The more compelling your subject line, the more likely it is to click — and to be clicked on.

✔ **Avoid cross-posting.** Cross-posting is the practice of posting the same message to more than one Usenet newsgroup. Not only does this confuse participants as to where they should send their responses without duplicating a lot of messages, it's also a favorite tactic of spammers — not the kind of folks you want to be associated with.

✓ **Don't even think of spamming.** Whereas spamming — posting identical commercial messages — is bad manners in e-mail and an ejectable offense in e-mail lists, it can lead to the equivalent of capital punishment in discussion groups, notably Usenet newsgroups. Imagine your e-mail account — and Internet service provider — being overloaded and shut down by *mailbombs,* rapid-fire return junk mail that sends thousands of messages in quick succession until the receiving server — the one that you use — chokes. Imagine *cancelbots,* automatic programs that erase messages, unleashed to seek out every newsgroup posting you've ever made and eliminate it. Imagine the *Usenet Death Penalty,* complete banishment from Usenet newsgroups, happening to your ISP because of your indiscretion. These things have all happened because of spam, and the Usenet Death Penalty was even applied for a brief time to CompuServe and UUNet, two of the largest ISPs, because of spams sent out by their subscribers. The bottom line: Just *don't* do it.

Now that you're ready to swear off salty luncheon meat forever — and discussion groups along with it — remember that discussion groups have power because of their reach and easy accessibility by Internet users. If you keep your postings on topic, helpful, hype-free, and appropriate, you can go a long way to increasing awareness of, and good feelings toward, your company.

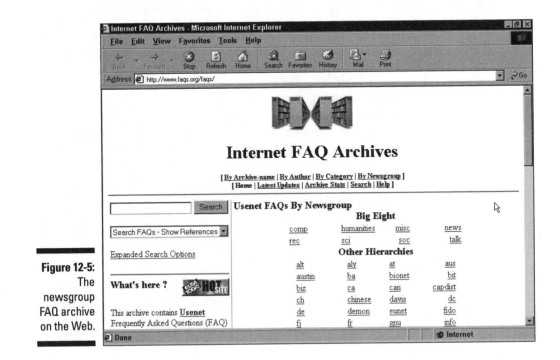

Figure 12-5:
The newsgroup FAQ archive on the Web.

A Few Words About Chat

If you're especially daring, consider marketing in *chat rooms* or *chat channels*: those ephemeral, and sometimes content-free, real-time discussions. (Content-free, you ask? Just go into a chat room populated primarily by pre-teens, all doing age- and gender-checks — and nothing else.)

Chat has exploded on the open Internet since it was popularized on America Online, in CompuServe's CB Simulator, and through the widely used Internet Relay Chat. It's a far more casual — and more rapid — method of moving ideas about over the Internet than e-mail, e-mail lists, or discussion groups. Essentially, chat is a real-time group discussion of a type similar to telephone conference calls or the 1970s phenomenon of Citizens Band radio. (Give yourself ten points if you remember any of the lyrics to the once-popular song, *Convoy*. But start worrying if you remember all of them.)

But chat's most attractive feature for participants — the ability to create discussions among ad hoc groups on the fly — also works against it as a marketing tactic. There is no persistence of discussion as there is in an e-mail list or discussion group. Either you participate in a chat at the precise moment it's going on, or you miss out. And those who don't participate may never experience your marketing brilliance (unless the chat is archived somewhere, and some are).

Before you speak up, check out a few chat resources:

✔ **eNow.** eNow (www.enow.com/website/index.html) is a chat search engine that monitors thousands of live chat rooms in real-time. Enter a search term or click a category and up pops a list of chats currently underway. eNow also lets you participate in the chats from its Chat Scanner interface, as shown in Figure 12-6.

✔ **Yack.** Yack (www.yack.com) is a guide to upcoming Internet events, including scheduled chats on a variety of topics on a wide range of Web sites.

✔ **America Online.** AOL's public Web site has a chat directory page (www.aol.com/community/directory.html) listing all chats using AOL Instant Messenger software, which is available free from the site. AOL doesn't require AOL membership to use AIM, but membership is required for AOL's internal chat rooms.

You can also find available chats from within popular Internet Relay Chat software programs (available from shareware sites) and on most Web portals.

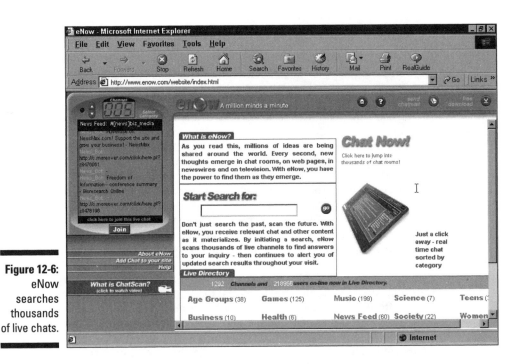

Figure 12-6:
eNow
searches
thousands
of live chats.

How might you or your company use online chat for marketing?

- ✔ **Take part in a scheduled online chat on an industry-focused Web site.** Make sure to identify yourself as representing your company. Participation helps build visibility and awareness (but only if you clearly identify yourself in your chat handle or screen name; unlike e-mail, chat has no sig files, as described in Chapter 9).

- ✔ **Offer yourself as a guest expert on a Web site that features chats in your area of expertise.** Many Web sites offer scheduled chats on various topics, some with featured guests. And because regular chats tend to chew through guests fast, if you have any credentials at all, odds are good that your offer will be accepted.

- ✔ **Monitor chats for news about competitors and your industry.** Using sites such as eNow, Yack, AOL.com, and chat schedules on Yahoo! and other portals, search for competitor names and find out when chats about your industry segment will be held. Make sure to monitor financial chats if your company — or if your competitors — are publicly held, because a lot of stock talk (good, bad, and fraudulent) goes on in chat rooms.

- ✔ **Integrate chat into your Web site.** This takes technical know-how or outsourcing know-how. But either way, chat features on your company's Web site can be used for interactive public relations (virtual news conferences) and regular discussions about your company's products and services, much like an e-mail list (see Chapter 11).

Keep in mind that because chat is real-time, the marketing style is subtle, informal, and, well, chatty. But avoid being long-winded; keep your comments brief. And if you're looking for a dos and don'ts guide, refer back to Chapter 9, because e-mail and chat share many of the same style characteristics.

Much more so than with e-mail lists or even discussion groups, chat is in-tensely anonymous: There's no guarantee that anyone is who he/she/it says he/she/it is or represents anything or anyone as claimed. So take with a grain of salt anything that's said with the force of fact in a chat room.

For more on the basics and mechanics of online chat, check out *The Internet For Dummies,* 7th Edition, by John R. Levine, Carol Baroudi, and Margaret Levine Young (IDG Books Worldwide, Inc.).

Chapter 13

Controlling the Message with Internet Advertising

*I*f you want to make a die-hard, traditional marketer nervous, suggest advertising on the Internet. For although print and broadcast advertising are well-developed centers of civilization, Internet advertising is still the wild frontier. It can sometimes be a challenge even getting two Internet ad experts to agree on the same terminology.

Yet advertising is a time-honored marketing tactic for creating demand in such a way that you, the advertiser, maintains control over the marketing message. And advertising online is more than the oft-maligned banner ad.

The three key things to keep in mind when planning Internet advertising are as follows: What do you want to accomplish? What ad vehicles are appropriate? How do you know when you've been successful?

What Are Your Goals?

Every ad campaign should begin with a clear set of goals. Following are two typical types of goals for Internet advertising:

▸ **Awareness.** Raising the visibility of your product or service for branding, introducing a new item, and/or reinforcing your offline advertising efforts. Awareness is crucial in the selling process; many prospects won't buy from you until they've heard of you a few times.

✔ **Action.** Encouraging actions such as clicking the ad, visiting a Web site, purchasing an item, or filling out a survey. Actions are great because they are much easier to measure than awareness. Also, any action-oriented efforts will make some impact on awareness as well.

Be as detailed as possible when setting the goals for your campaign — but also be realistic. Do you want to increase orders on your Web site by 5 percent? Boost recall of your company logo among aviation engineers? Increase the average add-on sale to your core product by $25 per order?

By being specific, you make measuring how well your campaign has done easier. By being realistic, you set achievable expectations and can more easily determine the appropriate amount to invest in an ad campaign.

If you have trouble coming up with clearly defined, measurable goals, beware. You may have fallen into one of the two dangerous Internet advertising traps:

✔ **Ego.** Massaging the ego of corporate officers or investors is a bad reason to advertise. Need proof? Just find a tape of one of the Super Bowl dot-com ad extravaganzas and then check out the results.

✔ **Pack mentality.** Your competition or colleagues are doing it, so it seems as though you should, too. As your (and our) mother said: "If your friends all jumped off a building, would you, too?"

If you don't have clearly defined goals, you really don't have a reason to advertise — but you may have a rationalization.

The "branding is advertising" trap

Ad agencies will often approach companies and say, "We can handle all your branding needs." They can't. Branding isn't advertising alone.

Good advertising may be the outward reflection of a well-thought-out branding effort. But building a brand means building a customer's emotional connection to a product, service, or company. *Brand attributes* — what qualities makes up a brand — are built by a combination of customer service, public relations, sales process, packaging, pricing, and the product or service itself. Advertising a logo or company name is not, by itself, "branding," anymore than buying a swimsuit is "swimming."

Internet advertising plays a part in your branding effort, but it shouldn't be all of your branding effort.

Driving the Right Ad Vehicle

Now that you've decided what you want to accomplish, what Internet advertising vehicles are available to get you there? The most popular — and established — are banner ads, site sponsorships, e-mail newsletter ads, and search engine keywords.

Banner ads

Banner ads are the nearly ubiquitous rectangular advertisements that run across the top or bottom of most heavily trafficked Web pages. As one of the oldest forms of Internet advertising, banner ads are also one of the few with some standards. The Internet Advertising Bureau (which you can find on the Web at www.iab.net) recognizes a standard ad banner as 468 pixels wide by 60 pixels high, as shown in Figure 13-1. This is not a lot of screen real estate — it's only about 10 percent of the screen area on a typical Web page — but it's enough for some text and graphics, often including simple animations. Some advertisers are also experimenting with *rich media* banner ads that include HTML graphics. Generally recognized alternatives to horizontal, 468 x 60 banners are taller *vertical banners*, smaller *buttons*, and full-screen *interstitials*.

Banners have fallen out of favor among some Web marketers because average *click-through rates* (CTR) — the percentage of ad viewers who actually click an ad — have dropped from 2 to 3 percent a few years ago to 0.5 percent or less now. However, average banner click-through rates aren't as important as several other factors: the *conversion rate* (the percentage of people who click through and take an action you're encouraging); how well a Web site your ads are on reaches your target audience (a better match usually means a better click-through rate); the quality of the ad graphics and copy (known as ad *creative*); and the quality of the Web site the ad banner clicks through to (a bad or confusing destination Web site can destroy the conversion rate).

Also, banner ads that aren't clicked still put your product name in front of a large number of people, much as TV and radio ads do. Debate continues between advertisers and ad space sellers as to how much this effect is worth. You need to figure out for yourself whether this "side effect" of banner advertising has value to you within a specific ad campaign.

Banner space can be purchased either from individual Web sites or through ad networks such as DoubleClick and 24/7 that represent a number of sites.

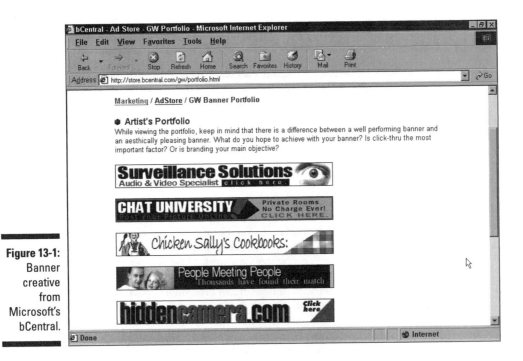

Figure 13-1:
Banner
creative
from
Microsoft's
bCentral.

Site sponsorships

Site sponsorships are a step up from banner ads, in terms of commitment, and involve sponsoring the content of the site. Heard of the Hallmark Hall of Fame or Mutual of Omaha's Wild Kingdom on TV? That's content sponsorship.

Sponsorships, because they're integrated into site editorial content, are not standardized in terms of duration or level of presence. But expect to commit to a sponsorship for from one month to a year at a flat rate. Sponsorships are most effective when the site's editorial content (and/or target audience) and your product or service are closely aligned: hiking-boot makers sponsoring an outdoor adventure site, for example.

If you're new to Internet advertising, don't make sponsorship of a site your first foray into online ads. Sponsorship deals, from site to site, can be very different and can be a significant commitment in terms of contract length and dollars. A better idea: Start with banner advertising. Typically, sponsorship packages include a package of banner ads. If you get your feet wet with banner advertising first, you'll see what works before you dive completely into a site sponsorship.

E-mail lists

E-mail discussion lists and newsletters (see Chapter 11) may allow the widest variety of advertising opportunities. They also have some of the most targeted audiences, because — unlike a Web site, which attracts all kinds of people — e-mail list readers identify themselves to the newsletter publisher when they ask to be signed up.

Advertising is generally limited to short text ads of four to eight lines each, as shown in Figure 13-2. If you need more space, look for some of the few e-mail newsletters that have longer sponsorship positions, or find an HTML newsletter that allows graphic ads much like banners. The key mechanism for delivering customers to you is a link to your Web site in the ad.

Newsletter sponsorships are usually based on a flat rate per advertising insertion and can be the best place for a new Internet advertiser to start. The ads are simple and straightforward (keeping ad creation costs down) and are very targeted.

Search engine keywords

Search engines and directories such as Yahoo! and AltaVista sell search keywords tied to ad banners — that is, your ad banner pops up when a search engine visitor searches for a particular word or term. So, if you buy the keyword "hiking" because you sell hiking boots, whenever a visitor enters that term, up pops your banner.

The more general the keyword and the more popular the search site, odds are the more expensive it will be to buy a keyword. But picking the right keywords to buy can provide very tight targeting when used in concert with good ad banner creative. Try to buy search keywords on a click-through basis; search sites will want to sell them to you by charging each time the ad is viewed, whether anyone clicks the ad or not. That way, the search sites make money no matter how well or poorly the ad works. Be ready to negotiate.

For more on the vehicles of traditional advertising, see *Marketing For Dummies,* by Alexander Hiam (IDG Books Worldwide, Inc.). Hiam covers print, radio, TV, and outdoor ads — all of which can mesh with your and Internet ad efforts.

Integrating online and offline marketing

If you're doing any offline (non-Internet) advertising, leverage your online and offline campaigns. Use any graphics, tag lines, offers, or other elements in your Internet ads to reinforce your other advertising and get the most bang for your buck. It's often said that it takes seven exposures to an ad to get a customer's attention. Why not make sure that Internet ads support that statistical goal?

The one exception to this integrated marketing is when you're testing a new logo, tag line, offer, or other concept. Then your Internet placements can serve as a test bed as long as you choose advertising vehicles that reflect your business's overall target audience.

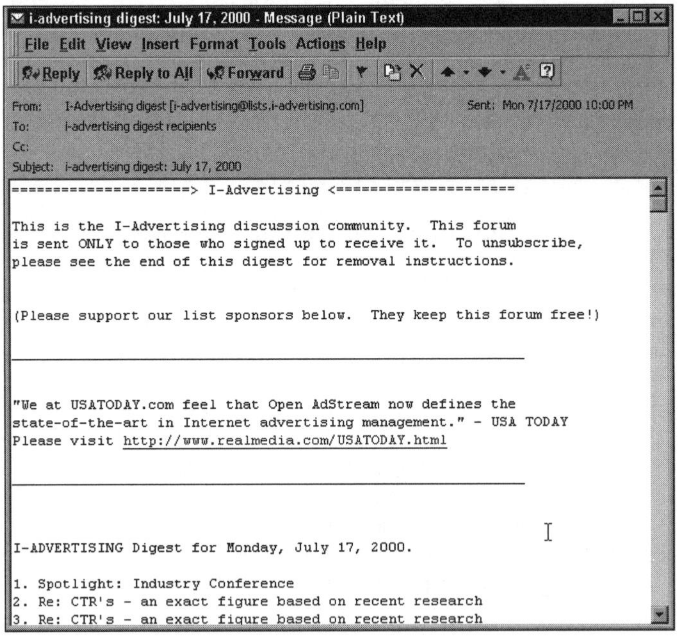
i-advertising digest: July 17, 2000 - Message (Plain Text)
File Edit View Insert Format Tools Actions Help
Reply Reply to All Forward
From: I-Advertising digest [i-advertising@lists.i-advertising.com]
Sent: Mon 7/17/2000 10:00 PM
To: i-advertising digest recipients
Cc:
Subject: i-advertising digest: July 17, 2000
=====================> I-Advertising <=====================
This is the I-Advertising discussion community. This forum is sent ONLY to those who signed up to receive it. To unsubscribe, please see the end of this digest for removal instructions.
(Please support our list sponsors below. They keep this forum free!)
"We at USATODAY.com feel that Open AdStream now defines the state-of-the-art in Internet advertising management." - USA TODAY
Please visit http://www.realmedia.com/USATODAY.html
I-ADVERTISING Digest for Monday, July 17, 2000.
1. Spotlight: Industry Conference
2. Re: CTR's - an exact figure based on recent research
3. Re: CTR's - an exact figure based on recent research

Figure 13-2: An ad from the I-Advertising e-mail discussion list.

Making the Ad Buy

What are the three most important words to remember when making an ad buy? Everything is negotiable.

That's because, more than in any other media, online ad inventory is elastic. You can cram only so many 30-second spots into an hour of TV, or inches of advertising into a newspaper. But when owners of a Web site decide that they want more ad inventory, they can just make a Web page longer or add more Web pages — at less cost than a print publication faces when printing and distributing more pages.

Much of that online inventory is going begging: A study by AdRelevance (`www.adrelevance.com`) found that nearly a fifth of all ad banners on popular sites were "house ads" promoting the site's own products and services rather than those of paying advertisers. So "negotiate" is the word to remember.

A few words about words

To make an informed Internet ad buy, you've got to speak the language (or, at least, realize that a language is being spoken). Some terms you'll come across:

- **Cost Per Thousand (CPM)** is the amount it costs to buy a thousand ad impressions. CPMs can range from $2 for undifferentiated run-of-site inventory to upwards of $100 for highly targeted sites and e-mail newsletters, meaning that each respective impression costs two-tenths of a cent or 10 cents. CPM is the most common way to price Internet advertising. (Why "M" for "thousand?" "M" is the equivalent Roman numeral.)

- **Cost Per Click (CPC)** is what an advertiser pays the site or e-mail newsletter for every individual click on his or her ad. CPC is generally disliked by those selling the ads because they get paid only if the ad performs, and ad sellers (accurately) point out that CPC compensation is dependent on factors out of their control — the quality of the ad creative and of the Web site the ad clicks through to. Yet the CPC model has picked up steam.

- **Impression** is one of the most fuzzy words in the Internet advertising lexicon. When you're buying CPM, you're buying per thousand ad impressions. On the surface, it seems that the definition should be clear: An impression is counted when someone sees the ad, right? But how and when that count is made is the subject of significant advertising community debate. Is it counted when the ad is requested from the server? Is it counted when it's completely delivered to the final pixel? As you may expect, ad sellers like to count them when they're requested from the ad server (even if the viewer clicks away before the ad loads) and ad buyers like to count them when they're fully delivered. Make sure that you know what you're paying for — the difference between the two counting methods can be 10 to 20 percent.

Size matters

When you plan an ad buy, two words you should remember in addition to "everything is negotiable" are these: Size matters.

The size of your ad buy, and the size of your company, matter a great deal to the company you're buying from. Basically, if you're a small fry, you pay top dollar for poor placement. If you're a bigger fish, you can cut a better deal.

What if you truly are a small fry? Follow the example of the pufferfish: Appear bigger than

you really are. Conduct yourself professionally; especially, don't appear overeager. Talk about your growth plans and the size of your target market, and describe your ad buy as a "first step" toward possible future business.

Don't get so caught up in your own hype that you spend more than you can afford. But do negotiate as if you were a much bigger business — which, if you do everything right, you will be.

Never buy an ad based on "hits." A hit is simply a request to a Web server for an element on a Web page. That request could be for a graphic, a text block, or a button and is a largely useless measure of the popularity of a Web site. Far better is to buy ads based on *page views* (the number of full pages that are actually served up by the site) or *unique visitors* (the number of individuals who come to a site). The site should be able to provide those statistics; ideally, the source of the numbers should a neutral, third-party Web site measurement firm. Adam Boettiger, founder and moderator of the popular I-Advertising e-mail discussion lists, has his own pointed definition of "hits": How Idiots Track Success.

The purchase process

To prepare for a Web ad buy, start at the Web site on which you're interested in placing ads. For an e-mail list, go to the list's home Web site or send an e-mail to the list moderator asking for advertiser information. Look or ask for a *media kit*, which contains current ad pricing on a *rate card*, with rates usually listed as cost per thousand (CPM) impressions, as shown in Figure 13-3. Then politely ignore it.

Rate cards have become one of the most popular works of fiction published online. Rarely are significant ad buys ever made based on rate card rates. But the key word is *significant:* I-Advertising's Boettiger noted in an interview with one of the authors (Frank) that a small ad buy may pay near the rate card price. In all other cases, the rate card is simply the starting point for negotiations. Boettiger adds that real pricing is based on market demand for an audience, not a site's ad inventory or what the competition is charging.

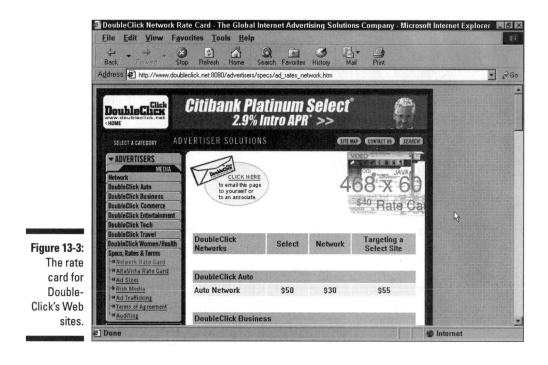

Figure 13-3:
The rate
card for
Double-
Click's Web
sites.

It's also possible to structure an Internet ad buy as a hybrid — balancing a
lower CPM with a modest CPC of, say, a dime or two per click-through. Or, if
you have a product, service, or Web site audience of interest to the site or
e-mail list with which you want to advertise, you could structure some or all
of the transaction as *barter*. But be careful: Generally, bartering occurs at the
rate card price, so make sure to adjust the value of what you're bartering
with commensurately.

Bartering banners on your site

Say, you muse to yourself, my Web site gets a
lot of visitors. Why not trade ads on my site for
my ads on other sites?

An easy way to get your feet wet is to join a
banner network, such as Microsoft's Link-
Exchange (adnetwork.bcentral.com). In
exchange for giving up some advertising inventory on your site, your ad banners appear on
other sites in the banner network — some
400,000 sites. A plus for LinkExchange is that it
can help increase traffic to your Web site. A
minus is that banner networks may give you
little control over the quality and type of banner
that you have to run on your site to get the additional exposure on other sites.

Still, joining a banner network is a small step
toward eventually selling advertising on your
own site without immediately requiring a media
kit, rate card, and ad sales reps.

I-Advertising's Boettiger says not to be afraid to ask for concessions — such as "bonus" impressions or over-delivery of what's contracted — if an ad sales rep balks at cutting the CPM. Here's the key question to ask the sales rep in negotiations: "How do I make you look good?"

Above all, keep in mind that doing an ad buy is still far more art than science, and many of its practitioners still don't agree on what art actually is.

When to call in a professional

If you're uncomfortable negotiating the media buy, need advice on setting ad campaign goals, don't know what a realistic budget is, or don't know how to create effective ads, an agency can help. Interactive ad agencies have sprung up like . . . well, like interactive ad agencies. Agencies and individual ad consultants excel at:

- ✔ **Cutting the deal.** They've done this before and likely are on top of the shifting sands of what's currently "standard" practice in a still nonstandard industry.

- ✔ **Getting the best rates.** Agencies may already have placed ads with the sites in your sights. Their existing relationship — and knowledge of how far to push — can be an asset.

- ✔ **Creating killer creative.** An ad campaign is no better than its worst creative — that is, graphics and ad copy — either on the ad or on the destination Web page. Agencies either have in-house creative teams or can recommend freelancers.

- ✔ **Test, test, test.** A good agency knows how to rotate and test which ads get the best response, helping ensure that only ads that pull the best are the ones that are running.

If you're a small or medium-sized company, look for an agency of similar size. Odds are that you'll get more attention from the principals, and the cost structure will come without the large agency overhead. You can find interactive agencies through referrals on discussion groups, advertising e-mail lists, or from colleagues. Or simply find an online ad campaign you like and e-mail the advertiser about the agency it used.

There are many things that are okay to do yourself: Oil changes. Window washing. But online ad creative isn't one of them, unless you already have experience doing it. The combination of skills — short, punchy copy writing, tiny yet effective graphic creation, and banner sizing and looping — are best left to people who do it for a living. A creative firm also can handle all the technical details of ads, such as knowing the maximum file size a site will allow, and acceptable color palettes. Do understand what your goals and your advertising call to action are. But leave implementation to either a free-lancer or an agency with experience in creating interactive ads so that your company looks good.

Still tempted to do it yourself? You can find a number of freeware and share-ware ad banner creation tools online. But recall that just as desktop publishing software was once credited with giving anyone the power to create incredibly ugly newsletters, many of the banner creation tools have done the same for interactive ads.

Measure by Measure

Ultimately, you'll want to know whether your ad campaign was a success. One simple — and effective — way to determine this is to calculate the *Cost Per Action (CPA)*.

Say that you bought a million ad impressions at $10 CPM. The ads had a click-through rate of 2 percent and a subsequent conversion rate — of, say, people filling out a form for more info — of 10 percent. (You have been tracking all these stats, or had your agency track them, throughout the campaign, right?)

Your CPA would be calculated by taking the total cost of the ad campaign and dividing it by the number of customers who took the desired action. To calculate the Cost part, multiply (1,000,000 impressions/1,000) by ($10 cost per thousand) for a total cost of $10,000.

To calculate the Action part, multiply (1,000,000 impressions) by (.02 click-through rate) by (.10 conversion rate) for 2,000 total actions (or just track total actions directly on your Web site, if you feel that you can identify their source).

Final CPA? Five bucks each, in this example: $10,000 total cost divided by 2,000 desired actions. With any luck, the value of each desired action was $5 or more. (If the desired action was to buy a $99 newsletter subscription, you're in good shape; if it was to fill out a form for more information leading to a $5 purchase, you probably overspent.)

CPA is most useful to determine the effectiveness of ad campaigns focused on generating a clear-cut action, such as completing a sale, filling out an online registration form, or attracting visitors to a Web page. But there's one wild card to keep in mind: A survey by the advertising services firm AdKnowledge showed that more than a third of Web site transactions involved customers who saw an ad, didn't click it, but later went to the site anyway to complete the desired transaction.

Advertising with AOL and CompuServe

America Online has more than 23 million members; CompuServe has several million more. Why not advertise with them? You can — but be ready to open your wallet.

Both AOL and its CompuServe service provide advertising opportunities that run the gamut from ad banners to long-term content partnerships. Neither, however, publicly posts its rates — though online forms on both services'

advertising information site Mediaspace (mediaspace.aol.com) imply an entry-level ad commitment of $3,000 per month. In 1997, AOL ad banners started at $1,000 per week; sponsorships, at $50,000; custom areas, at $300,000. AOL is much bigger now.

Upon reflection, forget opening your wallet. Open your bank.

CPA is not as helpful in determining the effectiveness of an awareness-focused campaign; for those types of campaigns, surveys on your Web site or pop-up window surveys on Web sites where you placed your ads may be more useful. An interactive agency may be able to help you with measuring the success of an awareness-oriented campaign.

No Internet ad campaign should be considered complete until you close the loop that begins with goals and ends with measurement.

Chapter 14

Spreading the Word
with Internet PR

*D*espite the high-tech communications made possible by the Internet, one of the best ways to market a product online is through word of mouth. And the primary marketing tactic for generating word-of-mouth buzz is public relations.

Whereas advertising gives you control over the message you want to convey, public relations gives you the awesome power to, well, influence. But unlike traditional PR, Internet PR provides a direct channel to your target audiences without always having to use the filter of the press.

In this chapter, we focus on how to understand and leverage the differences between Internet public relations and traditional PR. For a basic understanding of public relations in general, see *Marketing For Dummies,* by Alexander Hiam (IDG Books Worldwide, Inc.).

Whom Do You Want to Influence?

Public relations is first and foremost about relationships: relationships between the company and reporters and between the reporters and their audiences. And the first step in doing Internet PR is knowing what relationships you want to cultivate.

Targeting the right contacts

By now, you've targeted an audience for your product or service (Chapter 2). Now determine the Internet media these customers rely on for their information. Are they trade-group sites? Internet-only publications? Specific discussion groups or e-mail lists?

Next, figure out who decides what editorial content goes into each of these media vehicles. Check publication Web site "Contact Us" pages, and get the names of newsgroup and e-mail list moderators. Build a list of the key contacts you develop, or several lists if your products or services have multiple distinct audiences.

Finding the right Internet media contacts can require a fair amount of homework. For the right discussion groups, check Deja.com's Usenet Discussion Service (see Chapter 12). For e-mail lists, check Liszt and other e-mail list directories (see Chapter 11). For Internet-only publications, check directories like those in the News & Media category of Yahoo!.

Set your sights on realistic coverage goals. If you're the manufacturer of hiking boots, odds are you won't be profiled in *People* — unless your CEO is a celebrity. But you may be profiled in outdoor and adventure publications.

Keep in mind that print publications that cover your industry or appeal to your customers likely have Internet editions — and in many cases, those Internet versions have additional content not found in the offline version. For example, both Forbes.com (www.forbes.com), the online version of the eponymous business magazine, and newspaper industry trade site Editor and Publisher Online (www.mediainfo.com) feature significant amounts of material that you can't find in their print editions. These Web versions may have editorial departments that are separate from their print or broadcast counterparts, with a separate list of contacts.

Conversely, realize that some Web publications can't be influenced directly. Sites that rely on getting all their editorial content from other sources have no editorial departments of their own to influence. In order to reach them, you have to know what their sources of editorial content are: PR wire services (PR Newswire, BusinessWire), news wire services (Associated Press, Reuters), or specialized content sites (such as CNET for tech news). Then aim your influence ammo upstream.

Don't forget that your company's PR efforts may have more target audiences than the general marketing audiences for your products or services. Two common additional targets are analysts who follow your industry and the financial/investor press. Make a list for the online constituencies of each of these as well.

Using the right touch

After you develop a list of contacts, start slowly. Indiscriminately blasting out a press release via e-mail to your new contact lists is probably the best way to alienate reporters, e-mail list participants, and discussion group members. When researching editorial contacts, pay attention to how the contacts like to be approached — e-mail, telephone, fax, or not at all. Respect these wishes.

If you're not sure of the best approach, ask. Most reporters don't mind a very brief (one- or two-sentence) e-mail in which you introduce yourself, confirm that they cover what you think they do, and inquire as to how they would prefer to be contacted going forward.

There are fee-based Internet resources for finding editorial contacts and their preferences. Two of the best known are MediaMap (www.mediamap.com), shown in Figure 14-1, and Press Access (www.pressaccess.com). Yet the best place to start is on the Web sites of publications that you already know reach your target audiences. There's no substitute for first-hand research and relationship building.

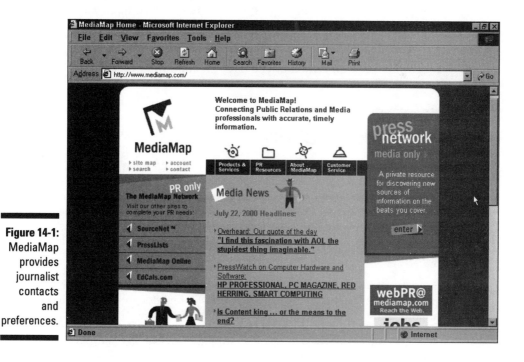

Figure 14-1: MediaMap provides journalist contacts and preferences.

Do be cognizant of the media outlet's news cycle. Sites with paper monthly, weekly, and daily counterparts have different deadline structures, as do broadcast media and Web-only media sites. Not every Web site is updated daily; the ones that are can be pretty hungry for new comments and breaking news, so plan accordingly.

Planning an Internet PR Campaign

Now that you know whom you want to influence, it's time to determine what you want to tell them.

As with any marketing tactic, your Internet public relations effort starts with a plan. Effective public relations is not just about grinding out an endless sausage of press releases. Good public relations is about getting the right messages to the right audiences — which may be conveyed by press releases or by other means.

This PR rule is even more true of Internet PR because of the speed at which a message can travel — and be posted — on news Web sites, public relations Web sites, and in discussion groups, sometimes with biting commentary.

In creating your Internet PR plan, determine what messages are important to your company and interesting to the press, how often you want to convey those messages, and whether you have the time and expertise to do it all yourself.

Messages are key

Before communicating with the press, ask yourself: What are your three key messages? There's a tendency in press communications to want to spew every tiny detail about your company. But face it — reporters, like anyone else, are busy people. Think about what's unique about your product or service that makes a difference to your target audience. Are you the fastest, the cheapest, the first? And why should anyone care? (That's the classic feature/benefit split.)

Then take those messages and simplify, simplify, simplify. Unlike advertising, in PR you don't control how the message will be interpreted and filtered. The simpler and cleaner the messages, the more likely they'll survive the media grinder. Realize that your message, no matter how pretty, will be reworded and possibly re-interpreted. So, it should be "the first widget that gets computer screens squeaky clean," and not "the first robust, scalable technology platform that utilizes industry standard architecture to polish monitor surfaces to 98.6% of their factory-manufactured tolerance."

Standing out in a crowd of releases

Sometimes, to stand out in a crowd of plain-text press releases, you have to be different. That was the tack taken by Bellevue, Washington's Wireless Services Corp. When the KMC Group, the company's PR firm, was stuck for an approach to announce the hiring of a new executive, it decided to go against the standard, serious grain.

"Guy with Funny Name Takes Job at Small Company," read the headline that came across the PR wire. "'We like Dave,' said President & CEO Steve Wood. 'He makes our things do stuff,'" the subhead continued. (The new executive's name was Dave Hoogerwerf.)

The beauty of this release? It was funny and unpretentious in a world of serious and puffed-up dot-com announcements. And it was brief: The entire release ran three paragraphs (including a company boilerplate that concluded, "The company is composed of 12 people in Bellevue, Wash., behind a Chinese restaurant and across from a Harley-Davidson dealership."). It followed the rules of most press releases, even while it tickled them. You still need to know the rules, even in Internet PR, before you can break them effectively.

Was this nonstandard standard press release effective? The *Wall Street Journal* mentioned it on its front page.

After you identify your key messages, repeat them in all your communications. And keep it to three messages, maximum. Anything else will get lost in translation because reporters have only so much space and time.

Excuse me, did you say something?

Your key messages are constants that permeate your news communications. But in order to make news, you can't just repeat your messages; you have to have a news hook. And nowhere is that more important than on the Internet, where timeliness is key.

Typical times to contact the press — online or off — are when there's significant company news in the eyes of your target audiences. Such news includes new strategic relationships, new products, executive-level personnel changes, and so on.

But you can't leave news to chance, because you want your company and products to appear in the news regularly. Your PR plan should indicate how often, on average, you want to contact each news media target audience (determined earlier in this chapter) with company news.

PR planning by pixel

If you need help doing public relations planning, a number of discussion groups, e-mail lists, and Web sites may be able to lend a hand.

The Online Public Relations site (www.online-pr.com) and PR Web (www.prweb.com) have numerous links to Web PR resources.

For e-mail discussion lists, try I-PR (www.adventive.com) and the Public Relations Society of America's Professional Practice Center Online list (www.prsa.org/ppc).

For discussion groups, the PR Network hosts its own (www.prnetwork.com). If you're a CompuServe or America Online member, the long-running CompuServe PR and Marketing Forum (go.compuserve.com/publicrelations) is chock full of useful tidbits. (AOL members simply enter their screen name and password at the CompuServe forum Web site to get access.)

Finally, Yahoo! and other directories, and community sites such as About.com (publicrelations.about.com) provide pointers on, and to other information about, online PR.

This doesn't mean that you must slavishly stick to this schedule, but it gives you something to shoot for in terms of resources and budgeting: "Contact industry analysts each quarter by e-mail," or "Pitch key editors on a feature story every six months," or "Distribute company press release every three weeks" may be targets.

How this changes in Internet marketing is that you can have many more meaningful, casual contacts with members of the news media by using e-mail. You can politely e-mail a reporter who does an industry round-up (and didn't include your company) with a brief introduction, for example. The key to any of these casual contacts is to keep them brief.

Internet PR agency or not?

You can do an awful lot of PR work yourself. But in some instances it makes sense to hire an outside public relations agency or PR freelancer to handle your PR:

✔ To assist with messaging and planning when you can't get enough objective distance from your own products and services.

✔ To ensure rapid turnaround of incoming press inquiries by e-mail or telephone; same day is a must, with a one-hour response the ideal.

✔ To develop press lists from databases of contacts they have developed from previous work or from specialized databases to which they have access.

> ✔ To leverage their existing relationships with members of the press and knowledge of how media outlets like to be approached.
>
> ✔ To write releases and other press materials, both online and offline, if you don't have the ability or time to do it well yourself.

Do you need one of the many new agencies that "specializes" in Internet PR? Probably not. As with everything from books to news, the Internet has rapidly become just another distribution channel and medium for press information. As more reporters have gone online, the PR professionals have followed.

But if all you get when you mention "discussion groups," "Usenet," or "e-mail newsletters" are blank looks, go elsewhere.

Getting Your Release Distributed

Although PR is more than just press releases, the press release is still the primary communications medium. And putting it on paper has rapidly diminished in impact and importance as reporters have turned to the Internet for research.

Ready for release

When writing your press release, keep the following Internet-inspired changes in mind:

✔ **Keep it short.** The equivalent of a page to page-and-a-half of printed text is more than enough. Take into account that your release may be posted, verbatim, on discussion groups and in e-mail lists (as we cover in Chapters 11 and 12). Brevity is the basis of good online communications.

✔ **Provide links to more information.** These could be links to a news area on your Web site for background too detailed for a press release or for downloading high-resolution product photographs and company logos.

✔ **Include URLs and e-mail addresses for your company.** The *boilerplate* at the end of the release should include where you're located, your URL, and a brief description of the firm. Don't forget press contact info — telephone numbers, e-mail addresses, and a physical address. If you expect the release to be controversial or of wide interest, include the cell number or even home phone number of the primary PR contact for your company.

Preaching to the choir

One of your most important audiences for PR is the employees in your company. Make sure that you distribute all press releases to everyone in your company so that everyone is kept up-to-date. Do the distribution in a timely manner; the press release should go out on company e-mail no later than when it's distributed to the news media. That timeliness prevents the morale-killing phenomenon of reading about your company's latest news online or in the paper before the company tells its employees about it.

And make doubly sure to tell everyone about press mentions; this can create the kind of morale boost that money can't buy.

Don't include anything in your press release that can't be reproduced as plain text — no special characters such as the trademark symbol (use "(TM)" in plain text instead), and no embedded graphics or HTML tags. Any nontext elements could get garbled in transmission and mess up your whole message. If it doesn't work in plain text e-mail, it shouldn't be in your press release.

Putting it on the wire

To get the release to reporters, you can (and should) maintain a in-house press e-mail distribution list (see Chapter 10 on how to set one up). But press-release distribution services, or PR wire services, will broadly circulate your release to reporters and editors. Most such services charge a fee, which can range from one hundred to several hundred dollars depending on factors such as the PR wire service you've chosen, desired geographic reach, and press-release length. Following are examples of the different types of PR wire services:

- ✔ **BusinessWire** (www.businesswire.com), as shown in Figure 14-2, and **PR Newswire** (www.prnewswire.com) are the two mainstays of traditional PR wire services. They are routinely scanned by major on- and offline news organizations as well as industry analysts for story leads, and they charge based on which of their targeted topic and geographic media lists you select.

- ✔ **Internet Wire** (www.internetwire.com) and **Internet News Bureau** (www.newsbureau.com) are examples of a new breed of Internet-only PR wire service. They tend to have smaller distribution than the traditional PR wires and may not be as widely read by offline news media, but they charge a lower, flat fee for distribution to all their subscribers.

✔ **PR Web** (www.prweb.com) is a free, advertising-supported PR service that posts press releases on its site and e-mails them to interested journalists. Other sites similarly offer free posting of press releases, such as **dbusiness.com's Release Tracker** (www.dbusiness.com), but these free sites generally don't provide details of who will get a press release.

BusinessWire, PR Newswire, and other major PR wire services feed their press releases raw to hundreds of other Web sites that then reproduce them verbatim — and these releases are also available for viewing on the originating PR wire service site. Distribution points include such large sites as Yahoo! and AltaVista, and online syndicators iSyndicate, Screaming Media, and COMTEX News Network. When you write your press release, keep this direct audience in mind: They could be customers reading about you in your own words. But the primary audience is still the analysts, reporters, and editors you hope to influence.

Stupid PR tricks

Want to know how to make a reporter into an enemy without any thought or effort? Don't put any thought or effort into your PR. There are several ways to irritate reporters with bonehead PR moves unique to the Internet:

✔ **Blindly add reporters to e-mail press release distribution lists without asking.** This is especially egregious if a reporter makes a one-time request or asks to receive limited information — for example, about a trade show in which your company is exhibiting — and you add him or her to your permanent PR distribution.

✔ **Include a press release as an attachment to an e-mail message.** Not only may you wrongly be assuming that the reporter has the right software handy to read the attachment (questionable if he or she is on the road and reading e-mail from a Web interface) but also quite a few reporters simply toss any attachments because they can harbor viruses — yes, even innocent-seeming Microsoft Word documents can harbor viruses.

✔ **Attach graphics or full press kits to an e-mail message.** You may have a high-speed connection and not notice the transmission time, but not everyone does; reporters can be working from home with a 28.8 Kbps connection. Plus, any attachment carries the threat of a virus.

✔ **Go on and on.** If you can't catch a reporter's attention in the first paragraph, you've lost him or her. No one likes to wade through paragraph after paragraph of self-congratulatory prose to see whether you'll ever make your point.

There are many more "don'ts," but these are among the most universally despised. ("Don'ts" applicable to all mass e-mail, such as letting all your e-mail recipients see the names of all the other people in your distribution list, are covered in Chapter 10.) For other tips and warnings, check out the Internet Press Guild's helpfully acerbic treatise, "The Care and Feeding of the Press" (www.netpress.org).

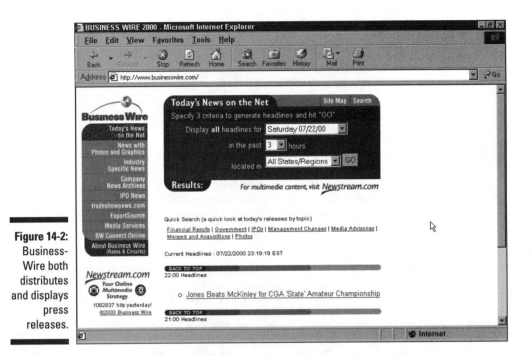

Figure 14-2:
Business-
Wire both
distributes
and displays
press
releases.

Tracking Your Released Release

Measuring public relations impact is tough in the physical world; on the Internet, it's a task reminiscent of the phrase, "Things are never so bad that they can't get worse." Whereas print and broadcast made it at least possible to count column inches and placement (where in a newscast or magazine a story was slotted), few accepted parallels exist online.

However, if you can't easily measure, you can at least monitor. As in most things marketing, two methods are available: Do it yourself or pay someone else.

Watching the wires

Monitoring PR on your own is as simple as visiting specialized search engines that track news sources and/or setting up *clipping services* on variety of sites.

Using these methods, you can track not only your own news coverage but also that of your competitors — providing a nice, fast tool for gauging comparative coverage and analyzing your competition.

✔ **News search engines** such as Powerize (www.powerize.com) and Northern Light (www.northernlight.com) offer free searching of a wide variety of publications. Northern Light takes searching a step further, organizing the results into neat topic folders. Although you may have to pay to see some of the individual stories, you can at least compile a solid list of where your company news was picked up.

✔ **Usenet newsgroups** frequently post press releases verbatim. Deja.com's Usenet Discussion Service (described in Chapter 12) is a powerful tool to search for your mentions and track them.

✔ **Clipping services** are available on a number of sites, including marketing research site DeepCanyon (www.deepcanyon.com), as shown in Figure 14-3, and AltaVista (www.altavista.com) at no charge. These services clip incoming news items and press releases for phrases, keywords, or categories of interest, and many alert you of a successful result by e-mail.

✔ **PR wire services** BusinessWire and PR Newswire both sell customized electronic feeds of their press releases, sliced by industry category or keyword, to nonjournalists. Subscriptions start at under $20 month.

A press release of yours posted by others in a discussion group or on an e-mail list offers you a great chance to observe how that online community reacts to the news. Feel free to chime in, too, with additional explanation if needed — after reading the tips on e-mail lists (Chapter 11) and discussion groups (Chapter 12).

If you've the money, you can use even more powerful publication search engines such as Dow Jones's and Reuters's Factiva (www.factiva.com) and Lexis-Nexis (www.lexis-nexis.com). But you'll pay for the privilege — on some databases, for both the news story you retrieve and the initial search to find it.

Pay for play

If you don't have the time — or the desire — to set up your own clipping criteria or search news search engines, that's where a professional clipping or monitoring service comes in.

Among the best known of this ilk are Luce (www.lucepress.com) and Bacon's (www.baconsinfo.com), both of which have a long history in the physical world and clip newspapers not available online. However, there is no shortage of Web-only newcomers, such as WebClipping.com (www.webclipping.com).

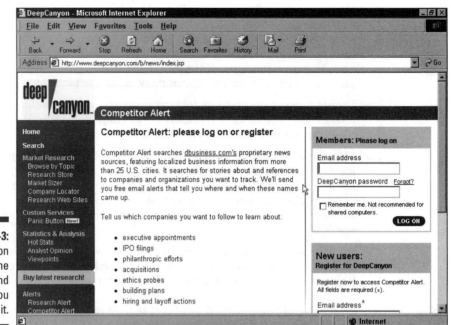

Figure 14-3:
DeepCanyon
clips the
news and
tells you
about it.

More information about professional clipping and monitoring services is available in the Green Book of PR service vendors on the Public Relations Society of America Web site (www.prsa.org), as well as from the Web sites and e-mail lists covered in "Planning an Internet PR Campaign," earlier in this chapter.

Part V
The Part of Tens

The 5th Wave   By Rich Tennant

"Yes, I think we should advertise with America Online. Besides, there is no Vladivostok Online."

In this part . . .

Summing up many of the most important points of this book is embarrassingly easy, but crucial — especially for marketing people who often like to see important points in the form of a quick list. We do so in the form of two chapters outlining the ten advantages and ten disadvantages of Internet marketing. (The rest of the book has the details to help you make your Internet marketing presence really work.) Our last chapter points out ten great *offline* marketing resources that will help you do your best marketing work online, offline, or both.

Chapter 15

Ten Advantages of Internet Marketing

● ●

In This Chapter

▶ Low barriers to entry exist

▶ Informational marketing works best

▶ Rapid responses are rewarded

▶ U.S. marketers have some advantages

▶ Geographic barriers are reduced

● ●

*I*nternet marketing is still only a fraction of marketing budgets for most companies. Despite all the attention that's paid to the Internet, figuring out how to use it properly for marketing, selling, customer service and more is still difficult. You may well need some ammunition to help convince others that you should be spending more time, and more of your company's money, on Internet marketing.

Following are ten of the most important advantages of Internet marketing — some of which we also look at in a different light in Chapter 16, "Ten Disadvantages of Internet Marketing."

Internet Marketing Has Low Barriers to Entry

A great advantage of Internet marketing is that it has low barriers to entry. You can begin building an effective Internet marketing presence with tools such as a basic business Web site (Chapter 5), an Internet e-mail list (Chapter 11), or presence in discussion groups such as newsgroups (Chapter 12) for a few hundred dollars and a moderate investment of time. Much useful Internet marketing work is done on the cheap. If your initial Internet work is successful, you can use your experience to justify building a larger, albeit more expensive, Internet marketing presence. For this reason, you want to always have one eye on the cost justification for your Internet marketing expenditures, as we explain in Chapter 8.

Internet Marketing Is Informational Marketing

Many people see marketing as an art that is less than completely honorable, and see marketers as people who are willing to stretch or even invent facts to make a sale. Needless to say, this perception does not lend itself to using marketing to build an enduring relationship with customers and potential customers.

Internet marketing has evolved in such a way that it avoids some of the disadvantages inherent in popular negative perceptions of offline marketing. Internet marketing has evolved into *informational marketing,* that is, a style of marketing in which you build a reasonable case for your product as the best, and for you and your company as trustworthy partners with the buyer in the purchase process. In Internet marketing, core marketing skills, such as finding and clearly stating the user benefits of product features, are valued over other disciplines such as fast-talking salesmanship or the glitz of advertising.

To find the write tone, if you'll excuse the pun, look at sponsored *advertorial* ("advertising" + "editorial") sections in *Forbes* and other business publications. The goal in advertorials is to deliver solid information that's just as true as anything in the magazine's articles, but written from the advertiser's point of view and selected to help build the case for purchasing the advertiser's product.

If you've been instilled with a tendency to express yourself in breathless superlatives over the years, as have many marketing people, you need to change your style on the Net — even in e-mail. Find someone who knows the online world and ask for a frank evaluation of the straightforwardness and clarity of your writing. Then edit your writing to remove anything that seems overstated or out of place.

If editing isn't your thing — or if you're a great editor of anyone except yourself — you may want to hire a pro to check your copy for you before posting. eLance, at www.elance.com, is one place to look for editing and other professionals who are willing to work on an hourly basis.

The Online World Enables You to Respond Rapidly

The ability to respond quickly — in many cases instantly, off the top of one's head — distinguishes the best marketers from the rest in offline marketing. The ability to respond rapidly is even more vital online — it enables you to build a one-to-one relationship with your customers and potential customers and gives people the impression they're getting factual information rather than a carefully crafted sales pitch. Marketers who aren't afraid to risk occasional criticism of timely, honest responses — for instance, mentioning a competitors' products as well as one's own in answering a question in a newsgroup, as described in Chapter 12 — can do a lot to advance the interests of their companies on the Net.

The Internet World Highlights Marketing's Role

One key reason that marketing in general is important is the link it establishes among products, customers, and sales. In the Internet world, this link gives Internet marketing an advantage over offline marketing in that Internet marketing is more immediate and obvious.

Tactical Internet efforts, such as redesigning Web pages for easier navigation, as well as strategic efforts, such as incorporating Internet sales into your site, are most often in the hands of the marketing department. Marketing is highlighted in the Internet world to such an extent that its importance in the rest of a company's efforts is brought to the forefront as well. The increased focus that the Internet brings on the importance of marketing may make it easier for people you work with to understand the importance of marketing input in other areas, such as product planning and distribution.

Be sure to keep track of your accomplishments in Internet marketing; they may impress a hiring manager or a potential client or customer down the road. A résumé with Internet marketing work alongside offline marketing work shows off your marketing versatility and your ability to stay on top of marketing trends.

Internet Innovations Are Marketing Opportunities

The Internet world is built on rapid change and continues to evolve at break-neck speed. These changes are good for you as a marketer, because each change brings you new ways to communicate with your customers.

Although the precursor networks to today's Internet existed more than 30 years ago, services such as Usenet newsgroups, online services, the World Wide Web, and wireless access have arrived steadily over time (some in just the last few years). The Web itself is changing rapidly as new standards and tools appear with dizzying rapidity. Each time new standards, tools, or technologies are introduced in the online world, examine them for opportunities to better communicate with your customers and potential customers.

The Internet Makes Research Easier

The online world is a tremendous resource for all kinds of research, as we describe in Chapter 2. Want to know what users are saying about your product? Scan Usenet newsgroups and other discussion groups for comments and then send e-mail, asking for details, to a few of the people who spoke out. Want to see what your competitors are planning? Check their Web sites and relevant newsgroups; you're likely to get valuable information such as their past press releases and upcoming events schedules. Sometimes secrets such as product release dates are hinted at, or even blurted out, by less-than-careful insiders.

Not only is online research informative, it's easy to share with others. Online information is freely available for others to verify — unlike things people might say to you over the phone or in person, though that kind of information remains valuable as well. Use online information to help convince others whenever you see a need for action.

As valuable as it is, online research is currently hampered by the fact that so many people, even in the relatively well-wired North American market, are not yet on the Internet. Another obstacle is the lack of information on many companies' Web sites. As the amount of information on company Web sites grows, online research will get easier and more valuable.

The Online World Is Forgiving of Misteaks

(Uh, aren't "misteaks" the feelings you have when you really want a top sirloin?) Compared to other marketing and publishing media, the Internet world is relatively forgiving of mistakes. If you make a typographical error in an e-mail message or a Usenet posting, few people are likely to care; it's more important to get a factually accurate and helpful response up quickly than to wait for editorial review. If you make a typographical error on a Web page, it's more embarrassing, and much more important to fix in a hurry. But you're still better off than with a printed piece, which you'd just have to throw out — possibly at great expense — if it contained typos.

Factual errors are different but still easier to correct on the Internet than elsewhere. If you make a factual error online, simply post the correct information and an apology for the earlier error, much as a newspaper would publish a correction. People on the Internet seem, in our experience, to appreciate the honesty displayed when an error is corrected in this manner.

Of course, no one wants to make errors on the Internet. Always use a spell checker when creating Web page content; the better Web page creation tools now include them, though it's amazing how often they seem to go unused. For other Internet services, use your best judgment. The larger the number of people who see a given communication, and the more official it is as opposed to being your personal response or opinion, the more important it is that you take the time to spell check and even grammar check the content.

Although nearly all Web page creation tools and even some e-mail programs have spell checkers, few have grammar checkers, which can catch subtle errors such as using the wrong version of a word when you right (misspelling intended). To use a grammar checker on your work, create your text in a full-featured word processing program, spell check it, grammar check it, and then copy and paste it into another tool for use on the Internet.

The Internet World Is Currently U.S. Centric . . .

The Internet itself was begun from a network funded by the U.S. military and expanded by further U.S. government funding supported by, among others, then Senator, now Vice President (as of this writing) Al Gore, who also coined the term *information superhighway* (but did not "invent the Internet," as he may have claimed). Most of the companies that dominate the creation of hardware, software, and services for the Internet are U.S. based, and the majority of frequent users are from the United States. So at this point in its history, the Internet is a U.S.-dominated medium.

The point of this is not that America or Americans are somehow superior; any American businesspeople who get smug today will have their heads handed to them by an overseas competitor tomorrow, as, for instance, U.S. automakers learned in the 1970s. The point is that a big opportunity exists right now for U.S.-based companies to take advantage of the current U.S.-centric nature of the Internet and get a head start on establishing themselves in cyberspace.

U.S.-based marketers need to be careful in using the word *American* to describe themselves and their companies; it turns out that Canadians, and to a lesser extent Mexicans and other South Americans, consider themselves American as well. "From the U.S.A" is more widely understood to mean what Americans — "there he goes again," to quote another Presidential candidate — are intending to mean.

The fact that the Internet world is U.S. centric makes life much easier for marketers based in the United States. They can hone their Net skills now, while the Internet is still led by Americans, and then expand their reach and influence as more and more citizens of other countries come online in the future years. (We don't know whether this is a *good* thing; it's just a fact of life that you can take advantage of if you happen to be based in the United States.) Some companies and professionals based in other countries will have a great deal of catching up to do as Internet use in their countries begins to take off.

. . . and English Centric

Because it's U.S. centric, the Internet world is also English centric. Again, this fact is a big advantage for U.S.-based Internet marketers. Companies and professionals that operate predominantly in other languages have a large barrier to operating successfully on the Internet. They must either operate only on the small part of the online world that's in their native tongue, or go through a constant translation process back and forth to English in order to operate in the mainstream of the online world.

Some people predict that the online world will become much more varied in its support for other languages, and that's no doubt true, but the authors of this book suspect that the great bulk of Internet content will continue to be in English for a long time to come. It may be that tens of millions of people who have other native languages will need to learn English to participate fully on the information superhighway, the same way that they do now in the sciences and some professions.

In the longer term, automatic translation services — the ability for computers to automatically translate one language to another — may make language barriers less relevant. (The AltaVista Web site at `babelfish.altavista.com` includes automatic translation.) For now, however, automatic translation isn't good enough to completely close the gap. If you work in English, take advantage of the current predominance of English in the Internet world to start getting your message out now.

Internet Marketing Removes Geographic Barriers

One of the most exciting but confusing things about the online world is the way in which it removes geographic barriers. In the online world, the challenges consist of getting people interested in what you have to say and helping them find you on the Internet. But reaching someone two time zones away costs no more than reaching someone next door. An international delicatessen in Ohio can now easily sell to customers in New York or New Delhi. (That's right, a new deli selling to New Delhi.)

Of course, operating in this new world requires a considerable amount of work and imagination to decide what makes sense and what doesn't. Should a local map store attempt to go statewide on the Internet? National? Global? As we mention in the previous two sections, you can get started with a U.S.-centric, English-only approach, but you also need to decide at what point you need to translate and localize content. Many vendors who've put up a Web storefront have been sadly disappointed by a poor response. Others have been successful beyond their wildest dreams.

You need marketing expertise and considerable self-restraint to use the online world to grow your business without courting disaster. That's why we suggest growing one's online presence gradually. But if your situation offers a unique opportunity to expand your geographic reach — for instance, if you have a lot of expertise, a lot of money, and a unique product — consider rolling the dice and making a bigger initial effort on the Internet.

Chapter 16

Ten Disadvantages of Internet Marketing

*I*nternet marketing has tremendous advantages. However, Internet marketing also has its problems — some of which are the underside of the good points we describe in Chapter 15. In this chapter, we tell you some of the monsters hiding in the Internet marketing closet — and show you how to shine a light on them and make them crawl farther back into the corner.

Internet Marketing Is Different

Internet marketing is definitely different from offline marketing. It's informational marketing with a vengeance — too much hype and your online readers and Web site visitors may not only turn you off, but turn on you. Internet marketing's costs are hard to estimate in advance, and their benefits are still unclear, whereas in offline marketing you have years of past experience to go on. And because of the fast pace of Internet marketing, on any day, a competitor who's one step ahead of you — or makes a lucky bet with the company's money — may get ahead of you.

Not only is Internet marketing different from other marketing work you've done, each Internet technology has its own kinks and culture. If you aren't already Net-savvy, you have a limited window in which to catch up; competitors who have a year or more of Internet experience may be much better able to take advantage of the medium than you are. If you don't at least start to get your hands dirty now, you'll fall farther behind. As an example of the different meaning of "experience" in the Internet world, the several years of Internet marketing experience that the authors of this book have, which would qualify us to be competent practitioners in many areas of offline marketing, are enough to make us minor gurus — "legends in our own minds," some might say — on the Internet.

What can you do about the problem of falling behind in Internet marketing? The solution is information and attitude. On the information side, this book, we humbly submit, is a good starting point for discovering what you need to know to get off to a running start in Internet marketing. Experience and other resources, including some described in Chapter 17 and the *Internet Marketing For Dummies* Internet Directory, will do the rest. Attitudinally, the solution can best be summed up in the Latin phrase *carpe diem,* or "seize the day." The Internet world is a huge opportunity for marketing; don't ignore the risks and difficulties of working in this new environment, but don't let them keep you from acting, either.

Internet Bandwidth Is Crowded

The Information Superhighway is like the U.S. highway system in more than just its name. Any free road tends to get overcrowded as people pile onto it; the traffic jams around our cities may well be matched by increasing frustration on the Net. The limiting factor is *bandwidth* — the speed of the connection between all the different routing and rerouting points on the Net, from the massive servers that host Web pages for companies such as IBM all the way down to the 56K modem built into someone's portable computer. And though many plans to increase Internet bandwidth — for the network as a whole and for specific kinds of users — exist, dozens of companies are also scheming to shove data down the newly enlarged *pipes* faster than you can say Napster, MP3s, and videoconferencing.

As a user, you probably understand that all these bottlenecks cause frustration. But how do they affect you as an Internet marketer? The answer is that you need to ignore the siren call of companies and individuals that tell you to use lots of large graphic images and multimedia files front and center in your online presence, especially on your Web site.

The solution to crowded network wires is KISS — Keep It Short and Sweet. Do experiment with multimedia to get your feet wet and liven up your Web site, but use a light touch, and always back up your multimedia information with static text and graphics that deliver the same message. That way, people who surf the Net with graphics turned off for speed's sake, or who don't wait for graphics to appear before surfing on to a new location, still get the message.

Internet Efforts Can Get Expensive

A full-scale Internet marketing effort with a Web site, newsgroup monitoring and response, and other efforts, as spelled out in the earlier chapters of this book, can get expensive. Such an effort for a company with, say, 10 to 100 staffers may require employing several people — usually a mix of employees and contractors. Some work on the site full time, others part time. Web site hosting costs are either paid to an Internet service provider (ISP) or handled internally. In high-wage areas, the total cost of keeping half a dozen people paid, insured, and housed in offices can approach a million dollars a year. (For employees, much of the cost is hidden as benefits and facilities expenses; for contractors, you write one check for your entire expense for that person.) So be ready to spend some real money if you expand beyond a CYA (Cover Your Assets) Web and online presence like the one we describe in Chapter 5 of this book.

A million dollars is a lot of money, but marketers have certainly been known to spend that and more. Spending that much money for an online effort brings up two special challenges. The first is that the expenses can sneak up on you — given that you can create a simple Internet presence in your spare time for a few hundred dollars, the large expenditures needed for a larger Internet presence can be a shock. The second is that, when all is said and done, not all of your target audience is likely to be online where your effort can reach them, as we describe in Chapter 2. You have to plan and budget carefully to avoid "sticker shock" within your company and to make sure that you still have enough money left to reach people offline as well.

The truly big spending, though, comes with online commerce. Carefully plan and budget your expenditures before selling online, and read *Selling Online For Dummies,* by Leslie Lundquist (IDG Books Worldwide, Inc.), to start getting an idea of what's involved.

Online Marketing Doesn't Reach Everybody

Your colleagues, the press, the analysts, and the core customers with whom you regularly work are likely to be connected. So you may think that your job of keeping all your customers informed, updated, and happy is done as soon as you put information on your Web site or answer a question in a newsgroup. Unfortunately, this just isn't so.

To avoid missing a big chunk of your customers, don't shut out people who are offline or have limited online capabilities. Design your online content, especially your Web pages, to be accessible to all. (If you can comfortably use your Web site with Netscape Navigator 2.0, which doesn't support recent advances such as Java, frames, and so on, then you can be assured that your site is accessible to the vast majority of Web users. You also have a leg up toward making your site accessible from handheld devices, set-top boxes such as WebTV and AOLTV, and so on.)

Your online audience is probably better informed than the offline world because people online tend to be very interested in news and information. However, make sure that both your online and offline groups have access to all the same information. (The GM BuyPower program, which provides people telephone access to the same information that other people get online, is a good example of providing equal access to both an online and offline customer base.)

Another technique is to make offline access information a part of your online presence. Examples of this include making information from your Web site available via a faxback service and adding a toll-free number to your sig (signature) file, as described in Chapter 9. Reaching out in this way helps your online customers pass on contact information to their unconnected friends.

Getting Online Can Be Difficult

If you've ever had problems connecting to your online service or ISP when traveling, you know that getting connected to the Internet when you need to can be all too difficult. Although getting connected can be hard enough for experienced computer users, the barriers to entry for people who don't yet use a computer are far higher: Between the decision to get online and actually being online lies a purchase of at least several hundred dollars as well as several hours of setup time. (Many people also have a large learning curve ahead of them before they can use a computer effectively.) So when you ask people to visit you on your Web site or otherwise get information from you online, you may be causing frustration for many people who would like to be in touch with you but can't get online right now or aren't online yet. So use a gentle touch when promoting your online presence, and provide alternate ways of getting information, as we describe in the preceding section.

The Internet Increases the Pressure on Marketing

In written Chinese, the character for crisis is a combination of the characters for danger and opportunity. So it is in marketing: The arrival of the Internet is a crisis, with many potential problems and many potential victories. Marketing is a fast-paced environment, and the Net makes it even faster. As a result, many,

many opportunities for "gotchas" exist. For instance, how many people knew, four or five years ago, that they should drop everything and register their best choice for a domain name before someone else beat them to it?

Coupled with the increased pace of change is the reality that marketing departments almost always seem understaffed, and the people who are on staff never seem to be given enough money to do the job. (One of the authors worked in an environment in which the marketing budget for a Fortune 100 company was cut to nearly zero one quarter — and then the next quarter's budget used the previous quarter's near-zero budget as its starting point.)

In marketing on the Internet, you may find yourself feeling as though you're always behind. Often, this feeling is brought about by the fact that dealing with something new or cool (like the Internet) can draw you away from your actual marketing goals. One way to overcome this potential stumbling block is to make a priority list and stick to it unless you have justification to change. If you stick to your priorities, you do a better job and you have a little energy left for the occasional tight deadline, such as adding the latest product ("What do you mean, you haven't added the new liver-flavored ice cream bars to the Web site yet? They hit store shelves yesterday!") to your marketing Web site.

Justifying the Cost of Net Marketing Efforts Is Hard

Measuring the impact of marketing expenses is always difficult, but at least some widely accepted rules exist for what's reasonable in offline media. Also, people in your company get a kick out of seeing and hearing ads on TV and radio. If the decision-makers in your company aren't entirely comfortable with the scale of effort needed to succeed on the Internet, they may not get as much of a thrill from a Web site, let alone a newsgroup posting. *Hint:* Don't suggest that they scan `alt.barney.dinosaur.die.die.die`, which is described in Chapter 12, or they might really think that the Internet is not something on which they want to spend a lot of their time — or the company's money.

The cost-justification effort is made more difficult by some of the costly processes that you may want to implement in order to make your online presence shine. These processes include:

✔ **Automating as many parts of your online presence as possible.** One example is using an e-mail autoresponder program to respond to e-mail messages sent to your Web site (Chapter 10). Automating your online processes costs time and money up front, and answering the messages individually doesn't seem to cost any money at all because the expense is hidden in people's salaries. (Not answering the messages costs even less — that is, in terms of hard dollar costs.) However, the opportunities you miss and the bad impression that you leave by not responding quickly to requests for information can be very expensive in terms of lost future sales.

✔ **Outsourcing work to consultants and companies that specialize in online work.** Although hiring outside consultants results in hard dollar costs in a form that many executives loathe — that is, medium-sized and large checks written to consultants — it can save you money in the long run. An outside consultant may be able to set up your marketing Web site in a couple of weeks, whereas doing it in-house may take months. (We explain outsourcing in Chapter 5.)

We strongly recommend that you adapt the advice in this book and your own experience into an ongoing effort to actively demonstrate the benefits of your online presence. Possible ways to demonstrate benefits include counting the number of times people click items in your Web site, counting downloads of files that you offer, polling your online visitors about the impact of your Web site on their buying behavior, and counting responses to special offers that you make on your Web site. Even when no one's asking, keep gathering information about the benefits of your online presence so that you're ready when they do ask.

Making Misteaks Online Is Easy

Any time that you do something new, you're bound to make mistakes. Typos are bad and embarrassing but easy to fix. The real challenge comes when you're put on the spot to answer tough questions — fast.

In the immediacy of the online world, you're often asked to explain complicated issues online almost to the minute the issues arise — why didn't your company ship a product on time? What are your plans for speeding up deliveries? When are you finally going to start doing customer service right? If you admit wrongdoing, you may embarrass yourself or others in your company; if you don't admit that you messed up, you can look ignorant, defensive, or clueless.

The approach we take online is to apologize a lot when we do anything that irritates a customer or partner, and always ask for clarification — is there some way you can perform a needed task with the current product? What happened to you when you spoke with our customer service department? The answers to these kinds of questions help you address real problems better and also lets the air out of wiseacres who may not even be customers or don't have any real problems with you but just like to throw bombs online.

When all is said and done, you have to ask others in your company to be tolerant of any mistakes that you and others make online, and you have to be tolerant of the mistakes that others in your company may make. The online world is a relatively new medium that's highly public and demands rapid responses — always a formula for potential embarrassment.

Some of our GenX friends — mainly people under 30 — have developed the habit of being very informal in sending e-mail, including typing in all lower case and not worrying about typos and punctuation mistakes. This seems to be taken as a sign that one is "cool" and being friendly by being casual in communications. Far be it from us to tell anyone what to do in his or her personal e-mail, but in business e-mail, you simply have to take the time to compose and check what you write, even for "whazzup"-type friendly messages. (The proper spelling of "whazzup" is w-h-a-z-z-u-p.) Otherwise, people will think you're an idiot.

You can reduce errors of judgment, as well as typing and other mistakes, by typing an answer and then reading it out loud to yourself. You may be surprised how your own words sound when you read them back to yourself. But whatever you do, mistakes happen — prepare to be flexible and get better at it as you go along.

Guilt by Association

Because of all the junk in the online world, including pornography, slander, libel, and hateful talk, many people have a bad impression of the Internet. The way that you conduct yourself and how you present your company online can do one of two things. You can reinforce people's negative stereotypes of the Internet, leading them to very quickly form a low opinion of your company, your products, and maybe even your parentage, or you can confound them by making a positive impression, and create a high opinion of your company and your products.

Like other media before it — Newton Minow, the chairman of the Federal Communications Commission called television a "vast wasteland" back in the 1960s — the Internet is bound to face criticism as it grows and develops. If you conduct yourself with class and professionalism online, you and your company can be seen as exceptions, even if the public at large believes that lies, half-truths, and junk are the online rule.

The Uncertain Future of the Online World

Usually, a fairly high degree of predictability exists between what happens one year and what happens the next. But the entire future of the online world seems continually up in the air. As a result, knowing how big a bet to put down on your online presence is hard.

Our answer to the rapid rate of change online is to move cautiously but quickly — cautiously in that you shouldn't make large investments at first, but quickly in that you can and should establish a modest, easy-to-use online presence as soon as possible. Then you can combine the advice you get in this book and elsewhere with your own increasing experience to create an online presence that works best for you and your own unique set of customers.

Chapter 17

Ten Offline Marketing Resources

*N*o matter how much the online world grows, most of the world's information will still be in books and magazines for the foreseeable future. This book's Directory (the section of yellow pages) has scores of great online marketing resources; this chapter is the source for some good offline resources. Several marketing classics and other resources listed in this chapter can help you to get a firm grasp of the essentials of marketing in any medium, online or offline.

Paying close attention to offline marketing vehicles such as television ads can help you sharpen and transfer your skills to the online world. As you gain experience in Net marketing, you look at traditional media — books, magazines, radio, television, and others — in a whole new way.

 All the books recommended in this chapter are available online through Amazon.com, the online bookseller, at www.amazon.com, or Barnes & Noble, the book superstore chain that has a large online presence as well, at www.barnesandnoble.com. (Be sure to check for a list of books and authors that were also purchased by people who bought the book you're interested in; you may learn even more.) Both of these Web sites are also great places to shop for books that may fit your specific job interests more closely.

Crossing the Chasm and Others

Crossing the Chasm by Geoffrey Moore (HarperBusiness) isn't about online marketing at all, but rather about the general marketing of high-technology products to mainstream customers. The online marketing world rests on a high-tech base and has the technology-oriented elite at its core. Therefore, the idea that a book on high-technology marketing would offer some valuable lessons for use in Internet marketing makes sense.

Moore's book definitely does make sense. Its successor, *Inside the Tornado,* by Geoffrey Moore (HarperBusiness), is valuable as well, but of the two, *Crossing the Chasm* is the classic. And Moore's *The Gorilla Game* (HarperBusiness) sums up the earlier two books and also contains valuable advice for investors.

The key lesson of *Crossing the Chasm* is Moore's insights into why most high-technology products fail to reach a broad market and instead stay stuck in niches — and how to get one's products unstuck. Reading *Crossing the Chasm* can help you to understand what you're doing online, why, and what to do next. If you don't look at any other offline marketing resource, look at this one.

Trade Associations

Every profession or industry that we can think of has a trade or professional association, from dentists to decorators to car dealers to computer companies. Many of these associations have marketing sections or groups that exchange marketing information and hold meetings. These associations are great resources for finding out what has and hasn't worked for others online in your industry.

If you're not familiar with all the associations that cover your field — national, regional, and local — talk with a colleague or check one of many directories of associations, available at most library reference desks. And if you want an online pointer to these offline associations, try the Yahoo! association listing online at www.yahoo.com/Business_and_Economy/Organizations/Trade_Associations/.

The trade association for marketing professionals across all industries is the American Marketing Association (AMA), more than 50,000 members strong. The AMA has local chapters in many cities and is another good way to compare experiences with others while building your online and offline marketing skills. You can find your local American Marketing Association chapter at www.ama.org.

Note the .org, for a nonprofit organization, not .com for a commercial entity, at the end of the URL for the American Marketing Association. (The domain ama.com was registered to a company called Imprint Media Communications in Louisville, Kentucky, in 1995, but is not in use as a Web site at this writing.) The American Marketing Association was sharp enough to beat the American

Medical Association, which of course has the same acronym, to the right URL for themselves! Chapter 4 describes how to choose and register the right domain name for your company.

Marketing: An Introduction and Marketing For Dummies

Marketing: An Introduction by Philip Kotler and Gary Armstrong (Prentice-Hall) is a marketing textbook that starts by looking at human needs as the basis of marketing — a good thing to think about in analyzing your Internet marketing efforts — and then covers all the basics of marketing, from market segmentation and public relations to designing new products. Reading all this with an eye to its application online is a mind-opening experience.

If the textbook approach isn't your cup of tea, an excellent marketing book written in the *...For Dummies* style may be more up your alley — if you don't mind our mixing British and American metaphors. *Marketing For Dummies,* by Alexander Hiam (IDG Books Worldwide, Inc.), is an excellent introduction to marketing and a valuable companion to this book.

Trade Publications

Another good source of trade-specific marketing information is your industry trade publications, whether they're weekly tabloids, monthly magazines, or the occasional newsletter. Articles frequently offer marketing tips or profiles of what other companies are doing. Your trade or professional association, or your colleagues, can point you in the right direction.

Also look at Internet-specific trade publications such as the weekly *Interactive Week,* the weekly *Industry Standard,* and the monthly *Internet World.* Go to a high-technology-oriented bookstore or the magazine section in a computer superstore, and you may see as many as a dozen such publications or more. These resources can help make you become familiar with what's happening online.

Marketing trade publications are also a good resource for online marketing. The American Marketing Association, mentioned in the "Trade Associations" section earlier in this chapter, puts out several publications, including *Marketing News,* the *Journal of Marketing, Services Marketing Today, Ad News,* and *Advertising Age.* As their names suggest, these publications are largely advertising-oriented but also cover trends that are generally useful to marketers as well.

Statistical Abstract of the United States and American Demographics

American Demographics is a magazine that addresses consumer trends and is therefore valuable to anyone in marketing. This magazine is also a useful aid to your thinking as you look at the differences between the demographics of the online world, as described in Chapter 1, and the demographics of the offline world. You can find American Demographics online at `www.marketingtools.com/publications/ad/index.htm`.

For definitive information on the U.S. population, the *Statistical Abstract of the United States* is available from the U.S. government in book or CD-ROM form. The *Statistical Abstract* is a great way to back up your plans and proposals with information that's about as authoritative as you can get in a fast-changing field like marketing. You can get the book from the American Demographics bookstore: Follow the link on the top of the American Demographics home page at `www.marketingtools.com/publications/ad/index.htm`.

News Radio

News radio is fairly analogous to the online world in general and the World Wide Web in particular. Basically, news radio stations are delivering information to attract listeners who then hear the commercials that pay the station bills. You can think of your Web site the same way: You're attracting people by providing information that interests them and also delivering your sales and marketing messages encouraging them to buy your product. Listen to news radio with an ear to understanding how it mixes many different kinds of information along with commercials in a way designed to keep you listening.

The writing style for your Web site may be improved if you borrow from the writing style for news radio — lots of short pieces of information, each capable of standing alone, with nothing extraneous in them. CNET news.com, which you can find online at `news.com`, is an example of a news radio-type approach translated to the Web.

Anything by Ries and Trout

If marketing had gods, Al Ries and Jack Trout would be right up there on Mount Olympus. All books written by this marketing duo are easy, fun reads full of marketing strategy tips with lots of real-life examples. Good titles include their classic *Positioning: The Battle for Your Mind* (Warner Books), as well as *Marketing Warfare* (McGraw-Hill), *Bottom-Up Marketing* (Plume), Al and Laura Ries's *The 22 Immutable Laws of Marketing* (HarperBusiness) and their recent *The 11 Immutable Laws of Internet Branding* (HarperBusiness). All are available in paperback and nicely challenge common marketing assumptions. They're worth reading — and rereading.

Any Big Magazine Rack

Imagine a big magazine rack with sewing thread used to connect information from one magazine to related information in others. By the time you were done connecting all the related pieces, you'd have, well, a web of information links. This idea was part of the thinking behind the creation of the World Wide Web, and you can see it in action today in any bookstore.

Most of the Web is very magazine like — pages of information mixing text and graphics, the text written in a compact style for easy skimming or scanning, and ads interspersed throughout. (One may argue that the Web has an advantage over magazines in the form of multimedia, but we've never seen a scratch-and-sniff insert on a Web page, so that's at least one "multi" medium where magazines have an advantage.)

You can pick out magazines you like and then compare them to your Web site. Look for layout and graphic design ideas in the magazine that you can apply to the Web. Find an article you like in a magazine and then compare the writing in it to the writing on your Web site; you may be able to find ways to improve the quality of writing on your Web site by using ideas you get from magazine articles.

Linking is the single biggest difference between the Web and magazines, given that no such thing as a hypertext link exists in print — you have to physically turn the pages to get somewhere else! Look at your Web site for ways to use linking that give your site an edge over magazines.

Permission Marketing

Seth Godin, author of the bestseller *Permission Marketing* (Simon & Schuster), is known as one of the best promoters on the Internet. The surprising thing is that he is not an in-your-face kind of marketer. His thesis is that Internet users have to actively consent to be marketed to or your marketing messages will bounce right off them.

His approach is very much in keeping with what both authors of this book have found to work: be low-key and invite the user in with information rather than hit them over the head with flash or hyperbole. *Permission Marketing* is a great tool for figuring out the right way to market on the Internet — or for helping convince your bosses and peers that a low-key approach is the best way to go.

Television Advertising

What do you do when you have 30 seconds of people's attention — *if* you can entice them not to click a button and surf away from you? TV has had this problem for decades, and the ways in which it meets (or fails to meet) this challenge are very educational for online marketers. Think of people giving your online messages their attention 15–30 seconds at a time — and realize that if they aren't enthralled at the end of each brief chunk of time, they go somewhere else. Study TV ads and then see whether you can apply the things that do and don't work for you, as a TV viewer, to your own online presence. (But expect people to be a bit surprised when they see you channel-surfing with your remote control to find commercials, rather than to avoid them!)

The Internet Marketing For Dummies Internet Directory

The 5th Wave   By Rich Tennant

"So far our Web presence has been pretty good. We've gotten some orders, a few inquiries, and nine guys who want to date our logo."

In this directory . . .

*W*here better to find out more information about Internet marketing than online? This directory, with its funky yellow pages, gives you a long list of online resources to use for your online marketing effort. We include search engines, technology resources, lists of mailing lists — all with a description of what you can expect to find at each address.

Surfing the Internet aimlessly for information regarding the marketing of your company, products, or services could result in using up your time, and we all know time is money. Therefore, this section of the book — set off with the stunning yellow pages — contains a collection of sites to help cut down on the time you spend searching and directs you to the information you need. Here are the main categories in this directory:

- ✔ Advertising
- ✔ Business Owner's Resources
- ✔ E-Mail Lists
- ✔ Government and Law
- ✔ Marketing
- ✔ Periodicals Online
- ✔ Search Engines and Directories
- ✔ Technology Resources
- ✔ Web Tools
- ✔ Miscellaneous

At the end of each category of sites, we include a section titled "Other Stuff to Check Out." Here you can find lists of URLs for additional sites that contain information related to the particular category.

About This Directory

For each entry, you may see one or more mini icons — micons — which provide a quick graphical reference to the site's characteristics. (No, "micon" is not a Web site for con artists.) Here is a list of the micons and what each one means.

Chat: Chat rooms are featured on the site.

Download: Software is available for downloading at this site.

$ Fee required: This site charges an access fee for some or all services.

Message Board: Discussion groups (see Chapter 12) are featured on the site.

Online Database: This site contains information in an online database.

Shopping: The site features online shopping opportunities.

Sign In: You're required to register here. This usually means no more than providing your name, address, and e-mail address for demographic purposes.

Advertising

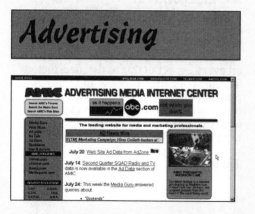

With television commercials, ads on the Internet, billboards, and the sides of buses, what isn't used for advertising? Each day you are likely bombarded with more than a hundred different ad messages that are trying to convey something to you. No business can survive unless it gets its message across to consumers. You have to do it, too, so here are a few sites to help get your message to your potential customers.

Advertising Media Internet Center

www.amic.com

A look into the world of advertising: This site is for anyone interested in the field of advertising. The time may come when you consider contracting an agency to handle the advertising campaign for your Web site. This site gives you information on the rates and trends for ad services. The Ad Talk & Chat section contains a list of forums and e-mail lists dedicated to a variety of marketing and advertising-related issues.

LinkExchange on Microsoft's bCentral

http://adnetwork.bcentral.com/

Display your company ad banner on Web sites: It's a banner-swapping service, through which your banner is randomly displayed on others' Web sites, and other people's banners are displayed on yours. For every two banners that you display on your Web site, you can display one of your own elsewhere on the Web. LinkExchange has more than 450,000 member sites in 32 languages. LinkExchange is a great way to get exposure and to advertise to people who otherwise wouldn't hear about your company. In addition, it provides free statistics on visitors who come to your site via your ad.

Submit It

www.submitit.com

 $

Register your Web site with multiple search engines: You want to give your Web site as much exposure as you possibly can. To do so, you must register your site by sending your company Web site address (URL) to as many search engines as possible. You *can* register your site individually with each of these search engines — a painstaking though acceptable procedure — or you can let Submit It do it in one shot. The site lets you list your URLs with 400 search engines and directories on the Web. You can even selectively register with search engines that may be specific to your product, market, or industry. And if that's not enough, the folks at Submit It offer a variety of fee-based services to promote your Web site.

Other Stuff to Check Out

www.admedia.org
www.bcentral.com
www.direct-web.net/index1.htm

Marketing is a crucial part of running a business — but not the only part. There are a ton of business owner's resources online. Maybe you prefer downloading business letters from the Web and finishing them yourself, as opposed to hiring someone else to do it. If you're the do-it-yourself kind of person, these are the sites for you to check out.

GreenBook Directory and the Focus Group Directory

www.greenbook.org/green.htm

Online directories of market research firms: The GreenBook and the Focus Group Directory are two distinct research-related directories on one Web site. They also give you the option to purchase both publications.

GreenBook is an international directory of market research companies and services. You can use this online version to look up companies and services according to multiple criteria, such as name, market specialties, industry specialties, research services offered, trademarked products and services, computer programs, and geographic location.

The Focus Group Directory, as its name suggests, is a geographical listing of companies that offer focus group facilities and recruiting, moderating, and transcription services.

Office of Minority Enterprise Development

www.sba.gov/MED/

For minority business owners: The federal government gives extensive assistance to businesses owned and operated by minority individuals. This site has information on every aspect of this assistance, including the application process and business-plan requirements. If you're eligible, you may want to cruise on over to claim a slice from this piece of the federal pie. Incidentally, the site carries an explanation of how you can determine whether you are qualified to receive federal assistance.

Service Corps of Retired Executives

www.score.org/

Get counseling via e-mail, and SCORE addresses: The Service Corps of Retired Executives (SCORE) is an organization of retired professionals who volunteer their time to help small businesses develop into successful companies. SCORE provides extensive expertise and valuable advice. And best of all, this service is free. Why hire a consultant who bills you by the hour when you can have someone who's "been there, done that" at some of the world's most prestigious companies — IBM, Kodak, General Electric — and can tell you how it's done, for free? The SCORE Web site is a wonderful collection of resources. Find a SCORE chapter in your town (see the listing at the site) and make the most of its services.

Small Business Administration

www.sba.gov

Business plans, counseling, and various services for the small business: The United States government created the Small Business Administration (SBA) to assist entrepreneurs in forming successful businesses. You can find out about a variety of SBA programs geared toward getting your business started, such as getting loans and keeping your business afloat, using various government-funded organizations such as Small Business Development Centers and SCORE (see previous listing). You can download software at this site as well as a sample business plan to guide your business. You

can even list yourself as a business in the nationwide business-card directory, categorized by state. You can also get the addresses of local SBA offices and information on how to get assistance if and when disaster strikes. (If good luck strikes, you're on your own . . . .)

Other Stuff to Check Out

http://smallbusiness.netscape.com
www.lowe.org
www.isquare.com
www.startupbiz.com

E-Mail Lists

So, you want to find out what some others in the marketing field have to say. Or maybe you've got something that you want others to hear about it. If so, an e-mail list might be of some interest you. An e-mail list is an online community of people sharing a common interest via e-mail, as we explain in Chapter 11. To send your message to all the subscribers on a list, you send it to a single e-mail address, which then automatically forwards your message to everybody on the list.

Remember, the process for signing up for e-mail lists can vary. Some of these lists require that you send an e-mail to a particular e-mail address with the word **subscribe** in the subject line or body of your e-mail message. Some e-mail lists require that you include **subscribe** in the Subject line, others in the body of the e-mail. Still other e-mail lists have you subscribe to them via a Web site interface. Each entry in this section explains how to subscribe to the particular list it describes.

AdPOWER Online

Get tips and ideas for effective ads and newsletters: AdPower Online is an online newsletter published by Drew Eric Whitman, a national advertising trainer, speaker, and consultant. The newsletter is informal but extremely informative. It is aimed at providing tips, ideas, and techniques to increase the response rate from your ads, newsletters, flyers, and whatever mode of communication you use to attract customers. Here's a tidbit from the newsletter: 60 percent of all people who read ads read the headline and no more. To subscribe, send an e-mail to

adpower@oaknetpub.com
In the body of the message, type **subscribe**.

Iconocast

Stats and attitude on the state on online marketing: Iconocast is a free e-mail newsletter helmed by Michael Tchong. Irreverent, edgy, and full of attitude, Iconocast is a great place to get round ups of all the conflicting statistics about Internet marketing — and some clear-headed analysis of what it all means and why there are contradictions. Plus, gossipmongers will enjoy the tidbits from Jaco at the end of each weekly issue.

To subscribe, visit the Web site at

www.iconocast.com

Internet Advertising

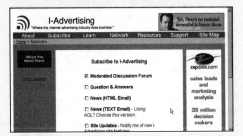

Wide-ranging debate and discussion of Internet advertising: Internet Advertising, or I-Advertising as the list is known to long-time subscribers, has some of the most intelligent exchanges of any e-mail list of its type. Moderator and founder Adam Boettiger knows his subject matter and keeps conversations moving along while simultaneously preventing topic creep and repetition. This list is especially useful for in-the-trenches, what-works-and-what-doesn't advice.

To subscribe, visit the Web site at

www.i-advertising.com

I-Sales

Online sales issues, success stories, and marketing trends discussed here: CNBC described this site as one of the best e-mail discussion lists on the Internet. It focuses on issues relating to online sales. Participants include those who are involved in the online sale of products and services. Examples of topics include order forms, methods of payment for products and services, success stories, and not-so-successful stories, too. The I-Sales Digest is sent to subscribers every day. The list has about 16,000 subscribers in more than 70 countries. The list is available in digest form only, which means that your mailbox receives only one message a day containing all the posts for that day. To subscribe via a Web-based subscription form, go to:

www.adventive.com

Market-L

Discussions on this list focus on marketing and advertising: The Market-L list is run by the Advertising Media Internet Center. The subscribers would like to portray the list as one with a laid-back atmosphere; one that is ". . . an unmoderated list populated by people whose jobs, fields of study, or hobbies are somehow related to marketing." You can expect to receive upwards of 50 messages a day. Topics may include education, politics, or religion, but with a marketing twist to them. To subscribe, send an e-mail to

listserv@amic.com

In the body of the message, type **subscribe Market-L**.

The e-mail list also maintains a Web site at

www.amic.com.

Mktseg

Find out how to target various market segments: This list focuses on targeting advertising and marketing toward specific market segments based on ethnicity, lifestyles, and other criteria. Topics discussed on the list include advertising material, media issues, research, database marketing, direct response, promotional issues, and educational material related to market segments. The discussion is among those whose interests lie in ethnic and lifestyle groups from a marketing point of view. What's encouraged is not just a technical discussion of marketing issues but also one related to things that have been tried and tested. To subscribe, send an e-mail to

listserv@amic.com

In the body of the message, type **subscribe MktSeg**.

Other Stuff to Check Out

Asian Internet Marketing

For subscription info, send a blank e-mail to

info@aim.apic.net

China Business List

To subscribe, send an e-mail to

cbiv-list-request@valueinfo.com

In the Subject line of the e-mail, type **subscribe**.

ClickZ Forum

To subscribe, visit the Web site at

www.clickzforum.com

Global Interact Network Mailing List (GINLIST)

To subscribe, send an e-mail to

listserv@msu.edu

In the body of your message, type **subscribe ginlist** *your name*.

Internet Times

To subscribe, send an e-mail to

internet-times@euromktg.com

In the body of the message, type **subscribe**.

Marketing Success

To subscribe, visit the Web site at

www.themarketingcoach.com/email.htm

Online Advertising Discussion List

To subscribe, visit the Web site at

www.o-a.com

Proposal-L

To subscribe, send an e-mail to

majordomo@ari.net

In the body of the message, type **subscribe proposal-l**.

Government and Law

The government is a great source of marketing information. Many U.S. government departments have Web sites, which are much more convenient to visit than going to a government office in person or trying to get through on the phone. Legal resources are also a good bet when planning your marketing efforts (if betting is illegal where you are, we didn't mean that). Check out the following low-hassle government and legal resources.

Consumer Information Center

www.pueblo.gsa.gov

Free advice from the federal government on health, career, food, travel, hobbies, and more: Remember that ad you used to see on TV telling you about free information from the U.S. government? It ended with the address of the place from which you could request free publications. You never wrote the address down because you thought you'd easily remember it. But two commercials later, it vanished from your memory. Well, that place now has a home on the Web, with a variety of information, ranging from auctions for seized property to consumer-related information. Complete texts of the publications are posted on the site so that you can download or print them and read them at your leisure.

Court TV Legal Help

www.courttv.com/legalhelp/business/

Legal help on a variety of subjects: Don't let the name fool you: It may sound corny, but the information on the Web site is anything but. The few links that this site offers are extremely useful. For example, the Forms and Model Documents link gets you to an archive of documents for a variety of business transactions and Internet commerce. You can download them and then edit them to suit your specific needs. You can also find helpful hints for dealing with lawyers, a legal research service, and information on intellectual property.

Federal Trade Commission

www.ftc.gov

Describes regulations and issues dealing with trade and business practices: The Federal Trade Commission is responsible for enforcing consumer-protection laws. Head straight for the Consumer Protection and Business Guidance sections, where you can find valuable information on various aspects of running a business, particularly with respect to compliance to federal trade laws, such as the Fair Credit Reporting Act and the labeling of products. You may be surprised at what you thought was legal but isn't. This site also includes information on subjects such as how to avoid Yellow Pages invoice scams.

FindLaw

www.findlaw.com

All your legal information needs are met here: FindLaw is one of the most comprehensive law sites on the Web. This site offers a forum to discuss your legal concerns, law reviews, links to almost every aspect of the law (Constitutional, corporate, commercial law, and contracts), state laws, a legal-news reference, legal forms and software, and mailing-list archives. If you're looking for a legal resource, you can find a link to it here.

International Trade Administration

www.ita.doc.gov/

Find trade statistics, export assistance, import regulations, and information on foreign trade zones: You can take advantage of the Internet's global reach to evaluate and pursue international markets for your products and services. The U.S. Department of Commerce International Trade Center provides a valuable service in this area. The Web site contains information on Export Assistance Centers in the United States and around the world, trade statistics, industries served by the organization, and also information on what you should take into account when considering the import of items. If you're involved in international markets, don't miss this site.

U.S. Business Advisor

www.business.gov

One-stop shop for your connection to the U.S. government: The U.S. Business Advisor is where you should go when you have questions related to federal government information, services, and transactions. It carries information on business transactions with the government, international trade, labor employment, and laws and regulations.

Other Stuff to Check Out

www.abanet.org
www.corporateinformation.com
www.freeedgar.com
www.laws.com
www.legal.com
www.micropatent.com
www.taxweb.com
www.uschamber.com

Marketing

Acquiring demographic information and marketing how-to info has never been this painless! The Web was seemingly *made* for storing statistics and suggestions that you can search and retrieve easily.

American Marketing Association

www.ama.org

$

The world's largest marketing association: The American Marketing Association bills itself as the world's largest professional society of marketers, with more than 45,000 members in 92 countries. Membership benefits are many. AMA holds meetings, seminars, and workshops for members to enhance their professional development. It publishes a variety of magazines, such as *Marketing News,* which features new ideas and developments in marketing, *Marketing Management,* a quarterly magazine featuring articles about marketing strategies, and *Marketing Research,* a magazine with articles on research methods and technologies.

ClickZ Network

www.clickz.com

Internet marketing information and opinion, served up daily: The ClickZ Network is a cornucopia of online marketing advice and tips, presented as a series of daily columns. Topics from guest writers and regulars run the gamut from affiliate and e-mail marketing to media buying and selling. (One of this book's authors has also been known to pen the occasional essay for ClickZ.) In addition to thoughtful and sometimes controversial columns, ClickZ has the ClickZ Forum, an e-mail discussion list debating issues raised in the columns. ClickZ clicks as a site to stay on top of the shifting sands of what's happening in Internet marketing.

DeepCanyon

www.deepcanyon.com

Market research resources from a variety of sources: Ever have trouble finding solid market-sizing numbers? You may find them here: DeepCanyon.com is a central point for finding all kinds of marketing information, from research reports to statistical data. One nice feature, Competitor Alert, scans news sources for competitor names and then e-mails you periodically with the results. DeepCanyon.com also has a rather extensive list of marketing links on the Web, neatly categorized.

The Direct Marketing Association

www.the-dma.org

Direct marketing practices, regulations, conferences, and seminars: If you're a direct marketer, — and, in a sense, everyone who uses the Internet for marketing is a direct marketer — this site deals with issues that may be useful to you. The site offers guidelines on ethical business practices, online marketing privacy principles, marketing by phone, and a news and events section. A government-affairs information section offers information related to privacy and consumer affairs, tax issues, current initiatives in Congress that affect direct marketing, key bills in legislatures, and a bookstore. A conference calendar highlights upcoming conferences and seminars.

International Data Corporation

www.idc.com

↘ $

Worldwide market research information on technology issues: International Data Corporation, the world's leading provider of technology data and a part of the same corporation as IDG, the publisher of this book, has operations in more than 40 countries. Its Web site won't let you down. You can find information on the North American, European, Latin American, and Asia Pacific markets, and much of it is available for free. Although the information contained here is related to the world of technology, you can find material on marketing and strategic planning, too. A free e-mail service can even inform you of new research results.

The Marketing Resource Center

www.marketingsource.com

One-stop shop for marketing tools, information, assistance, and associations: As its name suggests, this site is truly a resource for marketers, online or otherwise. It has a comprehensive collection of everything marketing: hundreds of articles on topics ranging from Internet and non-Internet advertising to marketing, home-based businesses, Web development, and Internet commerce. The Tools of the Trade section has a database with more than 2,000 worldwide marketing associations and a software library from which you can download business-related software. You'll also find a special section about marketing on the Net and links to government business sources. The Marketing Forum has bulletin boards on which you can share ideas and ask questions. The Eye on Business section carries a listing of business magazine and other news source Web sites. A very professional site.

Seven Myths of Internet Marketing

www.smartbiz.com/sbs/arts/bre2.htm

Useful marketing advice given in a concise manner: This site is a must-read for anyone thinking about starting an online business. It's a frank description of what you can expect from marketing on the Internet. It'll take you no more than five minutes to read, but they'll be the best five minutes you spend when planning your online-marketing strategy. For example, myth three states, "You can't advertise on the Internet." The author describes why this isn't necessarily the case, and how instead you ought to look at the issue of getting your message across.

Wilson Internet Services

www.wilsonweb.com

Message boards, online marketing newsletter, advice on Web site design, and e-commerce: This Web site, hosted by Wilson Internet Services, has useful information about marketing on the Web. Its Web Marketing Info Center has hundreds of articles covering almost all the questions you are likely to have about Web marketing. You can find information on banner-ad design, push marketing, e-mail marketing, Web-site promotion, Web-traffic analysis, international marketing, and demographics of the Web, as well as a Web-marketing checklist. The E-Commerce Research Room has a wealth of information, too. You may

also subscribe, for free, to the *Web Marketing Today* online newsletter. Lastly, at the Web Marketing Forum, you can exchange ideas with other Web marketers like yourself. The Forum has within it 21 subforums, classified by subjects ranging from strategies and trends to demographics, transactions, and ad revenue. Don't miss this site.

Other Stuff to Check Out

http://wdfm.com/promo/tenquest2.html
www.catalanoconsulting.com
www.census.gov
www.emarketer.com
www.focusgroups.com/
www.marketingtools.com
www.quirks.com/
www.researchinfo.com/
www.teleport.com/~tbchad/stats1.html
www.wolfbayne.com
www.worldopinion.com

Periodicals Online

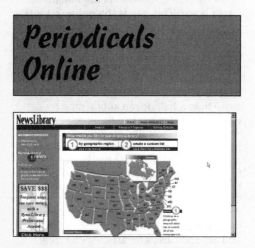

You don't need to go to your local library to get your hands on the latest copy of the *New York Times*, the *Wall Street Journal*, or magazines such as *Time* and *Forbes*. These leading publications — along with many others — are now available on the Web. Best of all, no ink to rub off on your hands!

Electric Library

www.elibrary.com

Online versions of printed media like news-papers and magazines: Electric Library is an online library of newspapers, magazines, radio and TV transcripts, and much more. Although the service isn't free, you can try it for 30 days at no cost. You do have to sign up with a credit card, though; you start getting billed after the free trial period ends. You can cancel the free trial subscription at any time to avoid getting billed.

Inc. Magazine

www.inc.com

Beats the printed version of the magazine hands down: This site is the online counter-part of the popular business magazine, but magazine articles form only a small amount of what's here. The Peer-to-Peer area is a great forum to share ideas, ask questions, and seek solutions to your dilemmas. It's been categorized into more than a half dozen subforums by topic, including Marketing, Technology Exchange, Networking by Industry, and Ethics. The guides to the Internet, Finance, and Biz Tech explain the fundamentals to the novice, with relevant links and informa-tion within each of them. The Virtual Consultant section has interactive work-sheets to help you make important deci-sions about profit margins, inventory, and expenditure. The articles covering International Business contain useful infor-mation that you may not have considered, such as obtaining a carnet. (Don't know what a carnet is? Stop by the site to find out.) Lastly, you can also find information on trade shows and conferences.

NewsLibrary

www.newslibrary.com

Newspaper archives from all over the United States: NewsLibrary is an archive of daily newspaper articles from more than 70 papers in 30 states. Among the more familiar names are the *San Jose Mercury News, Denver Post, Washington Post, Miami Herald, Baltimore Sun,* and *Minneapolis Star-Tribune.* Searching articles is free. Retrieving articles runs between $1 and $3 per article, depending on the newspaper.

Other Stuff to Check Out

www.businessweek.com
www.forbes.com
www.fortune.com
www.individual.com
www.wsj.com

Search Engines and Directories

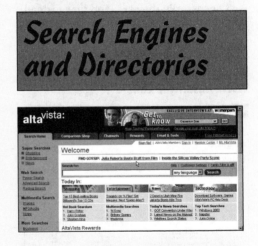

When you don't know where to find some-thing or somebody, these are the sites you turn to. Often searching for a term will make you end up with hundreds, thou-sands, or even millions of sites targeted to your search. Still, with some practice and patience, you can end up with some worth-while *hits* (successful searches).

AltaVista

www.altavista.com

Mother of all search engines: The AltaVista directory is among the largest on the Web. Its searchable index of more than 200GB (gigabytes — that's a lot of bytes) lets you find what you're looking for on the Web in less time than it takes to find a file on your PC. To make thorough use of the search engine, spend a few minutes with AltaVista's

Help feature and learn the commands that will help you narrow down your search and zoom in on your results. AltaVista even offers Babel Fish, a translation option with which the contents of a Web site can be translated into your language of preference. It's a very impressive service.

BigYellow

www.bigyellow.com

Yellow Pages on the Web listing millions of businesses: What you find on this site is a lot more than what you see in your local phone Yellow Pages directory. For one, BigYellow is a global directory of businesses, not just a local one. It includes more than 16 million businesses listed in more than 7,000 categories and all 50 U.S. states. In addition to business listings, you can look up the e-mail addresses of long-lost pals, their telephone numbers, and residential addresses, too. Lastly, BigYellow includes a home office section containing business advice.

Google

www.google.com

Search engine with a cache: Google.com is among the fastest pure search engines around, with few bells and whistles — it's basically search, search, and more search. But there's one nice additional feature: Google has a cache of its search results. So, after you find what you want, you can either directly go to the Web page Google has discovered, or click the "Cached" option to see it in Google's cache, with your search terms highlighted in yellow. This is especially useful if the Web page that Google has found has changed, moved, or simply disappeared. Google's cache is a historical record.

Lycos

www.lycos.com

Search engine and personalized e-mail addresses: There was a time when the Lycos site offered little more than a service to search the Web for information. These days it offers free e-mail, free Web access, free e-mail lists, and a lot more. Lycos also includes chat rooms on the site devoted to investing, news, sports, art, and entertainment. Lastly, a menu with almost two dozen categories allows you to go directly to links and information on a specific topic.

Yahoo!

www.yahoo.com

Most widely used library of Web site listings: Two graduate students at Stanford University started cruising the Web a few years ago and maintained links on their personal Web sites of all the sites they visited. Before long, this hobby became an obsession. Their graduate studies were put on hold, they became full-time Web cruisers, and they soon founded Yahoo!. Today, the Yahoo! Web site maintains one of the most comprehensive lists of sites on the Web. Sites are classified into more than a dozen categories with subcategories. The Business & Economy category currently has more than 600,000 sites listed within it, split over 35 main categories.

Other Stuff to Check Out

www.ask.com
www.bigfoot.com
www.dogpile.com
www.excite.com
www.hotbot.com
www.mamma.com
www.metacrawler.com
www.northernlight.com
www.powerize.com
www.smartengine.com

Technology Resources

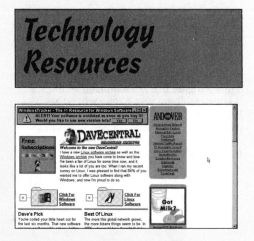

Whether you're in the market for hardware, software, or just some technical advice, you can find plenty of information online.

CNET's Download.com and Shareware.com
www.download.com
www.shareware.com

Collection of free software and shareware: Corporations think nothing of paying hundreds of dollars for software; however, regular people have to think twice about it. Before driving over to your friendly neighborhood computer retailer and donating a few hundred dollars to its livelihood, drop by these sites to see whether you can find something that will do what you're looking for. Most of what's here is *shareware,* which means that you can try it for free before you buy it. In addition to shareware, the site also carries *freeware,* which is — you guessed it — free software. To find all the freeware on the site, do a search for *freeware.*

DaveCentral Software Archive
www.davecentral.com

Handpicked shareware and freeware: Dave Franklin of DaveCentral doesn't just put up

any software on his well-respected site. The Windows and Linux software fan scours the Internet for new stuff, sometimes adding new shareware and free software daily. In addition, he highlights Dave's Picks — shareware he recommends and reviews — among the many titles in each category. A nice files-and-folders-like tree interface makes this site easy to navigate and easy to find what you're looking for. Discussion forums allow downloaders to exchange messages about what they like and don't like.

Hotmail.com
www.hotmail.com

Get a free e-mail account and check e-mail from anywhere: When the Internet revolution took off, everybody wanted an e-mail address. So everybody got one, and then two, and then three addresses. If you're wondering why anybody would need more than one e-mail address, you probably haven't been hit with junk e-mail yet. What you may want to do is have one e-mail address for official business and another one for random, potentially frivolous e-mail (because you never know when you might find something useful in all that junk mail). The former you guard carefully, and the latter you hand out freely. You can easily get a free e-mail account from Hotmail. And one of the greatest things about this e-mail account at Hotmail is that you can check e-mail from any computer, anywhere, that has access to the Web. Hotmail is a division of Microsoft's www.msn.com.

MicrosoftCorporation
www.microsoft.com
www.msn.com

Free software, technical information, and business resources: Hardly a day goes by that this company or its founder, Bill Gates, is not in the news. The largest software company in the world — with more than its share of millionaire employees — has a wealth of information on its Web site. Getting lost on this site is easy, but around every corner is useful information. Find free software, online technical support, and lots and lots of other goodies for managing a Web site and getting a business rolling. If the response time is slow, that's probably because a new version of some software has been released and a gazillion people are trying to download it at the same time. Don't worry; try again a little later.

TechWeb

www.techweb.com

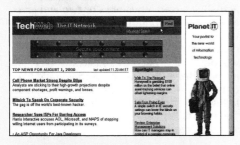

Technical news, financial data on thousands of companies: If you want to keep abreast of day-to-day events in the computer industry, this site is where it's at, especially if you have time for just one technology site. TechWeb carries technology news, stock quotes, product reviews, career listings, and a collection of profiles and financial data regarding 45,000 high-tech companies. You can subscribe to newsletters that are delivered to your e-mailbox every day and scroll through them to find out the day's top stories and the winners and losers on Wall Street. The site also has a small-business area (`www.techweb.com/smallbiz`) that contains a bookstore and a Small Biz Answer Desk manned by Dr. Net to answer your small-business questions. If you're interested in technology events, the technology event calendar has a comprehensive listing of worldwide events. You can download software, and if you're a Web developer, visit the TechTools area.

ZDNet

www.zdnet.com

Technical reviews of hardware and software: If you're in the market for a particular piece of hardware or software, visit this site for quality recommendations. The folks at *PC Magazine,* which is published by Ziff Davis, test more hardware and software in a month than any one person can use in a year. Their recommendations are unbiased and usually on the money. So before you spend that hard-earned cash on a computer that breaks down every time the clock chimes 12, check out this site. In addition to hardware and software evaluations, you can also find interesting articles on current trends in the computer industry and technical how-tos about using new technology. You can also browse through the *PC Magazine* archives of previous issues. And ZDNet has an extensive library of downloadable shareware, freeware, and demo/trial versions of software directly at `www.zdnet.com/downloads`.

Other Stuff to Check Out

www.broadpoint.com
www.netmoves.com

A tremendous number of great Web tool resources are out there — many are listed elsewhere in this Directory. Unfortunately, some Web tools sites have fallen out of date as technology has shifted. Others have "gone pro," moving out of the reach of beginners, or combined with non-Internet software development sites to create monolithic resources that are hard to find your way around in. Here are a few that have stayed current and are accessible by ordinary people.

CNET's Builder.com

www.builder.com

Builder.com is the CNET network site for Web site construction. It includes reviews of currently popular Web construction tools, graphics tips, and more. A lot of professional-level information is contained here, but the site is kept accessible to "the rest of us."

Slashdot

www.slashdot.org

What would happen if a bunch of computer geeks who felt absolutely no obligation to the rest of society — except a shared need to bash Microsoft — created a news and information site? You'd get slashdot. If you want to know what professional software and Web developers think, talk, and dream about, check out Slashdot.

The World Wide Web Consortium site

w3.org

You can track the ongoing deliberations of the World Wide Web Consortium as it builds the technical infrastructure for the Web at w3.org. If you're interested, you can even join one of the committees that contribute to the various aspects of Web infrastructure development. You can also research "from the horse's mouth" exactly what all those HTML tags do (and when they started doing it).

Miscellaneous

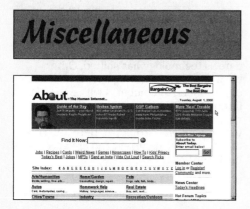

Here are some additional research-related sites. They didn't fit into a category listed previously but are sites that may be useful in your Internet marketing endeavors.

About.com, Inc.

www.about.com

Helpful information dished out by experts in their fields: About.com's approach to providing information on the Web is unique and refreshing. Like many other sites, this site provides a comprehensive listing of sites or areas of interests. But that's where the similarity ends. Each of the About.com's areas of interests is hosted by a Guide — a person who's an expert in that particular area. So, for example, a Guide who has actually started a business or two and gives a first-hand account of running a business, watching for pitfalls, and taking precautions hosts the Entrepreneur area. This is a wonderful approach that makes Web cruising a personal experience. And if you'd like to be a Guide in your area of expertise, just follow the Apply to be a Guide link and you'll be able to add your two cents for the world to see.

American Express Small Business Exchange

www.americanexpress.com/smallbusiness

Helpful information bundled with a sales pitch: This site, hosted by American Express, is part sales pitch and part helpful information. In addition to advertising the various services that American Express offers small businesses, the site has quite a good collection of information, including tips for business planning, expert advice handed out by a small-business expert, a business-to-business directory, and online classified ads.

Biz@dvantage

www.biz.n2k.com

Patent and trademark searches, company profiles, newsletters, and financial reports: Wow, what a site! Biz@dvantage is a comprehensive collection of business-related information. This site has it all: patent and trademark information, company profiles, business news, U.S. and international financial reports, industry newsletters, and worldwide research. It's unique in many of its offerings. For example, you can check whether your trademark will hold up well in more than a dozen European countries.

Business@Home

www.gohome.com

Get information on starting a home-based business: Business@Home is a site that provides valuable information on going out on your own and working from home. You can find information about finances, taxes, marketing, and family matters, along with a collection of home-based business-association links in Australia, Canada, the U.K., and the United States.

The Idea Cafe

www.ideacafe.com

Get help on starting and running a business: At the Idea Cafe, you can find the information you need to start and run a business — such things as financial planning, sources of capital, sales and advertising, protection of intellectual property, and sources of help from Uncle Sam. You can also read interviews with personalities such as Scott Adams, the creator of *Dilbert,* and Jerry Yang, a cofounder of Yahoo!. The site has lots of tips for running a small business — tips that you can't get from a textbook at the Harvard Business School, but only from someone who's actually done it.

International Business Resources on the Web

ciber.bus.msu.edu/busres.htm

Your source of information for international business: This site, at Michigan State University's Center for International Business Education and Research, is a good collection of sites related to international business. Sites are categorized according to a variety of criteria, such as geographic location, government resources, statistics, company listings, indexes of business resources, trades shows and seminars, market indicators, journals, research papers, and articles. If you plan on expanding into international markets, come here for your research needs and market leads.

NetMarketing

www.netb2b.com

Come here to put together your online marketing plan: How do you know whether your Web design and development budget is too small, too big, or just right? Has anyone told you that maintaining a site and keeping it current is far more work than the initial setup? Where do you go to get an idea of setup and maintenance costs? What about the incremental costs — adding things such as audio, video, databases, chat, and Java applets to the site? The folks at NetMarketing provide a valuable service in their attempts to answer these questions. The site also has a searchable KnowledgeBase containing tutorials, case studies, profiles, and articles on topics such as advertising, direct marketing, design, and technology.

Nua Internet Surveys

www.nua.ie/surveys/

Free survey results on business, demographics, social and technical trends: Now here's an example that all research organizations should follow: Make your research results available for free! That's exactly what Nua has done. Why? Because it feels that the quality and quantity of its information are a reflection of the organization. Its surveys are organized into categories such as Business, Demographics, Social, and Technical. This site is clearly not to be missed.

SmartBiz
www.smartbiz.com

Tips, services, and resources for anyone running a business: The SmartBiz site is a comprehensive collection of articles, Web sites, newsgroups, e-mail lists, tips, events, surveys, and statistics about starting and operating a business. The Super Store section contains a list of books, audio and videotapes, magazines, newsletters, and reports. The site isn't specifically geared to Internet marketing but does have some good business-related information.

Zona Research
www.zonaresearch.com

Reports on trends and technology related to the Internet: The Zona Research site does not have a ton of free material; the bulk of the material on the site is available only for a fee. However, before you order a report, you can read a profile or outline of the report to see whether it's what you're looking for. Place your order for a report directly on the Web.

Other Stuff to Check Out

www.companysleuth.com
www.dilbert.com
www.mediametrix.com
www.nielsen-netratings.com
www.pcdataonline.com
www.salesdoctors.com

Index

Notes

Notes

Notes

YOUR ONLINE RESOURCE

WWW.DUMMIES.COM

Discover Dummies Online!

The Dummies Web Site is your fun and friendly online resource for the latest information about *For Dummies®* books and your favorite topics. The Web site is the place to communicate with us, exchange ideas with other *For Dummies* readers, chat with authors, and have fun!

Ten Fun and Useful Things You Can Do at www.dummies.com

1. Win free *For Dummies* books and more!
2. Register your book and be entered in a prize drawing.
3. Meet your favorite authors through the IDG Books Worldwide Author Chat Series.
4. Exchange helpful information with other *For Dummies* readers.
5. Discover other great *For Dummies* books you must have!
6. Purchase Dummieswear® exclusively from our Web site.
7. Buy *For Dummies* books online.
8. Talk to us. Make comments, ask questions, get answers!
9. Download free software.
10. Find additional useful resources from authors.

Link directly to these ten fun and useful things at
http://www.dummies.com/10useful

For other technology titles from IDG Books Worldwide, go to
www.idgbooks.com

Not on the Web yet? It's easy to get started with *Dummies 101®: The Internet For Windows® 98* or *The Internet For Dummies®* at local retailers everywhere.

Find other *For Dummies* books on these topics:

Business • Career • Databases • Food & Beverage • Games • Gardening • Graphics • Hardware
Health & Fitness • Internet and the World Wide Web • Networking • Office Suites
Operating Systems • Personal Finance • Pets • Programming • Recreation • Sports
Spreadsheets • Teacher Resources • Test Prep • Word Processing

IDG BOOKS WORLDWIDE
BOOK REGISTRATION

We want to hear from you!

Register This Book and Win!

Visit **http://my2cents.dummies.com** to register this book and tell us how you liked it!

- Get entered in our monthly prize giveaway.
- Give us feedback about this book — tell us what you like best, what you like least, or maybe what you'd like to ask the author and us to change!
- Let us know any other *For Dummies*® topics that interest you.

Your feedback helps us determine what books to publish, tells us what coverage to add as we revise our books, and lets us know whether we're meeting your needs as a *For Dummies* reader. You're our most valuable resource, and what you have to say is important to us!

Not on the Web yet? It's easy to get started with *Dummies 101*®: *The Internet For Windows*® *98* or *The Internet For Dummies*® at local retailers everywhere.

Or let us know what you think by sending us a letter at the following address:

For Dummies Book Registration
Dummies Press
10475 Crosspoint Blvd.
Indianapolis, IN 46256

FOR DUMMIES™
BESTSELLING BOOK SERIES